THINGS CHINESE

中国风物

杜飞豹 杜白 编著

李念培 凌原 译

China Travel & Tourism Press

责任编辑： 谭　燕
责任印制： 韩君田
译　　审： 叶新如
设　　计： 吴　涛　庞卓娜
摄　　影： 杜飞豹　蒙　紫　等
（部分图片由中国图片网提供）

图书在版编目（CIP）数据

中国风物 = Things Chinese/杜飞豹，杜白编著；李念培，凌原译. —北京：中国旅游出版社，2002.3

ISBN 7－5032－1856－8

Ⅰ. 中...　Ⅱ. ①杜...②杜...③李...④凌...
Ⅲ. 文化—概况—中国—英文　Ⅳ. K203

中国版本图书馆 CIP 数据核字(2002)第 012578 号

书　　名： 中国风物

编　　著： 杜飞豹　杜　白
翻　　译： 李念培　凌　原
出版发行： 中国旅游出版社
（北京建国门内大街甲 9 号　邮编：100005）
印　　刷： 北京文高印刷有限公司
版　　次： 2002 年 4 月第 1 版
2003 年 9 月第 3 次印刷
开　　本： 889 毫米×1194 毫米　1/32
印　　张： 8.875
印　　数： 9001—14000 册
字　　数： 230 千
定　　价： 60.00 元

Introduction (前言)

There must be a reason behind the writing of a book. In this case, the idea for writing *Things Chinese* was inspired by a French friend visiting China.

Our job enabled us to take many foreign friends on tours in China. During such tours they asked a lot of questions, such as why the Chinese eat dumplings, post portraits of the Gate Guardian God on their doors and let off firecrackers on New Year's Day. Why should the tiles that cover roofs in Beijing come in yellow, green or black? What do the animal figurines that perch on roof ridges symbolize? Why the stone turtles are burdened with stone tablets? What's the purpose of the ceremonial columns in front of Tian'anmen Gate? Twenty years ago, a French friend told us that during his travel in China he was keenly on traditional Chinese culture but found it difficult to understand. He suggested that we write a book on Chinese culture.

In 1994, the English edition of *Things Chinese* were published. It soon became a hit with our readers, and that was why the book was reprinted twice. However, occupied by work, we did not have time to come up with a revised edition of the book.

Entering the new century the China Travel & Tourism Press decided to do a revised edition with more illustrations to give the book an entirely new look. Taking this opportunity we introduced 70 more Chinese cultural things in this book. So abundant is the Chinese culture and folklore that a single book like this can hardly cover both the width and depth of it. Given more opportunities, we will continue writing about it so as to do our humble bit for the dissemination of the Chinese culture.

We would like you to give us your valuable suggestions, so that we can make changes in the future.

Du Feibao and Du Bai
杜飞豹　杜 白
June 2001　Beijing

目 录
Contents

Introduction (前言)

1. Ancient Relics (古代遗物)

2. Folk Arts (民间工艺)

3. Architecture (建筑)

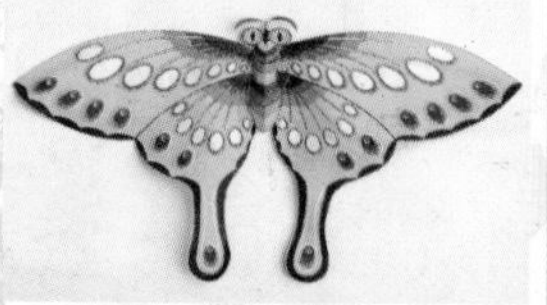
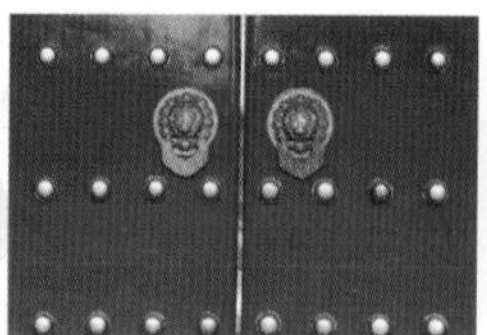

4. Calligraphy and Painting (书画)

7. Drinks and Snacks (饮食)

8. Lucky Things (吉祥物)

9. Entertainment (娱乐)

10. Medicine (医药)

APPENDIX (附录)

THINGS CHINESE 中国风物

Ancient Relics
古代遗物

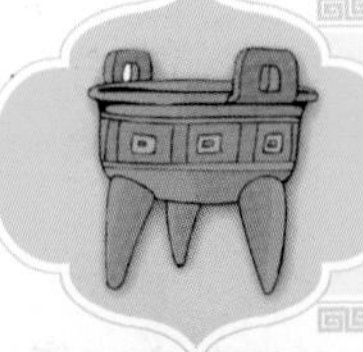

Counters

(算筹 *Suanchou*)

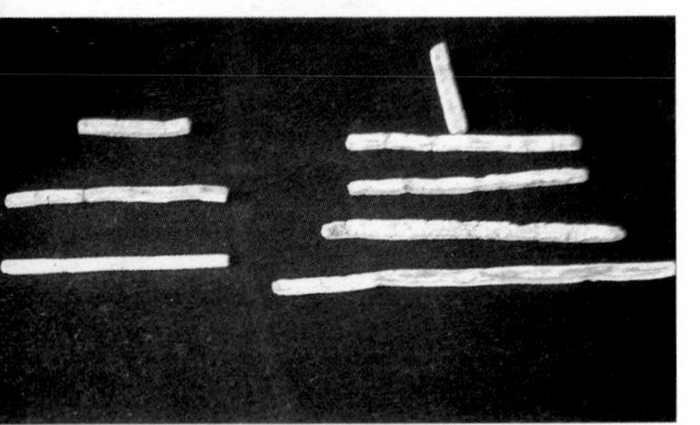

Before the invention of the abacus, counters or tallies were used in China in calculating operations over long ages. Historical writings indicate they were already quite widespread during the Spring and Autumn and the Warring States periods (770-221 B.C.).

The earliest counters were round sticks about 0.23 cm across and 12 cm long. Later on they became rectangular in cross-section and shortened to 7-8cm. The earliest counters thus far discovered were unearthed in 1971 in Qianyang County, Shaanxi Province. Dating from the Western Han (206 B.C.-25 A.D.), they total 30 in number.

Ancient counters, mostly made of bamboo and animal bone, are also found of iron, bronze, ivory and jade.

To express numbers with the unnotched tallies, ancient Chinese followed the decimal system. That is to say, the same stick placed at the unit's place meant "1", but placed at ten's place, meant "10". Arranged vertically, thus 𝍠, 𝍡, 𝍢, 𝍣, 𝍤, 𝍥, 𝍦, 𝍧, and 𝍨 (=1, 2, 3, 4, 5, 6, 7, 8 and 9), they were used to represent the figures at the unit's, hundred's, ten-thousand's and million's places. Arranged horizontally, thus 𝍠, 𝍡, 𝍢, 𝍣, 𝍩, 𝍪, 𝍫, 𝍬, 𝍭, 𝍮, 𝍯, 𝍰, and 𝍱 they would represent the figures at the ten's, thousand's and hundred-thousand's places. The two arrangements, alternating each with the other, could express any figure, no matter how long. In this way, 𝍩𝍨𝍰𝍣 would mean "1984". When a digit happens to be zero, it would be left blank.Thus, 𝍬𝍢 𝍧 would read "4308". The system proved easy to learn and master.

The counters represented at first only positive numbers. But as more complicated calculations were called for, tallies began to be made in two different colours with red ones standing for positive numbers and black ones negative numbers.

The counters, simple as they appear, were employed by the ancients not only to do the sums but also the extraction of square and cube roots, the solution of equations of higher degrees and the calculation of *pi*.

It is estimated that counter sticks were widely used in China for 1,500 years until gradually replaced by the abacus about the 15th century during the Ming Dynasty (1368-1644).

The Bronze Tripod or Cauldron (鼎 *Ding*)

The bronze *ding*, a cooking utensil in remote times, was used like a cauldron for boiling fish and meat. At first, about 5, 000 to 6, 000 years ago, the *ding* was made of fired clay, usually with three legs, occasionally with four that is why it is loosely referred to as "tripod" in English. It stands steadily and has a nice shape.

With the advent of the slavery system, China entered the bronze age, and the earthen *ding* was gradually replaced by the bronze one. In time, it assumed the role of an important sacrificial vessel used by the slave-owning aristocrats at ceremonies of worship.

Leading among the bronze *ding* that have been discovered to date, and by far the largest, is the "*Si Mu Wu*"*ding* which dates to the late Shang Dynasty (c.17th to 11th century B.C.). Weighing 875 kilograms, it is 133 centimeters high and rectangular in shape, standing on four legs. It was made for the King of Shang to offer sacrifices to his dead mother Wu. Exquisitely cast, it is considered a rare masterpiece of the bronze culture the world over. The *ding* of this historical period have a unique shape and are often decorated with patterns of animal masks and other distinctive features characteristic of the period. They are important material objects for the study of the ancient society concerned.

Towards the end of the slave society, the *ding* became a vessel which, by its size and numbers, indicated the power and status of its aristocrat owner. At rites, the emperor used a series of 9 *ding*, the dukes and barons 7, senior officials 5, and scholarly gentlemen 3. From the number of *ding* yielded by an ancient tomb, one can tell the status of its dead occupant.

Today visitors to palaces, imperial gardens and temples of the Ming and Qing courts can still see beautiful arrays of bronze tripods which were, in their time, both decorations and status symbols.

In the periods when Buddhism was the predominant faith in the country, the *ding* was also used as a religious incense-burner. Such burners, made of bronze, iron or stone in various sizes, can still be seen in many old temples. In Yonghegong, the famous Beijing lamasery, there is a large bronze *ding* with an overall height of 4.2 metres, cast with the inscription "Made in the 12th year of Qianlong" (1747). It was in this *ding* that Qing emperors, when they went to the temple for worship, were believed to have offered bundles of burning joss sticks.

Bronze tripods and cauldrons have always fascinated people with their heirarchical associations and their simple but stately forms. So there has always been a thriving craft devoted to the making of copies or imitations of them. Normally they are miniatures for table-top decoration often made of other materials such as jade, agate, lacquer and so on. They represent an important branch of Chinaís arts and crafts.

Musical Bells and Chime Stones

(钟与磬 *Zhong yu Qing*)

These are percussion musical instruments unique to ancient China. The *zhong* are made of bronze while the *qing* generally of stone. They may be played either individually or in groups. In the latter case, they are hung in rows on wooden racks and known respectively as *bianzhong* and *bianqing*. Struck with wooden hammers, they produce melodious sounds of various notes. In their time, they were the important instruments played — either in solo performance or in ensemble or as accompaniment —during imperial audiences, palace banquets and religious ceremonies.

1. Stone and Jade *Qing*

It can be easily imagined that the stone *qing* must have been one of the earliest musical instruments in China. During the Stone Age, the Chinese forefathers, working with stone implements, found out that certain sonorous rocks, when knocked, produced musical sounds and that, by knoking at rocks of different sizes, they could make music. So the earliest man-made chime stones were born out of those natural rocks. In 1973 a Shang Dynasty (c.17th-11th century B.C.) chime stone was discovered from the ruins of that age in Anyang, Henan Province. It is grey-coloured and has tiger patterns engraved on it, showing that it had been used by the imperial court.

The key step in the making of a chime stone is to give it the right note. Artisans learned long ago how to achieve this. If the pitch of a stone was too high, they would grind the two flat faces of the slab, making it thinner if the pitch was on the low side, they would grind the ends and make the slab shorter, until the right tone was arrived at.

The jade *qing* was made much later, following the same idea as for chime stones but using the more valuable jade as the material. In the Hall of Treasures of the

Forbidden City can be seen a chime consisting of 12 iade *qing*. They were made during the reign of Qianlong (1736-1795) of a precious black jade exquisitely finished on both sides with gold-painted dragons playing with balls. It is said that the twelve were chosen out of 160 pieces made at the time by the jade carvers of Suzhou, Jiangsu Province, involving 90,000 workdays and untold costs.

2. Chime of Bells *Bianzhong*

To make the chime of bells, an important metal instrument in ancient times, bronze was invariably used for the best acoustic effect. Early bells are called *yongzhong*, rather flat in shape and very much like two concave tiles joined face to face. Later, however, people stressed the beauty of their shape and gave them a more and more round body, at the expense of the tonal qualities.

It seems that there was no fixed number of bells for each chime. Judging by those unearthed to date, a chime may be very simple , consisting of 3, 6 or 9 bells, or very complicated, with 13, 14, 16 or as many as 36 bells.

The most elaborate ancient *bianzhong*, a set of 65 bells, was unearthed in 1978 in Suixian County, Hubei Province, from the tomb of the Marquis of Zeng dating from the Warring States Period (475-221 B.C.). Their total weight is over 2,500 kilograms, and they were found hung on a three-tiered rack. The biggest of the bells has an overall height of 153.4 centimetres and a weight of 203.6 kilograms. The whole chime, unprecedented disovery in the history of musical instrument ever brought to light —not only in China but in the world as a whole.

Although buried underground for over 2,400 years, the bells still produce fine tones. Ancient and modern music, including tunes from Beethoven's Ninth Symphony, revived ancient tunes of the Tang Dynasty and theme tunes of modern Chinese operas, has been played on them with satisfying results.

Careful study of the bells has revealed that they were cast according to the 7-tone scale with 5 semitones in between, completing a well-integrated system of 12 tones. The scale of the whole chime agrees with the modern 7-tone scale in C major, and its range covers 5 octaves, just two octaves less than the modern piano. What is more amazing, each bell can produce two different tones, a unique feature in percussion imstruments.

An inscription of 2,500 characters engraved on the bells tells of the musical theories and the names of the tones prevalent at the time as well as the positions where the tones can be produced. The unearthing of this set of bells has proved beyond all doubt the application of the twelve-tone equal temperament in Chinese music as early as the 5th century B.C. , providing one more evidence of the antiquity of the Chinese civilization.

The 65-bell *bianzhong* can be seen at the Provincial Museum of Hubei in the Central China city of Wuhan.

Another *bianzhong* worth seeing is one of 16 bells made of pure gold during the Qianlong period in the 18th century, now displayed in the Forbidden City's Hall of Treasures. Cast in unique forms and about the same size, the 16 bells are of a uniform height of 23.8 centimetres, but their weight ranges from 4,703 to 14,316 grams. Round in shape, they produce a rather monotonous ring, but they were meant during the heyday of the Qing Dynasty, to impress viewers with the wealth and extravagance of the imperial house. And they are indeed very much valued, being cast in dazzling gold and engraved with lively patterns of ball-playing dragons.

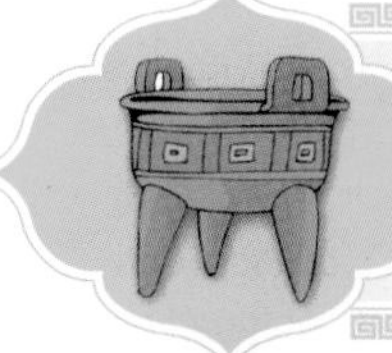

The Bronze Mirror (铜镜 *Tongjing*)

The bronze mirror, like its modern glass counterpart, was a household article of daily use in which to look at oneself. Its obverse side is so smoothly polished that it can reflect the image of the user's face. The reverse side is often cast with a knob and decorations, so it is also an art object. Most of the authentic bronze mirrors are finds from ancient tombs; some have been handed down from generation to generation in old families.

Ancient Chinese began to use bronze mirrors in very remote times, at the latest in the 11th century B.C. in the late Shang Dynasty, as evidenced by five of them discovered in Tomb No. 4 at the Yin Remains in Anyang, Henan Province.

The mirror became a popular object during the period of the Warring States (475-221 B.C.). The mirror of this period is often found to bear one or two rings of decorations, the usual designs being animal masks, flowers and leaves, dragon and phoenix...During the Western Han (206 B.C.-25 A.D.), the mirror became thicker, and the popular designs at the back were geometric patterns, supernatural beings, birds and animals. It was also in this period that simple, short inscriptions appeared, such as "keep me in mind, forget me not", "perpetual fortune, endless joy" or other words of good wishes. The form of the bronze mirror became more varied during the Song and the Yuan dynasties (10th-14th century). It may be round, oblong, lozenge or octagonal, with or without a handle. During the Qing (1616-1911), it was gradually replaced by the glass mirror.

Of particular interest is a bronze mirror dating from the Western Han. With a diameter of 11.5 cm and patterns at the back, it looks no differecnt from other mirrors except an inscription which reads: "With light from the sun, the world is greatly illuminated". The strange thing about it is that, when a sunbeam falls on its smooth surface, its reflexion on the wall shows the design and inscription on the reverse side as if the light had penetrated the bronze. This phenomenon of the mirror had puzzled people, including scientists, over long ages, and it was called the "magic mirror". A specimen of this mirror can be seen in the Shanghai Museum. Today, not only the strange reaction of the mirror to sunlight has been scientifically explained, but imitations have been made of it to amuse collectors.

Bronze mirrors, as usual funerary objects of ancient times, are often found in old tombs. They are placed near the head or chest of the dead or packed with combs in lacquer boxes or pouches within easy reach. Some of them are found at the top of the burial chamber or at the four corners of the coffin, suggesting a belief that the mirror had the magic power of warding off evil spirits.

The Bronze Drum

(铜鼓 *Tonggu*)

The bronze drum is not covered with skin but made entirely of hollowed bronze, and it is the most popular instrument among the ethnic minorities in the south and southwest of China. Its beginning may be traced to be bronze cauldron, a cooking utensil in ancient times.

It was used in its time as a sacrificial vessel at offerings and rituals, or as a percussion instrument to give the signals to summon the people of the tribe. In battles it was struck to direct the fighting. For this reason, it was in the possession of the clan headman or tribal chief as a symbol of ruling power. With the decline of chieftain dominance, the bronze drum usually fell into the hands of powerful or rich families.

Today the drum is still a favourite instrument with the Zhuang, Buyi, Dai, Dong, Miao and Yao nationalities of China. At festival celebrations or other important activities such as a horse race or a singing competition, the drum is usually

played to add to the fun.

Up to now, a total of 1,300 bronze drums, have been collected and unearthed in China, which are displayed in museums at various places. By far the richest collection of them is at the Museum of the Guangxi Zhuang Autonomous Region in Nanning, which has a special pavilion devoted to them.

The oldest bronze drum unearthed so far dates from the Warring States Period more than 2,600 years ago.

The average size of the drums of this type is about one metre in diameter, and most of them are decorated on the surface with cloud and thunder patterns, characteristic of ethnic arts.

The biggest bronze drum unearthed up to the time of writing saw the light in 1972 in Beiliu, Guangxi. It has a diameter of 1.65 metres, a height of 37.5 centimetres and a weight of 300 kilograms, and is now exhibited in Nanning Museum.

"As You Wish" (如意 *Ruyi*)

Visitors to Beijing's Forbidden City will notice a valuable exhibit called *ruyi* (formerly spelt as *juyi*) with a head like a shred of cloud and a long body or handle in the shape of a flat S. It may be made of any of a wide range of valuable materials: gold, jade, jadeite, crystal, agate, coral, agolloch eaglewood, bamboo, bone and what not. And the workmanship is often quite meticulous: it is carved with patterns in incision, low-relief or openwork and sometimes inlaid with silver, gold and gems. The designs may be simple or very elaborate but invariably convey messages of good wishes, such as "pine and crane" (standing for vigorous old age), "immortals wishing you longevity", "phoenix and peony" (standing for wealth, happiness and prosperity), and the like.

The *ruyi*, it is said, was born out of a common Chinese article of household use —the itch-scratcher. This is a stick about 1.5 feet long, with one end in the form of a miniature hand with bent fingers. Holding it, a man can scratch the itches on his own back and thus get a feeling of well-being. It is still used by some people in China today. Usually made of commonplace wood or bamboo, it is popularly called by the descriptive name *laotoule* ("old man's joy").

The itch-scratcher, being a joy, began to be made of more valuable materials for those who could afford it. But apart from being an art object, it continued to be used for its original purpose until sometime during the Qing Dynasty (1616-1911). It gradually became a pure ornamental object called ruyi ("as you wish"). The right place for the elevated and transformed itch-scratcher was now on the bedside table of the imperial sleeping chamber, by the side of the throne—to be appreciated daily by the emperor and his numerous wives. On every occasion of court celebrations, such as enthronement, royal wedding or birthday, the nobles and courtiers would be busy raising money and ordering whole sets of *ruyi* for presentation. On the 60th birthday of Emperor Qianlong (1700), for instance, the ministers presented to him 60 *ruyi* of gold filigree. Likewise, on the 60th birthday of the Empress Dowager Cixi (1894), she got 9 times 9 or 81 *ruyi*. (The number 9 × 9 symbolizes infinity or an endless long life.) The *ruyi* was also used by the emperor, when he chose a concubine out of a number of candidates, to point at the one catching his fancy.

The presentation of *ruyi* was not a one-way affair: it was often bestowed by the emperor upon his ministers or subjects. There is still a valuable collection of them in the Mansion of Confucius in Qufu, Shandong. They were given by various emperors to the descendants of the great sage.

It is still difficult to pinpoint the time of the first emergence of the *ruyi*, although no archaeological finds of them date from before the Qing Dynasty. They are much valued but commonly seen objects of decoration in the old Qing palaces, but outside of Beijing one rarely comes across them in provincial museums.

Sedans

(轿子 *Jiaozi*)

The sedan or sedanchair (*jiaozi*), a traditional vehicle of transportation carried by bearers, was called at the beginning *jianyu* (shoulder carriage), being a carriage that travelled on human shoulders. *Jiaozi* is its comparatively modern name.

In old times, sedans fell into two major categories: the *guanjiao* (official sedan) and the *minjiao* (private sedan). Those of the former type were used by the royal family and government officials, and they varied in elaborateness according to the status of the person carried inside, following strict rules laid down for different levels of the hierarchy.

Even for the emperor himself, he was to sit in palanquins or sedanchairs of different grades on different occasions: the ceremonial palanquin to go to a formal court of audience, the sedanchair when he made rounds of inspection inside the Forbidden City, the light sedan for hunts and excursions outside the capital, and finally the casual litter, a spare sedan accompanying him on his trips, into which he might want to change at any moment. For his everyday use in the palace, it was usually the casual litter. Then the furnishings also differed with the seasons: the warm sedan for winter and the cool type for summer. The two sedanchairs now on display in the Hall of Complete Harmony (Zhonghedian) of the Forbidden City are the casual litters used by the emperor for everyday purposes.

Sedanchairs for the ministers and lower officials varied in grandeur with their ranks. In all cases, an official sedan out in the street was heralded by the beating of gongs to clear the way and surrounded by a number of attendants. Common people meeting such a procession must keep quiet and step aside. The higher the official, the

greater the number of followers and sedan bearers. The latter might vary from two for a petty official to eight for a very eminent personage. The emperor himself might have as many as sixteen carriers.

Private sedans were of simple make, yet they were owned only by the landed gentry or urban rich. Built of wood or bamboo, they could be carried either on flat roads or along mountain paths. Some of the self-pampered potbellies inside, like the officials, were also accompanied by bodyguards walking by the side of the sedans.

There was yet another type of sedans for hire to the common people for use on weddings. They were called *huajiao* (flowery sedan) or *xijiao* (happiness sedan). The deluxe model of this type was covered by bright-coloured silks embroidered with gaudy designs of good luck and even decorated with sparkling gems. The run-of-the-mill model was also bedecked with colourful silk ribbons. In feudal times a bride was not to be seen by outsiders, so there was an elaborate "double-sedan" with a small one inside the outer one so that the bride could get into (or out of) the inner sedan indoors and then be carried into the outer sedan without exposing herself to public view.

Wedding sedanchairs continued to be in vogue for some time in certain regions after the founding of New China in 1949. Nowadays young people prefer the motorized sedan for their weddings, and the sedanchair has been relegated to the realm of history.

Ancient Figurines

(古俑 *Guyong*)

Most ancient figurines have come down as funerary objects. They have their origin in the institution of immolation or burying the living with the dead.

Immolation was practised in the period of slavery. In 1950, excavations made of a Shang Dynasty (c.17th-11th century B.C.) aristocrat's tomb at Wuguan Village, Anyang, Henan Province, brought to light the remains of 79 slaves who had been buried alive with their dead master. Besides, in 27 pits arranged in rows in front and at the back of the tomb were discovered, buried en masse, the skeletons of 207 other slaves beheaded in immolation.

The cruel custom of burying the living with the dead, though replaced by the burying of tomb figurines, lingered

on and was practised in isolated cases under nearly every dynasty. In the Ming (1368-1644), according to contemporary notes, a human sacrifice was entertained to a sumptuous temple to meet his last day before being led down to an underground temple to meet his horrible end. At the funeral of an emperor, palace maids were reportedly pushed, one after another, onto bed-like racks, and their heads into nooses, and were hanged after the racks had been removed. When Emperor Changzu of the Ming died in 1424, sixteen persons were buried alive with him. In the eastern and western "wells" on either side of the Changling Mausoleum (the largest of the Ming Tombs) are the remains of his immolated concubines.

After the Qin and Han dynasties, tomb figurines began to be used instead of human beings. And vast numbers of them, dating from the Warring States Period (475-221 B.C.) down to the Ming (1368-1644), have been unearthed. They are of various descriptions but most are made of pottery and porcelain, next come wood and lacquer, and occasionally jade. They represent people of different status and walks — court officials, generals, cavaliers, attendants, musicians,dancers and acrobats. As a rule, they are nicely modelled in different postures, constituting a valuable part of China's ancient art.

Jade figurines first appeared in China during the 8th to 3rd century B.C. A number of tiny jade figurines were unearthed in 1974 from a mausoleum of the ancient state of Zhongshan. Most of them appear to be females, though some are lads. They have their hair done up in buns on the head —double buns for women and single one for the boys. They all stand, holding their hands before the chest. The females are clad in tight-sleeved dresses, buttoned down the middle, and chequered long skirts. The hairdo and costume must be true-to-life reproductions of those prevalent in Zhongshan at the time.

The Qin (221-206 B.C.) and Han (206 B.C.-220 A.D.) dynasties are noted for the high quality and large numbers of pottery figurines they produced. In 1974 the famous terracotta warriors and horses of Qin Shi Huang (the First Emperor of the Qin) were discovered just east of his mausoleum. The excavation is still going on, and Vault No.1 alone is expected to yield 6,000 of them. The lifesized figures of men and horses are in neat battle formation, with the men holding real bronze weapons of the time and reflecting the formidable might of the legions of the First Emperor.

In the winter of 1980, another valuable find was made to the west of the mausoleum. Two bronze carriages, standing one behind the other, were discovered. Each was drawn by a team of four bronze horses and driven by a driver, also made of bronze. All figures are half life-size, weighing a total of 1,800 kilogrammes. They are the earliest, largest, most elaborate and best-preserved models of ancient bronze carriages, complete with animals and drivers, ever found in this country.

Each discovery at and near the Qin Shi Huang Mausoleum has caused—and will cause — a stir among archaeologists the world over.

Han Dynasty figurines show clear influences of the Qin, but are smaller in size. An impressive discovery was made a few years ago in a Han tomb at Yangjiawan, Xianyang, Shaanxi Province of a total of 3,000 painted pottery figures. Most of the standing figurines represent warriors, and some of them are equestrians. Compared with the human figures, the horses are more expressive: some stand quietly and others rear up with an unheard neigh. They must be truthful portraits in sculpture of the foot and mounted troops of the Han Dynasty.

With the flourishing of ceramics during the Tang, Song and Ming dynasties (10th-17th century), the tomb figurines of this long period are mostly glazed pottery and porcelain, among which the "tri-coloured glazed pottery of the Tang" is world-famous. Out of the ancient tombs of Xi'an and Luoyang have been unearthed many colour-glazed females, horses and camels. Noteworthy especially are the pottery camel drivers with their deep-set eyes, protruding noses and hairy faces, evidently Central Asians who plied the Silk Road with their caravans. The "tri-coloured Tangs" represent in effect a special handicraft art catering solely to the funerary needs of the aristocracy at the heyday of China's feudalism.

Wooden figurines have a much longer history which extends back to the Warring States Period (475-221 B.C.). They have been found in many ancient tombs of different ages and in different localities. The tomb of Zhu Tan, prince of Lu (the tenth son of the founding emperor Zhu Yuanzhang of the Ming), situated in Zouxian, Shandong Province, yielded in 1974 a total of 406 painted wood figures in the formation of a long funeral procession. It consists of three parts: musicians leading in front, followed by attendants and military officers in the middle, and civil officials bringing up the rear. The figures — a sculptured model of an early Ming (2nd half of the 14th century) funeral — are on display in the Provinical Museum of Shandong in Jinan.

Some wood figurines have been found in the Dingling Mausoleum of the Ming Tombs. They are few in number and crude in workmanship, showing that wood figures were already going out of vogue towards the end of the dynasty.

During the Qing Dynasty (1616-1911), paper figures appeared; they were not buried with the dead but were burnt at funerals to follow the dead to the nether world. After the fall of the Qing, tomb figures have fallen completely into disuse.

The Chinese Grandfather Chair
(太师椅 *Taishiyi*)

The *taishiyi* means literally the "Imperial Rector's chair" but has been loosely called by some old-time Western residents in China the "grandfather chair". It is different from its Western counterpart in that it is not upholstered but made of hard wood and with a straight back and arms. Rector's charis of various descriptions can still be seen in the imperial palaces and the mansions of former courtiers and officials. They can also be found in some old families among the people.

The name for the chair first appeared at the end of the Northern Song in the 12th century. A man, in order to please Qin Hui, the powerful and traitorous prime minister and Imperial Rector, presented to him a roomy, cross-legged chair specially made with a head-rest that resembled a lotus leaf, which he named the "Imperial Rector's chair". The novel design of the chair became the fashion among the upper strata of the Song officialdom, and the name stuck.

Down in the Ming Dynasty (1368-1644), the Rector's chair was reshaped, with its back and arms forming a semicircle.

The "grandfather chairs" commonly seen today are mostly handed down from the Qing Dynasty (1616-1911). With the armrests at right angles and with the back, they are generally made of rosewood, red sandalwood or padauk and often inset with marble bearing beautiful natural veins. In south China, some of the chairs may have seats woven with rattan skin for greater coolness.

As a rule, grandfather chairs are large in size, and in a saloon they are normally arranged in pairs with a teatable in between, creating a stately atmosphere.

The cross-legged chair of the Song, the

semi-circular chair of the Ming and the straight-backed armchair of the Qing, though different in shape and structure, are all called "Imperial Rector's chairs". They were made at the beginning for eminent officials, so they have always been reserved as the seats of honour for important visitors. When historical plays are staged, one of the indispensable props of certain scenes is the grandfather chair to highlight the features of the age.

The Sacred Way and Stone Statues
(神道与石像 *Shendao yu Shixiang*)

In the front part of imperial necropolises there is usually a "sacred way" or "divine road" for the spirits of the royal dead — in which the ancients believed — to walk on. This road is often lined with stone statues of men and animals as important decorations of the grounds.

The traditional name for the giant-sized statues of men, popularly called "stone men", is strictly *wengzhong*. It is said that a herculean giant by the name of Ruan Wengzhong lived in the Qin Dynasty (221-206 B.C.) and distinguished himself with great service in garrisoning the borders in Gansu and in fighting the Huns. After he died, Emperor Qin Shi Huang, to commemorate him, had a bronze statue carved in his likeness and erected at his palace in Xianyang. It is also said that, when Huns came to Xianyang and saw the statue, they thought Wengzhong was still alive. After that, all bronze men (and then stone statues) standing guard at palaces and imperial tombs came to be known as *Wengzhong*.

As for the stone animals, they have their origin in the following historical event:

Huo Qubing (140-117 B.C.) was a young military genius in the period of the Western Han. Distinguished in archery and horsemanship, he became an imperial attendant at age 17 and was several times sent on expeditions under his uncle Wei Qing, a famous commander, to fight the marauding Huns. He was given a command himself at 19 and twice led government forces to what was present-day Gansu and dealt telling blows to the Huns. He died at the age of 23 only. Emperor Wudi built for his beloved young general a magnificent tomb at Maoling and, to perpetuate the fame of his exploits in the northwest, had the mausoleum grounds landscaped like the Qilian Mountains where the battles had been fought. And as the mountain range is marked by rugged rocks that resemble wild beasts, so Huo's tumulus was strewn with grotesque rocks; furthermore, masons building the tomb sculptured many stone statues of animals—leaping and squatting horses, resting tigers, kneeling elephants, piglets and fish, bears and other wild beasts preying on sheep...Of the sculptures, the most renowned is one showing a Hun under the hoof of a galloping horse, a work of art aptly summing up the achievements of the young general in his meteoric career.

The group of statues are the earliest giant-sized stone sculptures known to stand in front of an ancient tomb in China.

Emperors in later epochs, taking their cue from this, had stone men and animals made for their own tombs, and they are now a common sight to greet visitors to imperial mausoleums of the Tang, Song, Ming and Qing dynasties.

The group of giant stone figures that stand on the grounds of the Ming Tombs near Beijing are the best preserved, the most true-to-life and most skilfully carved of their kind.

Erected where they are in A.D. 1435 (or the 10th year of the reign of the Ming Emperor Xuande), they consist of 12 human figures (civil and military officials and courtiers with meritorious records)and 24 animals (lions, camels, *xiezhi*, elephants, *qilin*, and horses — four of each, two standing and two squatting). The human figures were meant to imply firm and popular support to the imperial house, while the animals in different postures signified alternate day and night services to the dead monarchs.

Besides, different animals had each their symbolic significance:

The lion, ferocious in nature and lording it over the animal kingdom, symbolized awesome solemnity.

The camel and elephant, being dependable means of transport in the deserts and tropics, put together at the imperial tombs, were meant to suggest the vastness of the territory controlled by the court.

The *xiezhi*, a mythological unicorn which was supposed to possess a sixth sense to tell between right and wrong and which, when two men were embroiled in a fight, would gore the wicked one, was put there to keep evil spirits away.

The *qilin*,one of the four "divine animals" (the other three are dragon, phoeix and tortoise), was represented at the tombs as an auspicious symbol.

The horse, being the emperor's mount on many occasions, was of course indispensable.

Stele on the Back of Stone Tortoise
(石龟驮碑 *Shigui Tuo Bei*)

Visitors to China's mausoleums, temples and parks will come across many a stone stele standing on a stone pedestal in the form of a tortoise. Some of these stelae are well shaped out of high-grade smooth stone and bear inscriptions engraved in elegant calligraphy; the more important ones are sheltered by pavilions from weathering.

A stele of this type consists of three parts: the crown, the body and the pedestal. The crown is usually carved with a patern of *chi*, a mythological animal supposed to be one of the nine sons of Dragon. It has often been taken as a dragon's head, which it resembles.

The carving of inscriptions on stelae has a history extending a long time back. When a stele bears an inscription written by an emperor, it invariably has a stone tortoise as the base. Such inscriptions, whether written personally by emperors or by their ministers on their behalf, normally extol the emperors' virtues and achievements so that they might be remembered by posterity. Some stelae were erected for other purposes, too. A huge one standing in front of the hill in the Summer Palace bears an account of the building of the Hill of Longevity and Kunming Lake written in the hand of the 18th-century Qing Emperor Qianlong. The whole block, magnificently shaped and exquisitely carved, has an overall height of 9.8 metres with distinctive Chinese features.

Although ancient stelae were meant to bear inscriptions, yet a small number have nothing in writing on them at all. These are popularly called "wordless stelae", and most of those in front of the Ming Tombs fall into this category, though they are also named "stelae of divine achievements and holy virtues". The explanation for this can be found in a historical work devoted to the study of imperial mausoleums. Zhu Yuanzhang (1328-1398), founding emperor of the Ming, once said, "Stele inscriptions at imperial tombs have always been written by scholars to whitewash the royal dead; the practice should not be taken as the standard for posterity". So, the practice was suspended during the Ming (1368-1644), yet it did not prevent beautiful stelae from being carved and erected. For instance, the one at Dingling, the tomb that has been opened for visitors, is sculpted in low relief with six *chi* coiled round one another, so expressive that they seem to be fighting playfully on water for a big pearl. The huge stone tortoise at the base is no less a masterpiece of sculpture. Raising its head, it looks into the distance with almost real attention. Around the tortoise are carved images of prawns, crabs, fish and turtles, partly concealed in patterns of waves. All this provides the backdrop of a surging sea, which helps with its buoyancy the tortoise to bear the dozens of tons of stone on its back, while still doggedly forging ahead.

It may be necessary to point out that the animal under the stele is no tortoise at all as it is popularly supposed to be. Strictly speaking, its name is *Bixi*, the ninth son of the mythological dragon. It was born with such unparalelled strength that it could move the mountains and used to play havoc in the seas. Somehow it was tamed by the Great Yu, the legendary hero who fought the Flood, and helped him move obstacles and dig canals, contributing much to the conquest of the rampant waters. After the Flood had subsided, Yu was afraid that *Bixi* might slip back to his old ways and, to prevent this, made it carry a mammoth stone with an inscription praising its meritorious feats. This cost *Bixi* forever its freedom, as the heavy weight proved too cumbersome. In time, its image was confused with that of the mundane tortoise. Still it was supposed to possess extraordinary capacity for great weight and, for this, has been employed by emperors of all ages to bear their stelae. And for the Chinese who are accustomed to the sight of *Bixi* or the tortoise under the stele, it would be unthinkable to see anything else in its place.

One might be tempted to ask how the stelae, some of which are as tall as a dozen metres, were lifted up and erected on the back of the stone tortoises in the days when mechanical devices were unknown. The problem, legend has it, was solved at the suggestion of a deity who appeared to the Ming Emperor Chengzu in his dream. The emperor wanted to erect a monumental stele for his father Zhu Yuanzhang, founder of the Ming, but the stele was too big, and the workers were all at loss what to do. The god in the dream told the vexed emperor to use a method in which "the stele and the tortoise will not see each other". Enlightened by the cryptic message, the engineers and masons buried the stone tortoise and made a slope with earth, along which the stele was moved up and placed on top of the buried tortoise. With the earth removed, the stele was stood well in place. After that this became the standard operation for erecting stelae.

Tortoise-borne stelae are now regarded as important cultural relics, valued for the light they throw on historical events, studies of calligraphic arts and related subjects.

Tombstone and Buried Tablet

(墓碑与墓志 *Mubei yu Muzhi*)

The *mubei* and *muzhi* are two different things that serve the same purpose. The Chinese tombstone (*mubei*), like its Western counterpart, is an oblong piece of stone, erected vertically in front of the tomb and engraved with an inscription (*beiwen*). The *muzhi* is usually in the form of a square stone tablet which is buried in the grave with the coffin and placed in front of it. The practice of burying a tablet as part of the Chinese funerary rites appeared later than the tombstone.

The earliest Chinese tombstone had no inscriptions. They were but simple rectangular slabs with small holes, through which ropes were run to lower the coffin into the pit. Some of the very ancient tombstones still show vestiges of the holes on them.

The inscription, which appeared later, generally gives a brief account of the dead person, listing the major events he experienced and the lofty qualities he possessed to perpetuate his name to later generations. Important inscriptions or epitaphs, penned by eminent statesmen, men of letters or other public figures and engraved by master masons, are cherished as valuable relics important to the study of ancient literature, calligraphy and art in general.

Some inscribed epitaphs could be very

long. One such on a great stele dedicated to the Prince of Qi or Han Shizhong (1089-1151), a Song Dynasty general famous for his resistance against northern invaders, has a total of over 13,900 characters, the longest ever found on any tombstone.

Other tombstones carry no inscriptions at all. A typical one, and also the best known, is the tall stele standing at the front of Qianling Mausoleum in Shaanxi Province. The crown of the stele is carved in the shape of several intertwining dragons, and the sides are decorated with cloud-and-dragon patterns, but there are no words engraved on the face. This is the monument that Empress Wu Zetian (624-705, reigned 690-705) erected for herself. She refrained from singing her own praises, but preferred to leave it for later generations to appraise her merits and faults.

Inscriptions are bound to reflect the age in which they are written. Though the practice of erecting tombstones is as a whole falling into desuetude in New China, the few that have been built are completely new in content and form.

Towering aloft in Tian'anmen Square is the Monument to the People's Heroes. Its face is engraved with eight big characters, gilded and written in the hand of the late Chairman Mao Zedong, reading: "Eternal Glory to the People's Heroes". At the back is a memorial article authored also by Mao but written out by the late Premier Zhou Enlai. The stele is different from all tombstones of past ages.

It is a tombstone without a tomb, but a monument dedicated to all the heroes who have laid down their lives for the cause of the Chinese people. The monument is over 37 metres tall, and its pedestal, decorated on four sides with 10 sculptures carved in bas-relief on its white marble, is closed in by double-tiered marble balustrades. Simple and magnificent, it is also the grandest stele that China has ever built.

To bury a tablet with the dead person was an established practice among the people in old times. The tablet served a similar purpose as the tombstone but, being buried underground, could be preserved much longer.

There seemed to be no fixed form for the *muzhi* (buried tablet) at the beginning. Some were square at the bottom but round on top, rather like usual tombstones, but most are square. The earliest *muzhi* ever brought to light in China is the one Jia Wuzhong buried for his dead wife Ma Jiang in A.D. 106 during the Eastern Han. It is 46 cm high, 58.5 cm across and made of coarse stone, but the engraved text gives a rather detailed description of the dead woman. It is considered an archaeological treasure for its great antiquity.

During the Sui and Tang dynasties (6th to 10th century), the *muzhi* became finalized in form. As a rule, it consists of two square slabs of identical dimensions, placed one on top of the other. The top piece bears the name, native place and rank of the deceased, while the bottom one his epitaph or biographical account. Incidentally, the epitaph often written in rhyming prose, is also called *muzhi* or *muzhiming*. Occasionally, the top stone is sculpted in the shape of a tortoise with its head and legs stuck out and the name of the dead carved on its back.

A set of two buried tablets was unearthed in Shaanxi Province in 1971. It belonged to Yuchi Jingde (585-658), a famed general who helped found the Tang Dynasty. Both pieces, well preserved and finely carved out of smooth, finegrained stone, are square in shape, each measuring 1.2 × 1.2 metres with a thickness of 25 centimetres — the largest of such tablets ever unearthed.

Tombstones and buried tablets with their inscriptions, as part of the country's cultural legacy, are an important help to the study of various subjects — history, ancient geography, development of the Chinese script, the art of calligraphy and of course the dead themselves if they were important figures in their lifetime.

Picture of the Ultimate and the Eight Diagrams (太极八卦图 *Taiji Bagua Tu*)

The picture is a composite of the Ultimate and the Eight Diagrams, and is found even now in some Chinese temples. The picture of the Ultimate consists of a black and a white fish—also called the *yin* and *yang* fish. The picture of the Eight Diagrams is an octagon formed of eight combinations of three whole or broken lines.

☰ (乾) *qian*, sky
☷ (坤) *kun*, earth
☳ (震) *zhen*, thunder
☴ (巽) *xun*, wind
☵ (坎) *kan*, water
☲ (离) *li*, fire
☶ (艮) *gen*, mountain
☱ (兑) *dui*, lake

According to legend, the picture was created by Fuxi, an ancient Chinese sage.It is written in the ancient book *Zhou Yi* (The *Zhou* Book of Changes) that "Changes originate in the Ultimate; from the Ultimate issue the two spheres. From the two spheres issue the four elements, and from the four elements the eight diagrams". That was the basic theory of the Ultimate giving rise to the eight diagrams. By the Ultimate, the ancient meant the origin of all things and creatures.The philosopher Zhu Xi (1130-1200) of the Southern Song Dynasty said, "The Ultimate is the way of all things in heaven and earth". The two spheres refer to heaven and earth, or *yin*(feminine, negative) and *yang* (masculine, positive). The four elements are metal, wood, water and fire, which are everywhere. The eight diagrams symbolize the eight natural phenomena:sky, earth, thunder, wind, water, fire, mountain and lake. So the picture represented the ancient Chinese's earliest knowledge of the universe, which contained a simple dialectical materialist point of view.

What is more interesting is the picture of the Eight Diagrams, which are formed of *yao* (lines), namely, the *yangyao* (male line, whole line written as—) and the *yinyao* (female line, a broken line written as--.) The two forms are contradictory opposites and they form the eight combinations.

By taking two of them or doubling them, 64 combinations can be made.

It has been suggested that the German mathematician Wilhelm von Leibuiz (1646-1716) was inspired by the Chinese Eight Diagrams to create the binary system. If this was true, then the Chinese picture of the Ultimate and the Eight Diagrams made some historic contribution to the modern computer science.

In the early 1930's the Chinese scholar Liu Zihua, 27 years of age who was in France on a work-study basis, used the Eight Diagrams, without recourse to Newton's theory of gravity, to forecast the existence of the tenth planet of the solar system, and wrote a thesis entitled "The Eight Diagrams Theory of the Universe and Modern Astronomy", which won him the French national doctorate in 1938 and thrilled the world astronomist profession.

The Chinese picture of the Ultimate and the Eight Diagrams is still being studied by some Western scholars as a source of ancient science. It is certainly an important heritage of Chinese science and culture, though at times it was used for divination and other superstitious activities.

Sealing Clay

(封泥 *Fengni*)

In ancient China official and private documents were inscribed on bamboo or wooden slips. Before these documents were announced the slips were bound with a piece of thread and sealed with clay. The sealing clay was imprinted with the impression of an official or private seal to prevent illegal opening. The clay-sealing method, which was also used for the shipping of goods, gradually fell into oblivion with the invention of paper and silk fabrics. Since clay sealing was first discovered by historians in the late Qing Dynasty (1616-1911), it has commanded the attention of epigraphers and collectors. For archaeologists it makes excellent material for the study of history and ancient epigraphy and calligraphy.

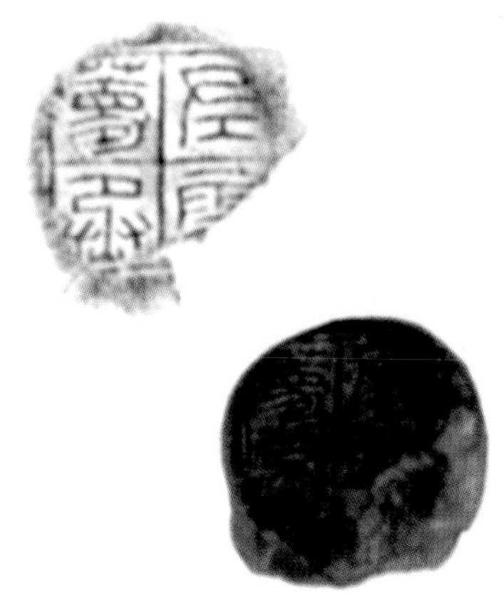

The Beijing Museum of Ancient Ceramic Civilization's collection of more than 1,000 pieces of sealing clay of the Qin Dynasty (221-206 BC) has been regarded as an archive for the study of the origin of the political system of ancient China.

Bi and *Cong*— Ancient Jade Carvings

(璧与琮 *Bi yu Cong*)

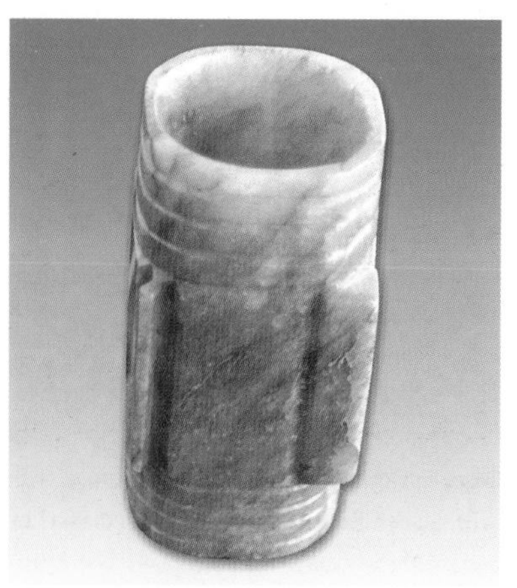

Bi and *cong* are both objects of art fashioned out of jade in ancient times. As symbols of good luck and the blue sky, they were used by aristocrats as ritual objects when attending audiences with the emperor, religious functions and funerals. Most often found in the tombs of the Shang, Zhou and Han dynasties, they also were used as jewellery.

Bi is a round flat piece of jade with a round hole in the middle. In 1936, 24 pieces of *bi* and 33 pieces of *cong* were unearthed from Tomb No.3 at Liangzhu Town of

Yuhang, Zhejiang Province.

Cong is a rectangular piece of jade with a round hollow to accentuate the ancient Chinese theory that heaven is round and earth square. During the Shang and Zhou dynasties, *cong* was a fashionable talisman of good luck which served as a ritual object for worshipping heaven and earth. When it was used as a burial object, it was placed on the deceasedís head and feet or around it.

Tally

(符 *Fu*)

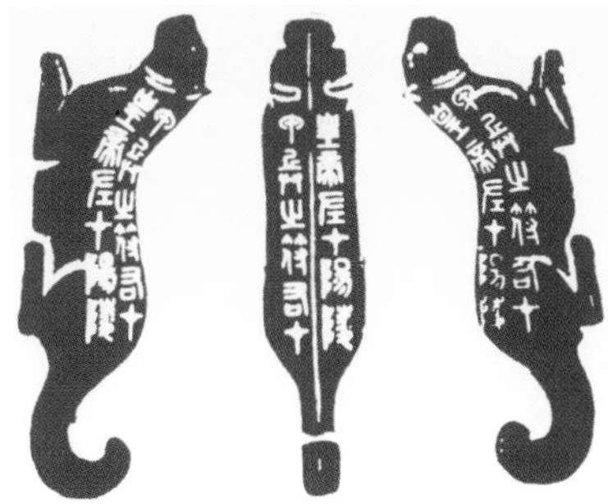

Fu, or tally, was a kind of talisman in ancient China. Before paper was invented in China, tallies were made from bamboo or wood. A tally consists of two pieces and is used to a general as imperial authorization for troop movement or other schemes. Among the populace, the tally was used as proof of authorization for exchanges of goods or leases.

In ancient China the official tally was made of gold, silver, jade or bronze in the shape of tiger, dragon, human figure, turtle, snake, fish, etc. Most of them, however, appear in the shape of a tiger. The "tiger tally" was used by an emperor for delegating his generals with the power to command and dispatch the army. A tiger tally is inscribed with a text on its back and consists of two parts, with the right part retained in the central government and the left part issued to a local official or a commander. Only when the tally was authenticated could the authorization take effect, a practice which was fashionable during the Warring States, Qin and Han periods.

To fashion a tally in the image of a tiger was also meant to indicate that with the emperor's authorization, the command should act as promptly and courageously as a tiger. By tradition the Chinese regard the tiger as a symbol of valour. Even today a crack force in the army is likely to be named "Flying Tiger Detachment". It is thus understandable for our ancients to use the tiger tally for the manoeuvring of soldiers.

Jade Clothes Sewn with Gold Thread (金缕玉衣 *Jinlüyuyi*)

According to an ancient Chinese belief, when a man had put on clothes made of jade pieces sewn together with gold thread when he died, his remains would never go rotten.

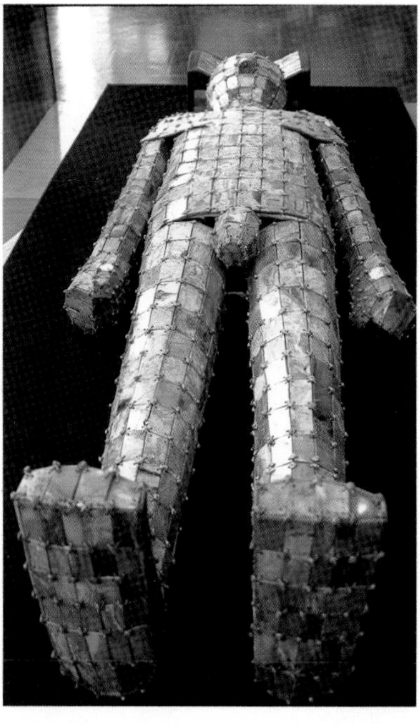

In 1968, Chinese archaeologists working in Mancheng, Hebei Province, found such clothes in a tomb buried with the remains of Liu Sheng, a princes of the Western Han Dynasty, and those of his wife, Dou Pass. Only a few teeth and a pile of bones were left of the remains, the jade clothes remained intact. Liu's clothes were made of a total of 2,498 pieces of jade, sewn together with lengths of thread that is 96 percent gold, 4 to 5 cm in length and 0.35-0.5 mm in diameter. There were also soft and sturdy gold ropes made by twisting 12 pieces of gold thread 0.08-0.13 mm in diameter. It took about 1,100 grams of gold to put Liu's clothes together. His wife's clothes were fashioned out of 2,160 pieces of jade and sewn with 700 grams of gold. Judging from the technology of today, it takes an entire decade for an artisan to finishing making such piece of jade clothes.

Bronze Ware

(青铜器 *Qingtongqi*)

The bronze ware were unique national treasures for China in ancient times for their impressive designs, classical decorative ornamentation, and wealth of inscriptions.

The ancient Chinese society fell into the Stone Tool Age and the Iron Tool Age. The earliest stoneware in China was found in 3000 B.C. The Shang and Zhou dynasties ushered China into the height of the Bronze Age. During this period the making of bronze ware reached its zenith. After the Spring and Autumn and Warring States periods China entered the Iron Tool Age.

Bronze is the alloy of copper and zinc or copper and lead that is bluish grey. The museums across China and some important museums outside China, have all collected Chinese bronze ware dating back to the Shang and Zhou dynasties. Some of them are part of the cultural heritage passed down through the generations, but most of them were dug up from underneath the earth.

Ancient Chinese bronze ware fall into three types: ritual vessels, weapons, and miscellaneous objects.

Ritual vessels refer to those objects employed by aristocrats in sacrificial ceremonies or audiences. Therefore there is something distinctively religious and shamanist about them. These vessels include food containers, wine vessels, water pots and musical instruments.

Bronze weapons come in such varieties as knife, sword, spear, halberd, axe, and dagger.

The miscellaneous objects refer to bronze utensils for daily use.

In ancient China the making of bronze ware was dominated by the imperial families and aristocrats. And the possession of such wares was regarded as a status symbol.

In comparison with counterparts in other parts of the world, the Chinese bronze ware stand out for their inscriptions which are regarded as major chapters in the Chinese history of calligraphy.

Ancient Coins (古币 *Gubi*)

The currency is a medium for the exchange of commodities; it was the inevitable outcome of such exchanges. In ancient China the currency came in different forms and was made variously from shells, jade, gold, silver, and paper. The following is a brief introduction to ancient coins in China.

Shell money. Shell money was the oldest form of currency in ancient China. As the shells were small and hard in texture, they came in handy as money. By the Shang and Zhou dynasties the use of shell money reached its zenith, and shell money became a symbol of wealth. Even today the Chinese like to call their most valuable objects "*baobei*", which is derived from the name of the Chinese shell money. In ancient China it was not uncommon to use shell money as burial objects.

Hoe-like Money. The hoe-like money was evolved from an ancient Chinese farming tool. In the early days it bore close resemblance to a hoe. Because the hoe is

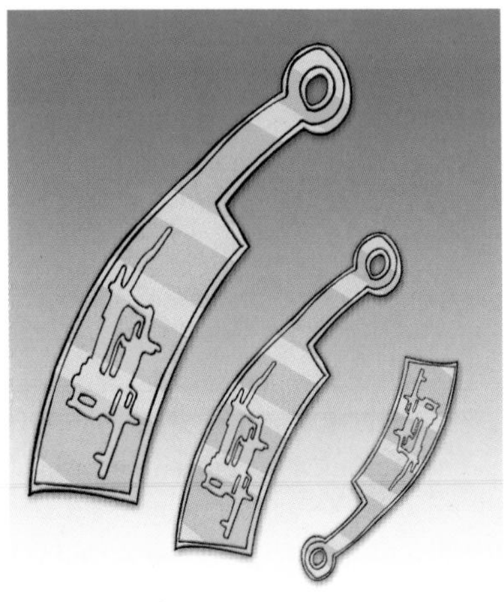

similar to the shovel. This is why the hoe-like money is also known as "shovel money".

Bronze money in the design of seashells. With the development of commodity exchange, the supply of natural shells as the currency ran out of supply. Imitation shell money made from stone, bone, ceramics and bronze was thus invented to make up for the shortage. But eventually it was bronze shell-shaped money that replaced natural shells. It was not until Qinshihuang unified the currency in 221 B.C. that shells finally were withdrawn from commodity circulation.

Knife-shaped money. Cast of bronze during the Spring and Autumn and Warring States periods, the money's knife-like shape was derived from a certain weapon from old days.

Bronze coin with a square hole in the centre. In the late Warring States Period, bronze coins with a round hole in the centre first appeared in china. The hole made it convenient to string the coins together. When Qinshihuang unified the nation and the currency, he had the round hole in the bronze coins changed into a square, as the round coin and its square hole is regarded as a reflection of the ancient theory that "heaven is round and earth square". Feudalism lasted for more than 2,000 years, however, despite the change of times and the currency, the round bronze coins with a square hole in the centre was in use for roughly the same duration. It was after the demise of the Qing Dynasty that they were gradually replaced with paper money.

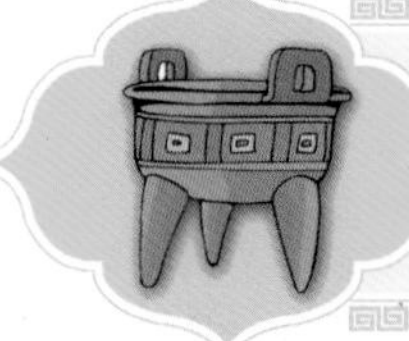

Hitching Post
(拴马桩 *Shuanma Zhuang*)

China has been a major agricultural country since ancient times. The use of horses as farm implements and means of transportation gave rise to hitching posts. The hitching posts of early days were made from timber. But are left to this day are mostly those made of stone during the Ming and Qing dynasties. Today, the hitching posts have long lost its practical value, but their artistic value is becoming increasingly appreciated.

The art of the hitching posts finds expression in the carving of the capital and neck of such a post. Round sculpture is integrated with relief and linear carving, and the motifs run the gamut from the Sakyamuni cult and Confucius preaching his doctrines to Lao Zi riding a buffalo, the Eight Immortals of Taoism, and the duke of Zhuang consulting some wise men. There are also such auspicious animals and plants as lions, unicorns, magpies, sweet-scented osmanthus, glossy ganoderma, and celestial grass. These motifs are mostly derived from historical tales, folk legends, celebrations and festivals, and traditional operas.

The hitching posts, besides their practical purpose for lassoing draft animals, also served to show off the prosperity of a family in old days. Some of them stand as tall as 3 metres—they were obviously not for hitching horses but served as symbols of a family's social status and cultural attainment.

THINGS CHINESE 中国风物

Folk Arts

民间工艺

Embroidery

(刺绣 *Cixiu*)

Embroidery, a folk art with a long tradition, occupies an important position in the history of Chinese arts and crafts. It is, in its long development, inseparable from silkworm-raising and silk-reeling and weaving.

China is the first country in the world that discovered the use of silk. Silkworms were domesticated as early as 5,000 years ago. The production of silk thread and fabrics gave rise to the art of embroidery. According to the classical *Shangshu* (or *Book of History*), the "regulations on costumes" of 4,000 years ago stipulated among other things "dresses and skirts with designs and embroideries". This is evidence that embroidery had become an established art by that remote time.

In 1958 a piece of silk was found in a tomb of the state of Chu of the Warring States Periond (475-221 B.C.). It is embroidered with a dragon-and-phoenix design. More than 2,000 years old, it is the earliest piece of Chinese embroidery ever unearthed.

The art became widespread during the Han Dynasty (206 B.C.-220 A.D.); many embroidered finds date back to that period.

Today, silk embroidery is practised nearly all over China. The best commercial products, it is generally agreed, come from four provinces: Jiangsu (notably Suzhou), Hunan, Sichuan and Guangdong, each with its distinctive features.

Embroidered works have become highly complex and exquisite today . Take the double-face embroidered "Cat", a representative work of Suzhou embroidery, for example. The artist splits the hair-thin coloured silk thread into filaments—half, quarter, 1/12 or even 1/48 of its original thickness — and uses these in embroidering concealing in the process the thousands

of ends and joints and making them disappear as if by magic. The finished work is a cute and mischievous-looking cat on both sides of the groundwork. The most difficult part of the job is the eyes of the cat. To give them lustre and life, silk filaments of more than 20 colours or shades have to be used.

Recently, on the basis of two-face embroidery have developed further innovations — the same design on both sides in different colours, and totally different patterns on the two faces of the same groundwork. It seems that possibilities hitherto unknown to the art may yet be explored.

Hair Embroidery

(发绣 *Faxiu*)

Hair embroidery, a traditional Chinese art, is a special needle-work of making patterns on silk with human hair as the thread. As Chinese hair is mostly black, it used to be known also as *moxiu* ("black ink" embroidery).

Today the art excels by far its past attainment in colour and in variety. The colour is no longer limited to black. Others —blonde, amber, auburn, white and grey — of various shades are also used, totalling dozens of tones, mostly collected from areas of ethnic minorities. Occasionally, to give the lips of an ancient beauty their usual rosiness, white hair may be dyed red. But on the whole, pictures embroidered with hair are in its natural hues.

To work with human hair is more difficult than with silk thread, for compared with the latter Chinese hair is stiff, slippery and brittle, breaking easily when stretched with exertion. It requires a well-trained skill but it is also rewarding in the end-product, which is elegantly neat, erosion-free, worm-resistant and fast in colour.

Tapestry Weaving

(缂丝或刻丝 *Kesi*)

Kesi is a special type of weaving peculiar to China. It is different from embroidery but rather similar to the making of tapestry.

It is done on a wooden handloom with raw silk as the warp and boiled-off silk as the weft. The weft threads are usually of dozens of colours and are separately reeled in many small shuttles. First the artisan makes on the warp a sketchy drawing of the pattern to be woven and then guides a shuttle with the weft thread of a specified colour across the warp threads — almost never throughout the entire width but only where that particular colour is needed. So, this is a form of weaving patch by patch. One could also say it represents an integration of the skills of silk-weaving and painting. It is necessary to make frequent changes of the shuttles (i.e. threads of different colours), and a small piece of work requires thousands of changes to finish.

The completed piece shows the design neatly and in equal exquisiteness on both sides.

The art has its beginnings in the Han and Wei dynasties but blossomed during the Song (960-1279), producing a great master in Zhu Kerou. The *Picture of Ducklings in Lotus Pond* woven by him, now kept in the Shanghai Museum, is considered a national treasure. The art of *kesi* was introduced to Japan during the Ming Dynasty (1368-1644). The belt for the Japanese kimono,which is woven in this way, is still called by the Japanese "Chinese Ming decorative belt".

Jade Carving

(玉雕 *Yudiao*)

Jade is loosely understood in China as the collective name for most precious stones, and jade carving in this sense constitutes an important part of Chinese arts and crafts. The love of jade ware, according to Dr. Joseph Needham, the noted British naturalist, has been one of the cultural features of China. Crude jade tools have been fornd among the archaeological finds dating back to the New Stone Age. There is, however, no evidence to indicate that neolithic people attached a great value to jade ware; they chose jade only because it was hard and good for making tools and fighting weapons. As time went on, people came gradually to appreciate the beauty of the stone, which after carving and polishing might be turned into things not only useful but also nice to look at.

In the historical epoch during which the slave society was replaced by the feudal society, jade ware became established as objects of pure decoration. Among the funerary objects unearthed from tombs of that long period are many jade articles used as personal ornaments or ceremonial vessels. The jade exhibits one sees today in museums of the country normally comprise vases, incense-burners, tripods, cups and wine vessels of various descriptions.

Large-sized jade articles began to appear in the middle of Chinese feudalism. There is today in the Round City of the Beihai Park a large jade jar the size of a small bathtub. It was used as a wine container by the Yuan Emperor Kublai Khan when he feted his followers. The 3.5-ton jar may hold as much as 3,000 litres of wine. It has a circumference of 493 cm and measures 70 cm high and 55 cm deep in the middle. The elliptic jar is well-shaped and engraved all round with clouds, waves, dragons and sea horses. It is the oldest jade object of a large size kept intact in the

country.

Another large piece worth mentioning is a jade sculpture dating from the reign of Qianlong in the 18th century. Entitled "Jade Mountain Showing the Great Yu Taming the Flood", it was sculpted after a Song Dynasty painting of a similar title. The masterpiece, standing 2.4 metres high and about 1 metre wide, depicts in vivid detail how the Great Yu, a heroic representative of the ancient working people, fought the Great Flood. According to historical records, the uncut jadestone, weighing more than 5 tons, was discovered in Hotan area, Xinjiang, took three years to be transported over the distance of 4,000 kilometres to Beijing, and some more years to be carved and polished into the national treasure that it is .

"There is a price for gold but no price for jade", says a Chinese proverb. Jade ware is often described as "worth a string of towns". An ancient story tells how King Zhao of Qin once offered 15 towns in exchange for the famous Ho's round jade. How is it that jade is so valuable?

First, its value lies in its scarcity. Precious stones are formed over long geological epochs and are hard to get, especially green jade, white jade and agate. Ancient people on a treasure hunt had to trek on the back of yaks in mountainous regions to get at the unhewn rocks containing the gems, exposed or half exposed, by the stamping of the animal's hoofs. Sometimes, precious stones were washed down by mountain torrents and were got hold of midway by men with the eye and luck. In any event, exposed stones grew scarce and people began to bore through the mountains to mine for precious stones, making them even more difficult to get.

Secondly, the value of jade lies in its hardness. Precious stones are divided by their hardness into two major groups: jadeites and nephrites. Jadeites are the ones with a solid texture and a hardness of degree 6 or above (on the basis of 10 for diamond). The more valuable varieties, such as green jade, may be as hard as degree 8 or 9. Jadeites are invulnerable to

steel cutting tools made of carbonrundum of diamond powder. Objects made of this hard jade are smooth, lustrous, glittering and translucent, and their grains are no longer visible to the naked eye.

Nephrites, on the other hand, being below degree 6 in hardness, can generally be incised and carved by burins. Their commercial values are much lower than jadeites.

Thirdly, the value of precious stones lies in their natural colour and hue. Some are as white as snow, others are brightly red, and still others alluringly green. Diamond, emerald, saphire and other gemstones can be processed into personal ornaments like rings and earrings whose colour will remain brilliant all the time. Some stones carry an array of colours which a master artisan can use to good effect. Even flaws in the stone can be turned into "beauty spots", for instance, an insect on a flower or a small squirrel on a tree, adding life and attraction to the entire piece of work.

Today there are jade workshops or factories in all major cities. Work which used to be done purely by hand has been partially mechanized. Although some operations have become faster with the use of simple machines, yet jade carving remains basically a handicraft art. And as raw materials are getting more and more scarce, the prices of jade ware will always be on the upward trend.

The Luminous Cup

(夜光杯 *Yeguangbei*)

Yeguangbei (literally, the night-glittering cup) is a special jade product of Jiuquan, Gansu Province.

Since very ancient times, the Qilian Mountains of Gansu have produced a beautiful jade of brilliant white, green, black and yellow colours. Local artisans grind and polish it into wine cups either of a pure colour or of mixed colours. They are of various forms, wine cups with stems, flat-bottomed cups, and cups with cut designs, all marked by a simple and elegant taste. They are all the more cherished because they stand sudden contact with extreme heat or cold.

Legend says that King Mu (c.10th century B.C.) of the Zhou Dynasty once drank with this cup and found it glittering snow-white in the moonlight. It was then named the "night-glittering cup". It became more famous after the Tang Dynasty poet Wang Han sang of it in the following lines:

Grape wine in luminous cups shine.
As we raise them to lips the pipa strikes

up fast.

Laugh not if we fall drunk on the battlefield.

Tell us how many ever returned from the war.

Jiuquan has today a well-established factory specializing in the making of such "luminous cups". Nowadays visitors to the town, apart from seeing Jiayuguan Pass, the western end of the Great Wall, all wish to make a tour of this factory, buying a few cups as a souvenir.

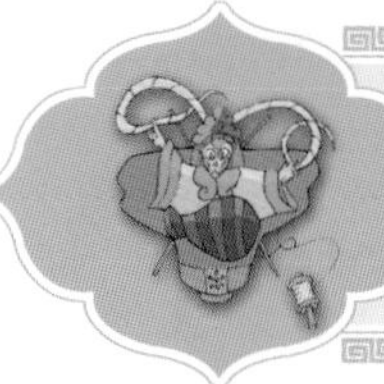

Ivory Carving

(牙雕 *Yadiao*)

Ivory scuptrue is an old art in China dating back to prehistoric times. From the ruins of the Yin Dynasty capital of 3,700 years ago knives and rulers made of ivory have been unearthed. *The Record of the Warring States*, a history written 20 centuries ago, tells of Mengchang, an aristocrat of the State of Qi, who "left his homeland for a tour abroad and, when he arrived in the state of Chu, presented an ivory bed...The bed was worth a thousand pieces of gold; the slightest damage would ruin the man who had to compensate for it."

As an art, ivory carving calls for meticulous care. The varying shapes and sizes and the position of hard core of the tusks must be taken into careful consideration together with the carver's own specialties, when he conceives the work he is going to produce. Normally, he will first hew out a rough shape before using his finer tools for the final chiseling and polishing of detail. For larger jobs a clay model will be moulded and found to be satisfactory before the ivory is worked on. A very large and complex piece of work comprises a number of parts sculptured separately and then assembled.

The Beijing Arts and Crafts Factory turned out in 1974 a large ivory sculpture entitled "The Chengdu-Kunming Railway". Measuring 180 cm long, 64 cm wide and 110 cm high (including the base) and weighing 318 kilograms, it took 5,000 work-days to complete. Rich in national flavour, it was presented to the United Nations Headquarters.

A gem in the art of ivory carving is the "latticed balls within balls", which has a history of barely a hundred years. To create this marvel, the master craftsman first shapes a piece of ivory into a perfect spherical ball and then bores through it at suitable intervals several conical holes, whose apexes meet exactly at the centre of the ball. Next, he marks the inside of each hole with lines to indicate the number of balls to be cut out. Only now is he ready to cut the balls of different layers, starting with the innermost. In spite of the holes, he cannot see anything but have to work by feels, relying on his years of experience and on a fine carver with a curved blade. The rest of the balls are cut out and carved successively from the inside out. Throughout the whole operation, any hair-thin mistake would ruin the entire work of art.

Up to the time of writing, the most complicated "latticed balls within balls" has been produced by the Daxin Ivory Factory of Guangzhou. Weng Rongbiao, a veteran master craftsman there, cut in 1977, out of an ivory block 15 cm across, a set of 42 latticed balls — one inside another, each ball movable inside its larger sphere and bearing pierced work of landscapes (pavilions and towers, clouds and mountains). And the innermost ball is as thin as paper!

Weng Rongbiao is from a family of four generations of ivory-ball carvers. As early as 1915, his father won international recognition at the International Fair in Panama with a set of "25 latticed balls within balls" carved out of ivory.

Microscopic Carving

(微雕 *Weidiao*)

The art of micro-carving refers generally to the engraving of infinitesimal characters on ivory or human hair. The artist engaged in this unique craft, when he applies the graver, cannot see the work he is doing but has to rely on feel.The art is therefore sometimes described as "carving by one's will".

There are in many cities of China such microsculptors, who can engrave on small grains of ivory poems, paintings and miniature seal marks in no less than 10 different colours.

Zhang Yunhu, a micro-callingrapher of Shanghai, on a piece of ivory 3 cm square, reproduced the whole anthology of *The Three Hundred Tang Poems*, totalling more than 10,000 characters. To the naked eye, the words are just rows upon rows of black needlepoint etchings.

In 1982, he came out with another marvel — the complete text in 14,000 characters of the *Constitution of the Chinese Communist Party* on a chip of ivory 2.8 cm square. This he did only in two weeks. Viewed under a microscope with a magnification of 100, the characters can be seen to be composed of elegant, clear and fine strokes.

Micro-carving on human hair is a new art developed only in recent years, being pioneered by Shen Weizhong, a member of the Suzhou Arts and Crafts Research Institute. On a hair several mm long and without the help of any magnifying apparatus, the artist can engrave poems or other texts by relying upon the feel of his fingers. To achieve this, he needs an absolutely quiet environment, in which, holding his breath and controlling his pulse by meditative power, he plies his art with a cutting wire thinner than the hair. To read the surprisingly neat characters on the finished work, it is necessary to magnify them several dozen times with a microscope.

Hair carving has been developed on the basis of fine-character carving, which has always been a Chinese tradition. Its rudiments may be traced back to more than 2,000 years ago. On the fragments of oracle bones of the Western Zhou period, unearthed in Guyuan, Shaanxi Province, have been found small carved characters the size of rice grains with hair-thin strokes. Archaeologists have also found on the much earlier Yin oracle shells miniature engravings the size of millet, legible only under 5-fold magnification.

Artists of today with their assiduous study and experiment have given the age-old art a new lustre.

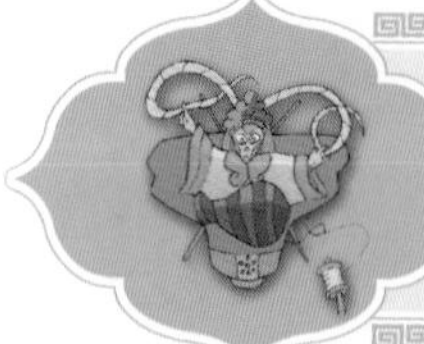

Clay Figurines

(泥人 *Niren*)

Clay figurines represent another type of folk art in China. They are much liked for their vivid and amusing expressions and, for this reason, make good indoor decorations and welcome presents between friends.

The principal material for making these figurines is porcelain clay. Though

this is found in most localities of China, the best is supposed to be that at Huishan Mountain, Wuxi. Normally, when people talk about clay figurines in China, they tend to think of those made at Huishan. Indeed, the earth from the paddy fields of the surrounding area is very fine and sticky, containing little sand. Moulded into figurines, it needs no firing but, after being dried in the shade for 3 or 4 days, is ready to be painted on. The finished products are very durable and will not crack in many years to come. A piece of work takes about half a day to complete, depending on the size and complexity.

The moulding of clay figures in China seems to have come from a long tradition. It is said that Sun Bin, famed strategist of the state of Qi who lived in the 4th to 3rd century B.C. during the Warring States period, in order to break an enemy formation, used clay figures for mock exercises. Because of this legend, Sun Bin has been regarded as the founder of the craft. Legend aside, the art can be traced in written history at least 400 years back to the Ming Dynasty. It was an age when Buddhism flourished in China, and an increasing number of pilgrims came to visit the temples on Huishan Mountain. In the vicinities of the hill began to appear handicraftsmen who hand moulded clay into images of the Goddess of Mercy, the God of Longevity and other deities to be sold to the visitors. Later on, the subjects became expanded to include toys, dramatic and everyday characters, plump babies and clownish figures. The clay figurines were sold as they were moulded, and many shops thrived on them.

Sharing the fame with Huishan in this field is a family in the northern port city of Tianjin. *Niren Zhang* (the Zhang family of clay figurine moulders) has been in the trade for four generations. They specialize in figures of popular tales and classical novels and are renowned for the drama and life they give their creations. They have also portrayed in clay men in various trades at different times, reflecting social life as genre paintings do. The family, regarded as a pride of the city of Tianjin, is also known abroad.

The God of Longevity (老寿星 *Laoshouxing*)

The God of Longevity, better known as *Laoshouxing* in the country, is a favourite subject with the Huishan clay figurine moulders of Wuxi. His image is also frequently seen in ivory and porcelain objects of art.

The god, created out of the human wish to live a long life, is distinguished by an abnormally large, protruding and deeplined forehead, white beard, long eyebrows, broad nose, square mouth with thick lips, and three holes in each ear. He is said to have lived a long time ago, being a man tranquil in nature and good at self-cultivation by meditation, knowing how to keep free from all cares and worries and to follow the course of nature in everything. For this reason, he lived a long life. According to legend, he showed no signs of ageing in his 767th year and ,when reaching the age of 800, he complained that he had not lived long enough. Later generations have made him the symbol of longevity, and well-wishers have often given a picture or a statue of him as a birthday present.

A colourful statue of *Laoshouxing* stands at the door of the reception room of the Huishan Clay Figurine Factory, Wuxi. As a clay figure, it is of a good size, being 1.10 metres tall and 60 centimetres across and moulded out of 300 kilograms of wet clay. When you visit the factory, he will most probably be still there, wishing you a long life with his characteristic smile.

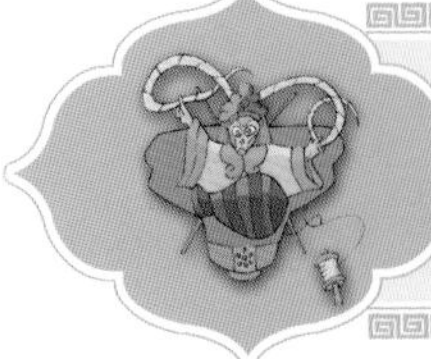

Dough Figurines

(面塑 *Miansu*)

Sculpture with dough is a folk art known to few countries, if any outside China.

It is interesting to see how a few coloured pieces of dough are turned in a matter of minutes into expressive and lively figurines by the trained hands of a folk artist, relying on no model. The figurines are generally about 8 centimetres (3 inches) tall, but recent innovations include figures as tall as 30 centimetres or tiny enough to be displayed in half a walnut shell.

The folk sculptor plies his trade with very simple tools:a spatula, scissors,a comb and a pointed stick, all of diminutive sizes.

The material used by him is prepared of two-thirds purified wheat flour and one-third glutinous rice flour. Mixed with water, the dough is kneaded well while bee-honey and glycerine are added. Cooked in a steamer under cover for half an hour, it will be ready for moulding. Other additives in the dough are a little antiseptic and repellent to make the finished figurines durable. The various colours in the dough are from mineral pigments that do not change with time.

Although the art has a history of some 2,000 years, few people specialize in today. Nevertheless, the works produced by the limited number of dough sculptors in the arts and crafts factories of Jinan, Shanghai and Beijing have aroused considerable interest in the collectors of China and abroad.

Ice Carving

(冰雕 *Bingdiao*)

Ice carving, a seasonal art in the far north of China, is also called "ice lanterns" and has its origin in local life. To prevent lights from being blown out by the winter wind, people started long, long ago to use hollowed ice blocks as lantern bulbs, giving the art its primitive form.

The citizens of Harbin, capital of the northernmost Heilongjiang Province, put on the first "ice lantern show" in the winter of 1963. By means of moulds they made various ice lanterns, in which they lighted candles. It proved a success and established a custom: since then an "ice festival" has been held every year lasting from New Year's Day to the traditional Lantern Festival (about mid-February), with the scale growing ever larger and the skills more and more perfected. Apart from the usual lanterns, pavilions, terraces, bridges and towers are built in ice to decorate the landscapes formed by sparkling mountains, crystal trees, glistening birds and animals, fish swimming in transparent pools...Ice sculpture is also found to be an artistic form suitable for reproducing scenes of well-known dramas and stories of science fiction often seen at the festival. Some works are of colossal dimensions: a pagoda may be built of up to 200 huge ice blocks, and it makes an impressive sight when lighted at night by hundreds of built-in coloured lamps. The ice show, with its translucent works and

sparkling lights, reminds visitors of the fabled emerald and crystal palace of the legendary Dragon King.

The main material for ice sculpture is obtained from the rivers. With the mercury constantly kept down at minus 20℃-30℃ in winter, the waters in the north provide an inexhaustible supply of ice.It is first sawn by workmen into blocks, and then the sculptors will put them to different uses according to thickness, strength and transparency. A large work is usually assembled of many component pieces.

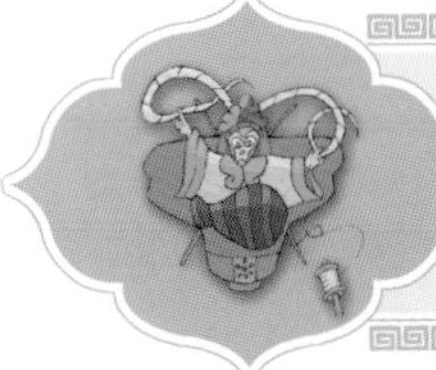

Butter Sculpture (酥油花 *Suyouhua*)

There is a special custom, among the Tibetans in Qinghai and Tibet, of making butter sculptures in winter. It is an art of moulding butter into various forms—human figures, flowers, fancy buildings, birds and beasts — to present certain scenes or depict popular episodes in Buddha's life.

The butter is made from yak or goat milk, suitable for moulding because it is snow-white, fine, soft and pliable, and mixes well with pigments.

Butter sculpture has a long history behind it. When Princess Wencheng of the Tang Dynasty was married in A.D. 641 to Songzan Gambo, leader of the Tibetan people, she took with her a gold statue of Sakyamuni, which was later enshrined in Jokhang Monastery in Lhasa. Several hundred years later, Tsong Kha-pa (1357-1419), founder of the Yellow Sect of Lamaism, offered to the statue a bouquet of flowers made of butter. This gave rise to a practice which spread to and flourished in Ta'er (Gumbum) Monastery in Tsong Kha-pa's homeland in Qinghai Province. Perfected over the years by the lamas of the monastery, the skills of fash-

ioning various figures in butter became an established art which, along with clay sculpture, mural painting and tanka embroidery, has contributed to the fame of the monastery.

A festival starting from the 15th day of the lunar New Year is held annunally at the monastery, displaying, besides paintings and embroideries, large numbers of coloured butter sculptures, attracting huge crowds of Tibetan and Han visitors.

As butter melts in heat, the craft is practised only in winter.

Lacquerware

(漆器 *Qiqi*)

Lacquer is a natural substance obtained from the lacquer tree which has its home in China, a country still leading the world in lacquer resources. Much of the country is suitable for growing the tree, but most of the output comes from five provinces —Shaanxi, Hubei, Sichuan, Guizhou and Yunnan.

Raw lacquer is the sap of the lacquer tree, which hardens in contact with air. A tree becomes productive 3-5 years after planting, and entails hard work on the part of the tapper. He can only get the latex in June and July each year and must tap it in the pre-dawn hours before the cockís crow and sunrise. For the sun would reduce the moisture in the air, stopping the flow of the latex.

Lacquerware has a long history which extends back to the remote ages in China. From the neolithic remains at Tuanjie Village and Meiyan Township (both in Wujiang County, Jiangsu Province) were unearthed in 1955 a number of lacquer-painted black pottery objects, two of which, a cup and a pot, were discovered intact and found to bear patterns painted in lacquer after the objects had been fired.They are the earliest lacquered articles ever discovered in China and are now kept in the Museum of Nanjing.

Before the invention of the Chinese ink, lacquer had been used for writing. Twenty-eight bamboo clips found in a Warring States (475-221 B.C.) tomb at Changtaiguan, Xinyang, Henan Province, bear a list of the burial objects with the characters written in lacquer.

Lacquerware is moisture-proof, resistant to heat, acid and alkali, and its colour and lustre are highly durable, adding beauty to its practical use. Beijing, Fuzhou and Yangzhou are the cities leading in the production of Chinese lacquerware.

The making of Beijing lacquerware starts with a brass or wooden body. After preparation and polishing, it is coated with several dozen up to hundreds of layers of lacquer, reaching a total thickness of 5 to 18 millimetres. Then, gravers will cut into the hardened lacquer, creating "carved paintings" of landscapes, human figures, flowers and birds. It is then finished by drying and polishing. Traditional Beijing lacquer objects are in the forms of chairs, screens, tea tables, vases, etc. Emperor Qianlong of the Qing Dynasty, an enthusiast for lacquerware, had his coffin decorated with carved lacquer.

Yangzhou lacquer articles are distinguished not only by carving in relief but by exquisite patterns inlaid with gems, gold, ivory and mother of pearl. The products are normally screens, cabinets, tables, chairs, vases, trays, cups, boxes and ashtrays.

Fuzhou is well-known for the "bodiless lacquerware", one of the "Three Treasures" of Chinese arts and crafts (the other two being Beijing cloisonné and Jingdezhen porcelain).

The bodiless lacquerware starts with a body of clay, plaster or wood. Grass linen or silk is pasted onto it, layer after layer, with lacquer as the binder. The origninal body is removed after the outer cloth shell has dried in the shade. This is then smoothed with putty, polished, and coated with layers of lacquer. After being carved with colourful patterns, it becomes the bodiless lacquerware of extremely light weight and exquisite finish.

Porcelain of Jingdezhen

(景德镇瓷器 *Jingdezhen Ciqi*)

Jingdezhen, formerly spelt Ching Teh Chen and known as the "Ceramics Metropolis" of China, is a synonym for Chinese porcelain.

Variably called Xinping or Changnanzhen in history, it is situated in the northeastern part of Jiangxi Province in a small basin rich in fine kaolin, hemmed in by mountains which keep it supplied with firewood from their conifers. People there began to produce ceramics as early as 1,800 years ago in the Eastern Han Dynasty. In the Jingde Period (1004-1007), Emperor Zhenzong of Song Dynasty decreed that Changnanzhen should produce the porcelain used by the imperial court, with each inscribed at the bottom "Made in the Reign of Jingde". From then on peole began to call all chinaware bearing such in scriptions "porcelain of Jingdezhen".

The ceramic industry experienced further development at Jingdezhen during the Ming and Qing dynasties or from the 14th to the 19th century, when skills became perfected and the general quality more refined; government kilns were set up to cater exclusively to the need of the imperial house.

The leading centre of the porcelain industry, Jingdezhen has been put under state protection also as an important historical city. With 133 ancient buildings and cultural sites, it is a tourist town attracting large numbers of visitors from home and abroad.

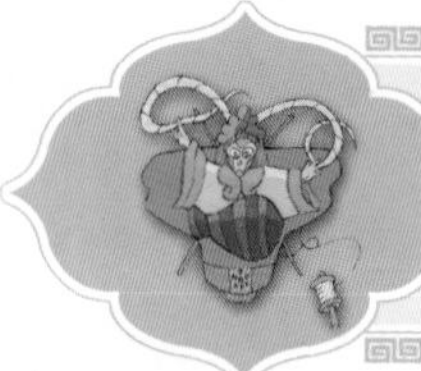

Cloisonné

(景泰蓝 *Jingtailan*)

Cloisonné, in which China excels, is known as *jingtailan* in the country. It first appeared toward the end of the Yuan Dynasty in the mid-14th century, flourished and reached its peak of development during the reign of the Ming emperor Jingtai (1450-1457). And as the objects were mostly in blue (*lan*) colour, cloisonné came to be called by its present name *jingtailan*.

A *jingtailan* article has a copper body.

The design on it is formed by copper wire stuck on with a vegetable glue. Coloured enamel is filled in with different colours kept apart by the wire strips. After being fired four or five times in a kiln, the workpiece is polished and gilded into a colourful and lustrous work of art.

During the Ming Dynasty (1368-1644), cloisonnewaré was mainly supplied for use in the imperial palace, in the form of incense-burners, vases, jars, boxes and candlesticks — all in imitation of antique porcelain and bronze.

Present-day production, with Beijing as the leading centre, stresses the adding of ornamental beauty to things that are useful. The artifacts include vases, plates, jars, boxes, tea sets, lamps, lanterns, tables, stools, drinking vessels and small articles for the desk.

A pair of big cloisonné horses have been made in recent years, each measuring 2.1 metres high and 2.4 metres long, and weighing about 700 kilograms. They took eight months to finish, involving the labour of hundreds of workers and 60 tons of coal for the firing. They represent the largest object ever made in cloisonné in the 500 years since the art was born.

Cloisonné ware bears on the surface vitreous enamal which, like porcelain, is hard but brittle, so it must not be knocked against anything hard. To remove dust from it, it should be whisked lightly with a soft cloth. Avoid heavy wiping with a wet cloth, for this might eventually wear off the gilding.

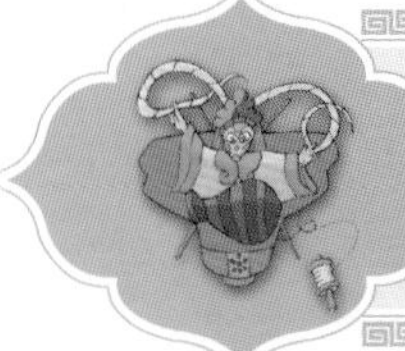

Potted Landscapes

(盆景 *Penjing*)

China is the homeland of the potted or miniature landscape. The art began about 1,200 years ago during the Tang Dynasty (618-907 A.D.) and has been known under various names. An indoor decoration of refined taste over long ages, it has been praised as "wordless poetry and sculptured painting".

The miniature landscape has become quite popular today and can be classified into two major categories: miniature rockeries and miniature trees.

The rocks used for the potted rockery are those that easily suck up water, such as sandstone, stratified rock and stalactite. A chosen piece is cut and carved into the shape of a mountain of rugged beauty, and placed in a flat pot with water. As the rock is moist, green moss grows on its surface. Some miniature tree may also be planted in a crevice of the rock, which is sometimes decorated with a little pagoda, bridge or pavillion. A tiny sail or two on the water will complete an enchanting landscape with mountain and river.

Miniature trees, the second category, are usually diminutive pines, cypresses, wintersweets, elms and bamboos which, with small leaves and thin branches, are slow in growth but vigorous in vitality. And the most valued miniature tree is made of old tree roots. They belong to trees that grow on mountain rocks in the wild. People fell the trees, leaving the roots as they are. New trees sprout and grow up and are felled again. This repeats itself but the roots remain, some as old as hundreds of years, assuming hardy and grotesque forms. Uprooted and transplanted in pots, they are further pruned and trained to have the gnarled branches of rugged grace or elegant vigour.

Potted landscapes have become a common sight in China—in parks, galleries, conference and reception rooms, even at public squares. Competitive exhibitions are held every year, and an increasing number of people are making it a pastime to introduce bits of nature in pots into their living and working quarters.

Batik

(蜡染 *Laran*)

Batik or wax printing is a folk art popular among certain ethnic minorities in Guizhou and neighbouring provinces.

It involves painstaking work but follows a rather simple process. First, beewax is melted in a bowl; then a special brass knife is used to pick up the liquid wax and make patterns with it as it hardens on the cotton cloth to be printed. The cloth is immersed completely in a jar of indigo bath so that the unwaxed parts take on colour. The dyed cloth is boiled to melt off the wax and leave clear patterns in white on a blue ground.

Batik offers ample scope for artistic imagination in the making of patterns. Those commonly seen are floral, geometric and spiral designs, but folk painters may also follow their artistic inclinations and draw flowers, birds, beasts, insects or fish. The patterns in all cases are enchantingly simple with rich local flavour.

In the process of printing, the dye penetrates fine cracks naturally formed in the solidified wax, leaving hair-thin blue lines on the undyed white designs and enhancing the charm of the end product. And as the fine lines differ, no two pieces of cloth are identical even though they may bear the same pattern.

In the ethnic areas, batik is used extensively on many cloth articles, from dresses, skirts, kerchiefs, belts to handkerchiefs, pillows, pillow slips and bedcovers, from tablecloths, curtains, tapestries to handbags, satchels and cushions.

With the development of tourism in China, batik articles are growing in popularity as attractive souvenirs of certain Chinese provinces.

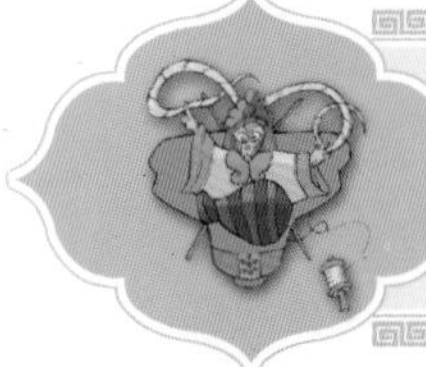

Paper-Cuts

(剪纸 *Jianzhi*)

The making of paper-cuts is another popular folk art in China. A piece of paper can be turned in the hands of an artisan, with the help of a knife or a pair of scissors, into any of a wide variety of patterns — landscapes, flowers, birds, animals and human figures. These simple works of art may be displayed in wall frames or pressed under glass table-tops to grace the room with their elegant lines and pleasing images.

Paper-cuts fall into two categories:

1)The monochrome scissor-cut: This is cut from a single piece of paper with a pair of scissors. It requires imagination and dexterity on the part of the artist. A master in this field is Wang Zigan, member of the Shanghai Arts and Crafts Research Institute, who has practised the craft for more than 50 years since the age of 13. It is a delightful experience to watch him at it — turn the scissors this way and that, cutting through a large piece of paper and producing, in a matter of minutes, a picture of a crowing cock with a group of grazing lambs. To cut such a picture or any other from a vast repertory, he needs no draft or model, but his work is always done in smooth and flowing lines and with expressive figures.

2)The patterned paper-cut: For this, patterns or models are first made by the master, and then the workers do the cutting accordingly, not on one sheet of paper but through a pile of some two dozens, producing as many paper-cuts at a time. The cutting tools used are knives of various sizes, some as long as 14 cm, others as thin as needles.

It is difficult to tell since when the art of paper-cutting began in China. Excavations made in 1949 at the ruins of the ancient city of Gaochang in Turpan, Xinjiang, unearthed paper-cuts showing a pair of horses and a pair of monkeys. They date back 1,500 years to the period of the Northern and Southern dynasties (420-589). They are the earliest speciments of ancient paper-cuts that have been discovered.

In the old days, people of certain regions used to cut red paper and imitation fold foil into chickens, dogs, sheep, pigs, cattle and horses or pictures of "peaches of immortality" and "high-ranking person on fine horse" and decorate their offerings to the gods with these by way of praying for prosperity and happiness. Today, on festivals or festive occasions such as a wedding, paper-cuts are still made and pasted on doors, windows, walls, rice jars and stoves to brighten up the house and add to the jubilance.

There is yet anoter kind of paper-cuts especially made as patterns for embroidery work.

The art of paper-cutting has experienced considerable development since the founding of New China. Research societies have been set up in a number of areas and the number of lovers has been on the increase. The folk art, it seems, has a more splendid future in store.

Basketwork on Porcelain
(瓷胎竹编 *Citai Zhubian*)

This is a national art with a tradition of barely 100 years. It is very fine basketwork woven with thread-like bamboo strips round a porcelain vessel as the body. If the latter is compared to a beauty, the basket will be her elegant and close-fitting dress; it not only protects the vessel but also enhances its appeal.

To weave such a basket involves a process of a dozen steps or more. The bamboo must be flawless on the surface and at least 2/3 of a metre long between the joints. Thread-thin strips are drawn from it, averaging about one kilogram from every 100 kilograms of bamboo. Then the handicraftsman weaves the strips, next to the surface of the porcelain, into a basket of close-knit and even-arranged warp and weft without showing any ends or joints. The basket, in some cases, is woven with pictures of various figures, bringing the art to an even higher level of ingenuity. Even if the porcelain inside should be broken, the basket itself would still remain a fine piece of art worth keeping.

The Shadow Show

(皮影戏 *Piyingxi*)

The shadow show or leather silhouette play is a type of drama which has its roots in China.

Legend has it that Emperor Wudi (156-87 B.C.) of the Western Han was depressed with the death of his favourite concubine Lady Li. To help him get over the sadness, an occultist sculptured a wooden figure in the likeness of the lady and projected its shadow on a curtain for the emperor to see, bringing him consolation with the belief that the shadow was her spirit. This has been thought to be the beginning of the shadow show.

Today's shadow puppets are made of leather instead of wood for the simple reason that leather is much lighter, easier to manipulate and carry round. The process for making the puppets is as follows: Sheep or donkey skin with hair removed is cleaned and treated chemically to become thin enough to be translucent. Coated with tung oil and dried, it is carved into various parts of dramatic figures. The trunk, head and limbs of a puppet are separately carved but joined together by thread so that each part may be manipulated by operator to simulate human movements. The leather puppets are painted with various colours to show their different qualities—kind or wicked, beautiful or unly. During the performance, the "actors" are held close to a white curtain with their coloured shadows cast on it by a strong light from behind. Moved by guiding sticks, they play the roles, accompanied by music, with their parts or singing done by the operators. The plays can be quite dramatic and, when it comes to fairy tales or kungfu stories, the "actors" may be made to ride on clouds or perform unusual feats, to the great enjoyment of the audience, especially children.

The shadow show became quite popular as early as the Song Dynasty (960-1279) when holidays were marked by the presentation of many shadow plays. During the Ming (1368-1644), there were 40 to 50 shadow show troupes in the city of Beijing alone.

In the 13th century the shadow show became a regular recreation in the barracks of the Mongolian troops. It was spread by the conquering Mongols to distant countries like Persia, Arabia and Turkey. Later, it was introduced to Southeastern Asian countries, too.

The show began to spread to Europe in the mid-18th century, when French missionaries to China took it back to France in 1767 and put on performances in Paris and Marseilles, causing quite a stir. In time, the *ombres chinoises*, with local modification and embellishment, became the *ombres francaises* and struck root in the country.

As present, more than 20 countries are known to have shadow show troupes.

Some people may have gone too far in alleging that the Chinese shadow show heralded the cinematic industry, but it certainly has contributed its bit towards enriching the world's amusement business.

Today, when the motion picture and television have become wide spread throughout the world, foreign tourists in China are still keen to see a performance of this ancient dramatic art.

Shadow puppets are also available from certain shops as art souvenirs of the country.

The Puppet Show

(木偶戏 *Mu' ouxi*)

The puppet show (*kuileixi*) is better known as *mu'ouxi* (play of wooden dolls), in the country, which has its roots in remote times. It is said that King Mu of the Zhou (c.10th century B.C.) of oral history, on his way home from a big hunt on the Kunlun Mountain, saw a choral dance performed by Yanshi, a skilled carpenter, with wooden dolls made by himself. However, it was not until the Han Dynasty that the

puppet show was mentioned as a full-fledged form of amusement. Still, that puts it at least 2,000 years back in Chinese history.

As in most other countries, three types of puppet shows are presented in China: the rod-top puppet, the marionette and the glove puppet of these, the first type is most populer in China. The puppet generally less than a metre tall, is made with true-to-life features. It is raised overhead at the top of a stick by the puppeteer with one hand and manipulated by him with the other hand moving a pair of wire rods. This type of puppets generally do not show their feet.

One of the basic skills required of the operator is to be able to hold high the puppet, which weighs 2 to 3 kilograms, with one arm and to keep it either motionless or moving steadily on the same level as dictated by the scenario. Only on this basis may the puppet be convincing in its other dramatic actions.

The marionette appears on stage in full view of the audience. It is of a more complicated structure, with the head, shoulders, waist, hands and feet all jointed, movable and controlled by separate wires. During performance, it is operated from a concealed operating bridge high above the puppet.

The glove or hand puppet, rather like those in a Punch and Judy show, is also called "bag puppet" (*budai mu' ou*) in China. About 20 cm long, it is the smallest of the three types. Its dress is in the form of a small bag, from inside which the puppeteer's hand manipulates its postures and movements.

The Kite

(风筝 *Fengzheng*)

The kite, a Chinese invention, has been praised as the forerunner of the modern aeroplane. In the pavilion of aircraft of the National Aeronautics and Space Museum, Washington D.C., a plaque says, "the earliest aircraft are the kites and missiles of China".

The kite is mainly, but not only, a plaything. It has contributed to science and production.The first planes were shaped after the kite. In 1782, Benjamin Franklin, noted American scientist and statesman, studied lightning and thunder in the sky with the help of a kite and then invented the lightning rod. Kites are still used by some fishermen to lay bait in the sea to attract fish, or by photographers to take pictures of bird's-eye view from high altitude.

The earliest Chinese kites were made of wood and called *muyuan* (wooden kites); they date as far back as the Warring States Period (475-221 B.C.) at least two millennia ago. After the invention of paper, kites began to be made of this new material called *zhiyuan* (paper kites).

Instead of being playthings, early kites were used for military purposes. Historical records say they were large in size; some were powerful enough to carry men up in the air to observe enemy movements, and others were used to scatter poropaganda leaflets over hostile forces. According to the *Records of Strange Events* (Du Yi Zhi), an ancient work, when Xiao Yan, Emperor Wudi (464-549) of the Liang Dynasty, was surrounded at Taicheng, Nanjing by the rebel troops under Hou Jing, it was by means of a kite that he sent out an S.O.S. message for outside help.

During the Tang Dynasty (618-907), people began to fix on kites some bamboo strips which, when high in the air, would vibrate and ring in the breeze like a *zheng* (a stringed instrument). Since then, the popular Chinese name for the kite has become *fengzheng* (wind *zheng*). The kites made today in certain localities are fixed with silk strings or rubber bands to give out pleasant ringing in the wind.

It was also believed, for instance, during the Qing Dynasty (1616-1911), that flying a kite and then letting it go, apart from the pleasure in itself, might send off one's bad luck and illness. Consequently it would bring bad luck if one should pick up a kite lost by other people. This may be dismissed as superstition but may not be altogether without reason: think of the good it will do to a person, ill and depressed all the time, if he or she could go out into the fields and fresh air to fly a kite.

Certain enthusiasts enjoy flying kites during the night. They hang small coloured laterns on the line with candles burning inside, which go up high in the air to decorate the night sky with strings of glimmering lights, adding much to the fun.

Chinese kites fall into two major categories: those with detachable wings and those with fixed wings. The former can be taken apart and packed in boxes. Easy to carry about, they make good presents. The second category refers to those with fixed, non-detachable frames; they fly better and higher, given a steady wind. Classified by designs and other specifications, there are no less than 300 varieties, including human figures, fish, insects, birds, animals and written characters. In size, they range from 304 metres to only 30 centimetres across.

It is no easy job to make a kite that one can be proud of. For the frame, the right kind of bamboo must be selected. It should be thick and strong for a kite of large dimensions in order to stand the wind pressure. For miniature kites, on the other hand, thin bamboo strips are to be used.

The second step in the making of a kite is the covering of the frame. This is normally done with paper, sometimes with silk. Silk kites are more durable and generally of higher artistic value.

Painting of the kite (the third step) may be done in either of two ways. For mass-produced kites, pre-printed paper is used to cover the frames. Custom-made kites are painted manually after covering. Many of the designs bear messages of good luck; a pine tree and a crane, for example, mean longevity, bats and peaches wish you good fortune and a long life, and so on.

In 1983 a large-scale kite-flying competition was held in Tianjin. A "dragon-headed centipede" of a hundred sections, with a total length of a hundred metres, flown up by a squad of 5 or 6 young men of the Tianjin Fine Arts Factory, thrashed and danced about in the air. A Japanese enthusiast sent up a 300-metre-long kite of a string of 270 sections. These and other successes attracted large crowds and won thunderous applause.

The well-known Weifang (Shandong Province) Kite Festival has become an annual feature in the country, drawing hundreds of participants each April from home and many foreign countries.

As early as two dozen years ago, a film entitled *The Kite* was jointly made by Chinese and French studios, which sings of Sino-French friendship through the "adventures" of a kite.

Fancy Lanterns

(彩灯 Caideng)

Fancy lanterns, a special handicraft product of Chinese tradition, are widely used for decorations in the country on festivals and holidays, on weddings and other personal celebrations.

On the whole, they consist of a frame made of metal wire or bamboo strips covered with paper or thin gauze and then painted over to be attractive. There is also a kind with a collapsible redwood frame that can be taken apart and folded up when not in use; it makes a good tourist souvenir.

Many types of traditional lanterns fit with the description of "fancy"; those commonly seen include palace lanterns, lanterns with revolving figures, gauze lanterns, wall lanterns and glass silk lanterns. Those hung on the Tower of

Tian'anmen are red gauze lanterns of an unusual size. In old times they were commonly called *qishifeng deng* (the lantern that enrages the wind) because, coated with fish glue, it was windproof while allowing the candle light to shine through. Today, of course, electric lights have long replaced the candles.

Outsanding among various lanterns is the one with revolving figures known as *zouma deng* in the country. It usually looks like a pretty paper pavilion with upturned eaves and corners. It is ringed by a number of coloured figures of men and animals, or a panoramic landscape of mountains, rivers and flowers, either painted on or cut in paper, that revolve like a merry-go-round.

This kind of "roundabout" latern may be traced to the Tang and Song dynasties about 1,000 years ago. The figures or pictures stand on the circumference of a wire frame which is fastened at the centre to a vertical shaft pasted with paper vanes. Propelled by the heated air from the lit candle, the vanes turn the shaft, making the frame with the figures revlove. Today this kind of lantern has become more elaborate and beautiful, but the basic structure remains the same. It shows that the Chinese already grasped in ancient times the principle of transforming the current of hot air into mechanical revolution.

A series of special postage stamps of various lanterns was issued by the Chinese postal authorities in 1981. Totalling six pieces, they show fancy lanterns of different shapes: a flower basket, a coloured ball, dragon-and-phoenix, a treasure box, grass-and-flower, and a peony plant. The designers, employing techniques of traditional "fine brushwork", gave the pictures a dazzling brilliance and brought them to life.

Firecrackers

(鞭炮 *Bianpao*)

The sound of firecrackers is a distinctive feature on Chinese festivals and joyous personal occasions.

Firecrackers are called by various names at different times and in different parts of the country. At the very beginning, crackers were used to scare away wild beasts, especially a legendary unicorn called *nian*, which appeared regularly at the end of winter or beginning of spring, wreaking great havoc among the people. That was long before the invention of gunpowder, and people burnt dry bamboo sticks to produce the explosive sound. So the first firecrakers were called *baozhu* (cracking bamboo), which is still the name in some books.

Incidentally, *nian*, the name of the animal which appeared at yearly intervals, came to mean "year". And the custom of letting off firecrackers at the New Year has become deep-rooted in all parts of the country. The beginning of the custom can be traced in written history to at least 2,000 years ago.

When gunpowder was invented in China, it was used to fill in bamboo tubes and,when lighted, produced loud explosions. Firecrackers came to be called *baozhang* (exploding sticks), a name still used in certain regions. According to the Song Dynasty work *Origins of Things*, the first scientist who used gunpowder in crackers was Ma Jun of the period of the Three Kingdoms (220-265), which puts their beginning at 1,700 years ago.

Baozhang led to the earliest crackers of gunpowder rolled in paper, which could

give out single explosion only. The double-bang *ertijiao* and stringed firecrackers *bianpao* came as later innovations. The "double-bang" is a tight paper roll composed of two powder-filled chambers; the first explosion bursts the bottom chamber and sends the cracker up into the air and then the second explodes, making a loud and far-reaching report. Modern times have witnessed further improvements of the traditional firecracker. Colour-luminescent chemicals are added into gunpowder, and the firework shells fired up by cannons explode high in the air, covering the night sky with magnificent displays of colourful splendour.

Enthusiasts for firecrackers have always been youths and children. Given the excuse and occasion — New Year, a wedding, a victory scored by the national team at an important world sports event, the opening of an international festival, etc. they will resort to firecrackers to express their jubilation. And the custom seems to have been spreading fast to other nations.

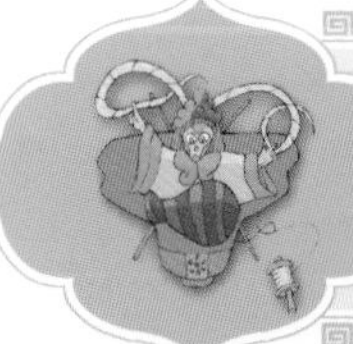

Celadon

(青瓷 *Qingci*)

Celadon, a famous type of ancient Chinese stoneware, came into being during the period of the Five Dynasties (907-960). It is characterized by simple but refined shapes, jade-like glaze, solid substance and a distinctive style. As the celadonware produced in Longquan County, Zhejiang Province, is most valued, so it is also generally called *Longquan qingci.*

Its Chinese name, *qingci*, means "greenish porcelain". Why then is it known in the West as "celadon"?

Celadon was the hero of the French writer Honoré d'Urfe's romance L'Astrée (1610), the lover of the heroine Astrée. He was presented as a young man in green and his dress became all the rage in Europe. And it was just about this time that the Chinese *qingci* made its debut in Paris and won acclaim. People compared its colour to Celadon's suit and started to call the porcelain "celadon", a name which has stuck and spread to other countries.

Now, new products of *Longquan qingci* have been developed to radiate with fresh lustre; they include eggshell china and underglaze painting.

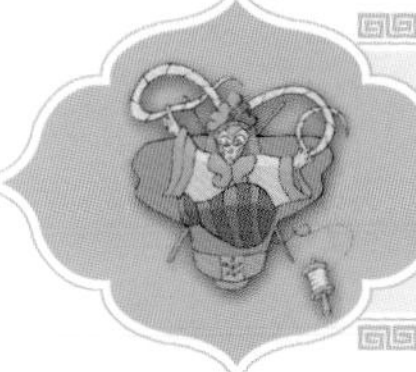

Red Ware
(紫砂陶器 *Zisha Taoqi*)

Yixing, Jiangsu Province, known in China as the "Pottery Metropolis", produces a much-valued red ware or boccaro ware. Teapots of this category made there were appraised as the best vessel there was, already in the Song Dynasty a thousand years ago.

Yixing earthenware is generally marked by simplicity and exquisite craftsmanship; it is also appreciated for its practical utility. The material, called *zisha* (purple sand), is abundantly available in the locality. Although not as white or as fine as kaolin, it needs no glazing and, after firing,the product is solid and impermeable, yet porous enough to "breathe". A Yixing teapot enhances the tea brewed in it in respect of colour, perfume, and taste. Its walls seem to absorb the tea and keeps its fragrance. In summer it keeps the tea overnight without spoiling. With hot tea inside, it does not scald the hand, purple sand being a slow heat-conductor. But in winter it may serve as a handwarmer and may be left on a low fire to make certain types of tea which need simmering. To the Chinese connoisseur, it is the "ideal teapot".

The purple sand of Yixing may also be made into other utensils. The earthenware steam cooker is a casserole which cooks with steam and appears on the dining table as a serving dish as well. Drinking vessels and coffee sets of red ware are also welcome to users because they are good in preserving the flavour of the beverages. A boon to flower lovers, the red ware flower pot absorbs excessive water, helps the soil "breathe", keeps the roots from rotting, and generally ensures the plant a healthy growth.

What makes the Yixing earthenware all the more attractive is the tasy designs it bears. Artisans cut or incise on the unburnt bodies pictures of birds and fish, flowers and animals, Chinese characters and seal marks all in the traditional style, thus turning utensils of practical use into works of art with national features.

Technical innovations attained in recent years have made it possible for the "Pottery Metropolis" to turn out many refractory kitchen utensils such as steamers, rice cookers, and pots, pans and dishes used for roasting. They can stand drastic change of heat and may be used on any kind of fire to cook food by boiling, steaming, roasting or frying. Thus new uses have been developed for the traditional earthenware.

Tri-Coloured Tang

(唐三彩 *Tangsancai*)

Tangsancai refers to the tri-coloured glazed pottery of the Tang Dynasty (618-907 A.D.), a painted earthenware which appeared in the wake of celadon. It is called "tri-coloured" because yellow, green and white were normally used, although some pieces are also in two or four colours. Developed on the basis of the green and brown glazed-pottery of the Han Dynasty, it represented a peak in the development of Chinese ceramics and was already well-known in the world in its time.

Unearthed tri-coloured Tangs are usually horses, camels, female figurines, dragon-head mugs, figurines of musicians and acrobats, and pillows. Of these, the three-coloured camels have won the greatest admiration. They are presented as bearing loads of silk or carrying musicians on their backs, their heads raised as if neighing; the red-bearded, blue-eyed drivers, clad in tunics of tight sleeves and hats with upturned brims, reproduce true-to-life images of men from Central Asia of that time as they trudged along the Silk Road to the tinkle of camel bells.

The tri-coloured glazed pottery of the Tang Dynasty was developed some 1,300 years ago by drawing on the skills of Chinese painting and sculpture and employing on the bodies the techniques of clay-strip forming and incising. The lines thus produced were rugged and powerful.Then glazes of different colours were painted on and, while chemical reactions took place in the process of firing in the kiln, they dripped naturally so that the colours mingled with each other and formed smooth tones.

The tri-coloured Tang flourished during a rather short period of time (the 8th century)of the dynasty, when pottery pieces of this category were used by the aristocrats as funerary objects. So the finds today are limited in number and are considered to be rare treasures, valued for their brilliant colour and life-like shapes.

Imitations now produced in Luoyang, Xi'an and other cities of China are well received as tourist souvenirs because of their close resemblance to the authentic works.

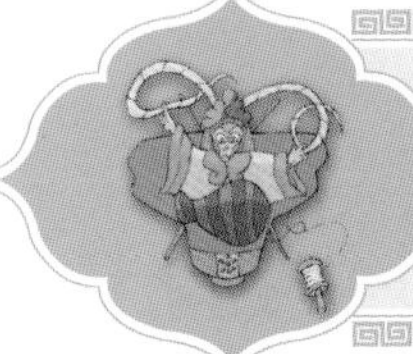

Eggshell China

(薄胎瓷 *Botaici*)

A gem of Chinese ceramics, eggshell china is remarkable first of all for its extraordinary thinness. Yet it is appreciated also because it is spotlessly white, translucent, and sonorous when tapped.It is made mainly into bowls, vases, cups, lampshades and articles for use in the study. Whatever form it assumes, one may appreciate through its paper-thin wall the coloured painting on the other side, like watching the moon through flimsy clouds, or green hills through a thin mist with the beauty enhanced by a veiled effect.

The "eggshell" has as its forerunner *yingqingci* (shadowy celadon), which was produced as early as in the Northern Song Dynasty (906-1127). Present-day production excels the past in both quantity and quality. Recent successes at Jingdezhen include a 75-cm-tall vase and a large bowl 25.7 cm across, sizes thought impossible to mould in eggshell china in the past.

To make such "insubstantial" utensils, an exacting craftsmanship is called for. It requires the best and carefully selected kaolin, mixing of ingredients according to strict prescriptions and repeated tempering of the clay, before the potter moulds the paste into bodies. Then a master craftsman will wield various cutting tools to shape them finely into eggshell thinness and have them fired in the kiln at a high temperature of over 1,300℃.

Of these processes, the most difficult part is fine-moulding, which finalizes the form of the utensil. A veteran master, relying solely on his sense of hearing and touch, decides on the thickness of the wall, holding his breath when he applies his knife, as a slight slip would result in a ruined body.

Eggshell porcelain is not for use but for interior decoration and it is deluxe ornament, too.

Silhouette Carving

(影雕 *Yingdiao*)

The silhouette carving, which is a branch of the Hui'an school of stone sculpture in Fujian, derives its name from its photo-like artistic effects. For its exquisite craftsmanship it is extolled as a wonder of China.

Using a variety of tiny chisels ranging in size from nails to needles, the artist consults the details of a photograph while carving on a piece of bluestone about two inches in thickness, forming patterns and images by varying the size, depth and density of the chisel points and alternating realism with abstraction. A piece of silhouette carving can be as large as more than 100 square metres and as small as 4 to 5 square cm.

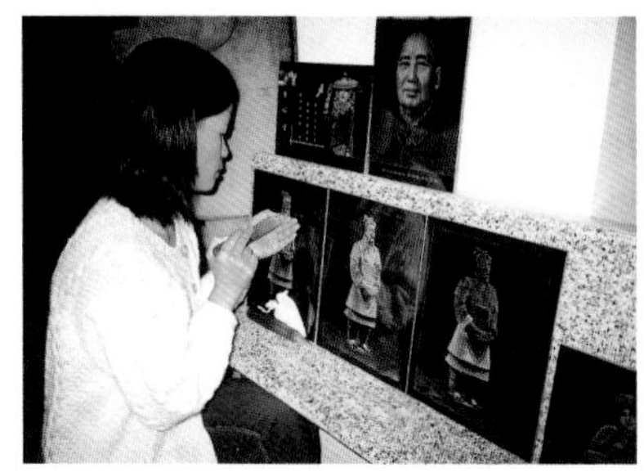

The silhouette carvings made in the Hui'an County Stone Carving Factory are often selected as gifts for diplomatic occasions and shown in exhibitions abroad.

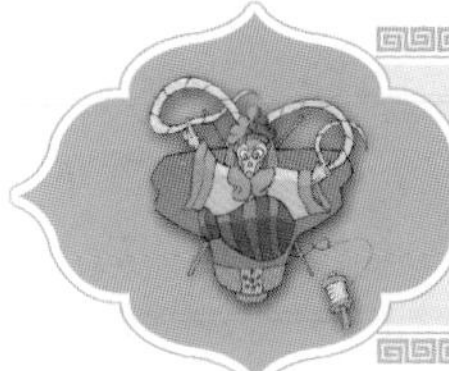

Silk Flowers

(绢花 *Juanhua*)

These are artificial flowers made of fine woven silk in exact imitation of natural ones in respect of colour and shape. They are made in several steps: starching and dyeing of the material, shaping and pasting. The art of making silk flowers is believed to have originated in the imperial palace; such flowers are therefore also known as gonghua, or palace flowers.

In a famous painting of Palace Ladies by Gu Kaizhi (c.345-406) of the Jin Dynasty, the ladies are shown to be wearing flowery ornaments artificially made, showing that silk flowers have had a history of at least 1,500 years.

Silk flowers may be worn as personal ornaments or given away as presents of good taste and personal touch. Needless to say, they are welcome substitutes in seasons when fresh flowers are hard to come by.

Brick Sculpture

(砖雕 *Zhuandiao*)

Bricks carved with patterns in relief were used for decorative purposes on the exterior of old houses-mansions of officials and the rich, shrines and temples, landscape buildings in parts. They are also found on the entrance gates, windows and screen walls in houses which once belonged to big business and the landed gentry, "to bring honour to the owners and their ancestors".

Carvings on bricks may cover a wide range of subjects. Usually seen are human figures drawn from popular legends, dramas and folklore, most of them lifelike and spirited. Animals and plants are also favourite subjects, mostly those portending power and good luck or representing certain lofty qualities, for example, dragon, phoenix, plum, bamboo, crysanthemum and so on. Other carvings represent attempts to reproduce traditional paintings on bricks. Apart from the sculpted pictures, they are often complete with inscriptions and seal marks.

This particular art of sculpture was done on a kind of carefully polished blue brick. It was called fangzhuan (square brick) in the Ming Dynasty and jinzhuan ("gold" brick, see a preceding article of this title under ARCHITECTURE) in the Qing Dynasty. This brick was fine in texture and most suitable for carving, but as it was also brittle, the work might be easily ruined by a slip of the carving tool.

The large numbers of brick-carvings which we can still see today are impressive with their vivid figures, their composition in depths and on varying levels, giving a feeling of three dimensions and appealing with an impact not found in frescoes.

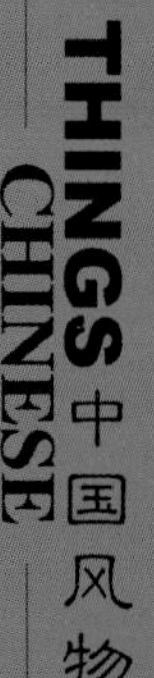

Architecture 建筑

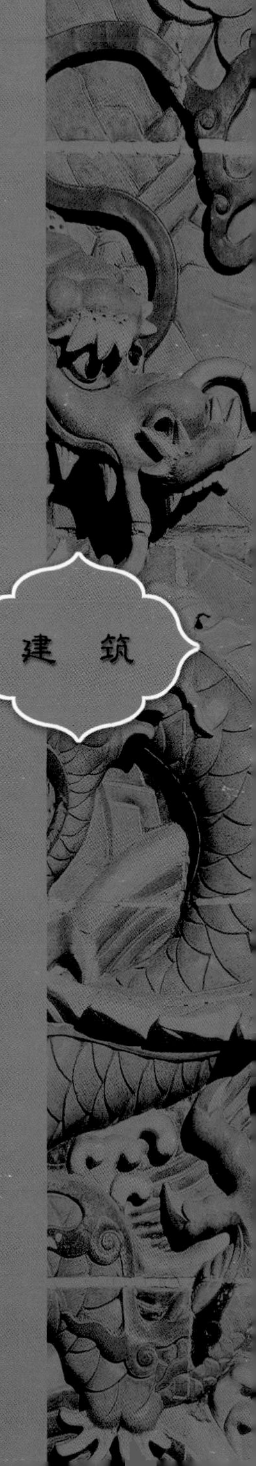

Palace

(宫 *Gong*)

The Chinese word for "palace" is *gong* which, however, may refer to anyone of several different things.

In the earliest Chinese writings it meant no more than an ordinary house. After the founding of the Qin Dynasty (221-206 B.C.), *gong* came gradually to mean the group of buildings in which the emperor lived and worked. From about the same time, the Chinese palace grew ever larger in scale. The Efanggong (or Epanggong, according to the purists) of the First Emperor of Qin, according to an authoritative source, measured "5 *li* (2 1/2 km) from east to west and 1,000 paces from north to south." The Weiyanggong of the Western Han Dynasty (206 B.C.-25 A.D.) had,within a periphery of 11 kilometres, as many as 43 halls and terraces. The Forbidden City of Beijing, which still stands intact and which served as the imperial palace for both Ming and Qing emperors (1368-1911), covers an area of 720,000 square metres and embraces many halls, towers, pavilions and studies, measured as 9,900 bays. It is one of the greatest palaces still existing in the world. In short, the *gong* grew into a veritable city and is often called *gongcheng* (palace city).

Apart from the palace, other abodes of the emperor are also called *gong*. So, the Yiheyuan Park used to be the Summer Palace; the Mountain Resort at Chengde and the Huaqingchi thermal spa near Xi'an were both *xinggong* or "palace-on-tour". Then there is another type of *gong* called *zhaigong*, where the emperor prepared himself with ablution and abstinence before he offered sacrifice at a grand ceremony. There is one such *zhaigong* on the grounds of Beijing's Temple of Heaven.

Inside a great *gong*, certain individual buildings may also be called *gong*. The Qing emperors used to live at *Qianqinggong* (Palace of Heavenly Purity) in the Forbidden City, whereas the living quarters of the empresses were at *Kunninggong* (Palace of Female Tranquility). The imperial concubines of various ranks inhabited the six *gong* or palace quadrangles on either side of the central axis of the Forbidden City. When the monarchs or their spouses died, they were buried in *digong* (underground palaces).

The name *gong* is also used for religious buildings of great dimensions. The Potala in Lhasa is a *gong* to the Chinese; the lama temple of Beijing is *Yonghegong*. The temples of Taoist priests are generally called *Sanqinggong* (palace of triple purity).

For thousands of years in old China, the word *gong* was reserved exclusively for naming imperial and religious buildings. With the passage of time and political changes, many of the old *gong* have been opened to the general public for sightseeing. Furthermore, a number of buildings have been named *gong* or palace. For instance, *Taimiao* or the Imperial Ancestral Temple in Beijing has been renamed the "Working People's Palace of Culture". On West Chang'an Jie, a comparatively new building serves as the "Cultural Palace of National Minorities". Similar *gong* or palaces have been built in many cities of the country for the cultural, scientific and recreational actvities respectively for workers, youth and children.

Hall

(殿 *Dian*)

The *dian* is the largest single building in traditiolal Chinese architecture and is generally referred to as *dadian* (grand hall). It is also called *zhengdian* (central hall) as it is invariably built on the axis of an architectural complex.

Corresponding to the rigid ranking system of feudal times, there were strict regulations about the building of palace halls. The *dadian* was the grandest of all buildings, being symbolic of the supreme power of the emperor.

The most famour Chinese *dian* are three: *Taihedian* or the Hall of Supreme Harmony in Beijing's Forbidden City, *Dachengdian* or the Great Hall in the Confucius Temple of Qufu, and *Tiankuangdian* or the Hall of Celestial Gift in the Daimiao Temple at the foot of Mt. Taishan. Of the three, the Hall of Supreme Harmony in Beijing is the greatest and most splendid. It measures 28 metres high,11 bays wide and 5 bays deep, totalling 55 bays. Its double-eaved, four-sloped roof is covered with yellow glazed tiles. From each end of the main ridge, which is straight and level, fork down two corner ridges, which curve slightly and turn up at the lower corners, presenting a beautiful skyline. All the ridges are decorated with *wenshou* or zoomorphic ornaments, adding a mystic flavour to grandeur.

At the centre of the ornate interior,the emperor's throne,gilded in gold and carved with dragons,stands on a platform flanked by six huge columns also entwined with gilded dragons. The caisson ceiling high above carries a dragon carved in relief playing with pearls and has a big glass-ball mirror hanging down from the centre.

Taihedian is the main hall of the palace,where grand ceremonies took place and important edicts were read and issued during the days of the emperors. It represents the most sumptuous example of the traditional art of Chinese architecture.

Other halls deserving to be called *dian* were mostly buildings where imperial sacrifices took place. *Tiankuangdian*, mentioned before, was the hall in which the emperors worshipped the God of Mt. Taishan. *Qiniandian* in Beijing's Temple of Heaven, famous for its unique structure, was where the emperors prayed for good harvest and has been known as the "Hall of Prayer" among Westerners. For the worship of their ancestors, the emperors used to go to a great hall in *Taimiao*, the Imperial Family Temple lying to the east of Tian'anmen Gate.

The above example suffice to show that the name *dian* or *dadian* was reserved only for certain buildings related to the supreme ruler.

Ornamental Pillar

(华表 *Huabiao*)

A well-known architectural ornament in China is the *huabiao*, often seen on the grounds of palaces, imperial gardens and mausoleums. It is also seen at some crossroads to mark the thoroughfares.

There is a pair of such ornamental pillars carved out of marble standing in front and behind Tian'anmen, the Gate of Heavenly Peace, at the centre of Beijing. Each pillar, entwined by a divine dragon engraved in relief, carries a plate on top,on which squats an animal called *kong*. This creature in Chinese mythology is supposed to be born of the dragon and good at keeping watch. It is generally referred to as the "stone lion". The four *kong* at Tian'anmen have different names, the two in front facing south and with their backs to the wall are called *wangjungui* or "looking out for the emperor's return". Their duty, it is said,was to watch over the emperor's excursions and call him back if he was too long absent from the palace. The couple inside the gate facing north are called *wangjungchu* or "looking out for the emperor's progress", and their job was to supervise how the emperor behaved in the imperial palace. If he should indulge himself and neglect court affairs, the stone lions would remind him of his duties and tell him it was time to go out among the people.

These popular explanations reflected the naive wishes of the people for an emperor who would listen to advice and work really for their good.

The *huabiao* has a long history behind it and can be traced back to Yao and Shun, legendary sage kings in remote times.To solicit public criticism, it is said, they erected wooden crosses at marketplaces so that the people might write their complaints and wishes on them. These wooden posts were replaced during the Han Dynasty (206 B. C.-220 A.D.) by stone pillars, which grew more and more decorative and ornately carved until they became the sumptuous columns to palace gates.

Screen Wall

(影壁 *Yingbi*)

Foreign visitors may have noticed the isolated wall either outside or just inside the gate of a traditional Chinese house to shield the rooms from outsider's view. Known as a "screen wall" in English, it is called *yingbi* or *zhaobi* in Chinese. It can

be made of any material—brick, wood, stone or glazed tile.

The *yingbi* dates back at least to the Western Zhou Dynasty (11 century B.C.to 771 B.C.). Archaeologists have discovered in recent years from tombs of that period in Shaanxi Province what remains of a screen wall. It measures 240 cm long and 20 cm high. This is the earliest known wall of its kind in China at the time of writing.

In ancient times, the *yingbi* was a symbol of rank. According to the Western Zhou system of rites, only royal palaces, noblemen's mansions and religious temples could have a screen wall. Apart from keeping passers-by from peeping into the courtyard, the screen wall could also be used by the visitor, who would get off from his carriage and, standing behind the wall, tidy up his dress before going in. It was not until much later that private houses (mainly the quadrangles of bungalows in the northern parts of the country) began to have screen walls.

The most exquisite of all ancient screen walls are three "nine-dragon walls" built of glazed colour tiles.The largest of these, 45.5m × 8m × 2.02m, is now in the city of Datong, Shanxi Province. It originally stood in front of the princely mansion of the thirteenth son of Zhu Yuanzhang,first emperor of the Ming Dynasty. Sculpted on it in seven different colours are nine dragons flying in clouds. The most splendid of the three is the one which belonged to a palace of the Ming Dynasty and now stands north of the lake in Beijing's Beihai Park. It is a mosaic of glazed colour tiles showing on each side nine curly dragons in relief. An observant visitor could also count 635 dragons of smaller sizes on the ridges and roof tiles of the wall. The third of these walls stands opposite the gate Huangjimen in the Forbidden City and is well-known to sightseers. All the three mentioned above were built during the Ming Dynasty (1368-1644) and all used to stand in front of the entrance to a courtyard, making a component part of the architectural complex and adding to the magnificence of the buildings.

Besides these, there are also screen walls with one, three or five dragons to be seen in different parts of the country.

There is a screen wall in each of the side palace courtyards of the Forbidden City. Whether made of wood, carved out of marble or built with glazed tiles, it is invariably a fine piece of work with designs symbolic of good luck.

Certain screen walls found in the eastern provinces of China bear the image of a strange animal called *tan*, either carved in brick or painted in colour. According to local belief, this animal was so greedy that it wanted to devour the rising sun on the sea, meeting its own death by drowning. The picture serves as a reminder that greed leads to self-destruction.

In the vicinity of the Five Dragon Pavilions (*Wulongting*) in the Beihai Park of Beijing, there is a so-called "iron screen wall", a relic from the Yuan Dynasty of the thirteenth century. At first glance,it appears to have been cast of iron but actually it is a piece of volcanic rock. Carved on it in vivid style are, on one side, lions playing with a ball and, on the other, a legendary unicorn; it is noted for its antiquity and simplicity of execution.

Glazed Tile

(琉璃瓦 *Liuliwa*)

The glazed tile, as a high-grade building material in old China, was used exclusively on palace buildings of the imperial house of the big mansions of nobles and high officials.

The glaze was normally in one of four colours: yellow, green, blue and black. Tiles coated with it not only add splendour to the buildings but, in old times, carried a political significance.

Yellow tiles were reserved for use on the roofs of royal palaces, mausoleums, imperial gardens and temples. This, it is said, was because yellow is the colour of the Yellow River, once believed to be the cradle of the Chinese civilization. Probably for the same reason the earliest leader of the alliance of the tribes in prehistoric legend was named *Huangdi* or the Yellow Emperor, whose descendants all Chinese are supposed to be. In the meantime, the ancients believed that the physical universe was composed of five elements — metal, wood, water, fire and earth, and the yellow colour represented earth which lay at the centre of the universe.Yellow, therefore, was taken as

the cardinal colour of the core and became the royal colour to be used exclusively by the rulers.

It can be seen that the colours of the roof tiles indicated the positions of the people who lived in the house. Even in the same part, as for instance the Summer Palace of Beijing, differently coloured tiles were used for different houses. The groups of halls and pavilions used by the monarch and his family, visitors will notice, have yellow roofs whereas the quarters for the court officials have green roofs. As for other structures erected for landscaping or for the accommodation of people without a senior rank, they have as a rule black tiles.

Tiles of yellow glaze, however, also cover certain halls which were not built for the imperial family, as for instance temples dedicated to Confucius and Guan Yu*, worshipped for his bravery and loyalty, but this was because they were canonized by emperors of later dynasties as their equals and given posthumous titles as such.

Colours on ancient buildings were not only status indicators but in certain cases carried other implications. One example is Wenyuange, the imperial library in Beijing's Forbidden City which, amidst many yellow roofs, stands under a roof of black tiles. The reason: books were liable to catch fire, black was supposed to be the colour of water, and a black-coloured roof would mean ever-ready water to put out fires.

Another example is the buildings of the Temple of Heaven. They were roofed with blue tiles, for the evident reason that blue is the colour of Heaven.

Incidentally, mention should be made of the red enclosure walls that invariably go with the yellow roofs of imperial palaces. Red has always been the colour of happiness and festivity in China; even today red lanterns and red streamers are still dominant features on occasions of public enjoyment. Red walls, however, could only be built for palaces and temples and, in combination with the yellow glazed roofs, they were meant to play up the atmosphere of solemnity and happiness.

* A famous general of the period of the Three Kingdoms (220-280 A.D.)

The Number "Nine" and Imperial Buildings (“九”与皇家建筑 *"Jiu" yu Huangjia Jianzhu*)

It may not be common knowledge among western visitors that the number "nine" carried a special significance in old China. Ancient Chinese regarded odd numbers as masculine and even numbers as feminine. "Nine", the largest single digit unmber, was taken as representing the "ultimate masculine" and was, therefore, symbolic of the supreme sovereignty of the emperor. For this reason, the number "nine" (or its multiples) is often employed in palace structures and designs. A noticeable example is the number of studs on palace gates. The studs are usually arranged in nine rows of nine each, totalling eighty-one. This is even true of the marble gates of the "underground palace" of the Dingling Mausoleum in Beijing: 81 (or 9 × 9) studs were carved out of the stone. If the visitor goes to the Temple of Guan Yu in Luoyang, he will also find on the red gate nine rows of nine wood studs each. This was because Guan was given posthumous honours of an emperor.

Ancient palaces generally consisted of nine courtyards or quadrangles; so does the Temple of Confucius in Qufu, Shandong Province — a magnificent architectural complex worthy of an imperial household and testifying to the importance attached to the great sage by the courts of various dynasties.

The buildings of the Forbidden City of Beijing are traditionally measured as having a total floor space of 9,900 bays —some even say 9,999 bays, which may be an exaggeration. The picturesque towers guarding the four corners of the palace compound havc each 9 beams and 18 columns, and the three famous screen walls (in Datong and Beijing—see above article) have nine dragons on each.

The number "nine" was sometimes combined with "five" to represent imperial majesty. The great hall on Tian'anmen is 9 bays wide by 5 bays deep.

There is a seventeen-arched bridge in the Summer Palace of Beijing. This, too, has much to do with "nine". Count the arches from either end, and you will find that the largest span in the middle is the ninth.

An extreme example of the "game of nine" is perhaps the Circular Mound Altar (*Huanqiutan*) in the Temple of Heaven. Site for the Ming and Qing emperors to worship Heaven, the altar is in three tiers. The upper terrace is made up of nine concentric rings of slabs. The first ring or innermost circle consists of nine fan-shaped slabs, the second ring 18 (2 × 9) slabs, the third 27(3 × 9)... until the last or ninth ring, made up of 81 or 9 × 9 slabs.

The number "nine" is not only used on buildings. The New Year dinner for the imperial house was composed of 99 dishes. To celebrate the birthday of an emperor, the stage performances must comprise of 99 numbers as a sign of good luck and long life.

Stone Baluster Head

(望柱头 *Wangzhu Tou*)

Important halls, towers and pavilions in the old palaces of China normally stand on terraces. These are bordered with marble balustrades; so are many historic bridges of stone. The upright posts or balusters supporting them, called *wangzhu* in Chinese, have heads sculpted in the shapes of dragons, phoenixes, lions, flames, and so on. They are not only highly ornamental but served to reflect hierarchical ranks.

Dragon-and-phoenix images on baluster heads were exclusive to imperial buildings. These legendary creatures, carved with clouds, are often placed on top of the stone posts around audience halls, palace gates and halls of worship. They are, however, found in the greatest concentration around the group of buildings known as *San Da Dian* (The Three Great Halls) in Beijing's Forbidden City. These halls stand majestic on a terrace of three tiers, each of which is surrounded by a white marble balustrade. The 1,460 balusters, viewed from a distance, look like a "Stone Forest" and give the halls an ethereal loftiness. This arrangement is unique to "The Three Great Halls" as the site where the emperor held grand ceremonies, received his ministers and issued important edicts. For people of a lesser rank to use this magnificent layout or the dragon-

and-phoenix motif would be a crime punishable as high treason.

The differentiation of status is most noticeable on the five bridges spanning the Golden Water River just inside *Wumen*, the Meridian Gate of the Forbidden City. The middle bridge, i.e., the one used by the emperor, has balusters topped with carved dragons and clouds, whereas the other four have on the baluster crowns designs of flames as ornaments and symbols of illumination. For the lesser buildings on the palace grounds, the decorations for stone baluster heads are generally *ruyi**, pomegranates, lions and others which signify good luck, happiness and longevity.

At the eastern end of the Golden Water River there is a baluster whose head could be used as a siren. Carved in the Qing Dynasty(1616-1911)in the form of fire-flames over a lotus blossom, the post has an opening running from the top to a string of beads under the flower. In case of an emergency, the guard could blow into the top hole and the baluster head would sound warning alarms like a horn.

* An ornamental object as a symbol of good luck.

Stone Lions

(石狮 *Shishi*)

In front of the gates of traditional buildings — palace halls, old government offices, mansions and other houses of style —one can still see a pair of lions standing guard.Carved out of stone*, they are a male and a female, with the male on the left, his right paw resting on a ball, and the lioness on the right, her left paw fonding a cub.

The lion was thought to be the monarch of the animal kingdom, and its images represented august power and formidable prestige to keep all quarters in awful submission. The ball played by the male lion symbolized the unity of the empire, and the cub below the female thriving offspring.

Use of the lions was not the exclusive privilege of the court. Other personages of rank could also have them in front of the main entrances to their houses, with their ranks indicated by the number of lumps representing the curly hair on the head of the animal. Lions with 13 lumps, the highest number, guarded the houses of officials of the first grade, and the number of these lumps decreased by one as the rank of the official went down each grade. Officials below the seventh grade, however, were not allowed to have stone lions.

At the dawn of history China had no lions, whose habitat was Africa and West Asia. Official contacts with countries to the west were established after Zhang Qian (?-114 B.C.) was despatched to Central Asia as a special envoy by Empoeror Wu of the Han Dynasty. In A.D.87, when Emperor Zhang of the Eastern Han reigned in China, the King of Parthia presented a lion to him; the next year, another was presented to the Chinese court by a Central Asian country known as Yuezhi to ancient China.

The existence of stone lions may have preceded that of real ones. It is believed that the earliest stone lions were sculpted at the beginning of the Eastern Han Dynasty (25-220 A.D.) with the introduction of Buddhism into China. Sakyamuni (founder of the faith), it is said, was seen after his birth "to point to Heaven with one hand and to Earth with another, roaring like an lion,'Between Heaven and Earth I alone am supreme'. " Elsewhere it is also said that "Buddha is a lion among men." "Buddhists admiring the lion for its mighty swiftness made it the mount for the Bodhisattva Manjusri." In short, the lion is regarded in the Buddhist faith as a divine animal of nobleness and dignity, able to keep off evils and protect the Truth.

For the same reason, it was a custom to use figures of the lion to decorate certain structures, especially stone bridges. A most prominant example is the *Lugouqiao* or Marco Polo Bridge near Beijing. Adorning the heads of its stone balusters are 501 lions of varying sizes and postures.

As further proof of the general liking for the animal, the knobs of seals are often sculpted in the form of lions.Among folk dances, the lion dance which was known as early as the Han Dynasty has remained popular ever since.

* Some may be cast of iron or bronze (and gilded, as in the palaces).

Door Studs

(门钉 *Mending*)

The main entrances to ancient palaces, temples and mansions have doors with studs arranged in rows. Like other decorations on traditional buildings, the studs served to indicate ranks in the feudal hierarchy.

Door studs go back a long time in history. To keep off aggression, heavy city gates were built and braced on the surface with iron plates, which were fastened on by means of studs. This system lasted for thousands of years.

The door studs on the gates of the Forbidden City were made of brass and plated with gold. Lustrous, they add to the splendour and magnificence of the imperial palace. All the gates used by the emperor have 9 × 9 or 81 studs, as the number nine represented the supremacy of the monarch. Other titled personages, princes and barons had fewer studs on their gates, such as 9 rows 7 each, 7 × 7 or 5 × 5; those who had lower ranks had studs made of iron.

An interesting question arises with regard to the Donghuamen gate of the Forbidden City which, unlike the other principal entrances, have 72 studs instead of the usual 81. The explanation lies in a historic event. At the end of the Ming Dynasty, the capital fell to Li Zicheng, leader of a famous peasant revolt in 1644. And it was by Donghuamen that Chongzhen the last Ming emperor left the palace and then hanged himself at Jingshan (Hill of Prospect, popularly known as Coal Hill). The Qing house which replaced the Ming regarded Donghuamen as inauspicious, decided to use it for the exit of imperial hearses and cut down the number of its studs at the same time.

Knocker Base

(铺首 *Pushou*)

The two-leafed gate of a traditional Chinese house has a pair of ring knockers, whose base, called *pushou*, serves also a decorative purpose.

The knocker-bases for a private house are fixed only on the outermost, more solidly-built gate. They are normally simple discs made of iron or brass. People who call at the house will tap one of the rings lightly, which will hit the base to produce clear percussions. In answer to the sound, the people of the house will come to open the door to greet the visitor. When the owner of the house goes out he can lock up the gate by fastening the knocker-rings together.

The knocker bases on palace gates, naturally, are much more elaborate. Made of gold-gilded brass, they are in the form of tigers, lions, turtles, snakes or other animals which were supposed to possess magic powers or unequalled strength. The

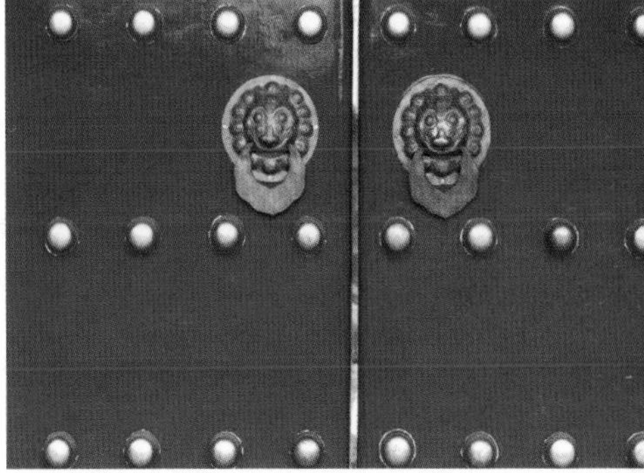

consummate art with which they were carved also contribute to the splendour of the edifices.

Pushou first appeared in China during the Han Dynasty (206 B.C.-220 A.D.) and have had a history of 2,000 years. Today they still decorate the houses newly built in the countryside, but they are disappearing in cities where modern multistoreyed buildings are being constructed in increasing numbers.

Water Vat

(大缸 *Da Gang*)

In the courtyards of palaces and imperiral gardens water vats are seen standing not far from the main buildings. In their time they were filled with water against

the emergency of a fire. In winter they were covered and wrapped around with quilts and, when necessary, heated from below with charcoal to prevent the water from freezing. There were in the old days 308 such vats in the Forbidden City of Beijing; now only a little over 200 are counted.

The water vats were not only fire-fighting installations but part of the adornments that made up imperial magnificence. In the Ming Dynasty (1368-1644) they were mostly made of iron or bronze, but they became much more elaborate and finely made in the Qing (1644-1911), being of gold-plated brass and adorned with rings and side knobs in the form of animal heads.

These water vats fall into different grades. Flanking the front of such important halls as Taihedian (Hall of Supreme Harmony), Baohedian (Hall of Preserving Harmony) and Qianqingmen (Gate of Heavenly Purity) are huge vats, each weighing 3,392 kilograms and measuring 1.6 metres in diameter. Near less important buildings, the vat weighs 2,166 kilograms and measures 1.28 metres. Still less important pavilions and towers have iron or bronze vats of yet smaller sizes.

Visitors to the old imperial palace today can no longer see the gold-plated brass vats as they were in their time.This is because the gold plate was scraped off with bayonets by troops of the Eight-Power Allied Forces which invaded China in 1900.

Dougong Brackets
(斗拱 *Dougong*)

The *dougong* is a system of brackets unique to traditional Chinese architecture. These brackets, arranged like baskets of flowers, are set under the overhanging eaves, adding to the sumptuous magnificence of the buildings.

Thanks to them the ancient Chinese edifices are so graceful with their upturned eaves and at the same time so well constructed and enduring.

The *dougong* bracket is a structural member found between the top of a column and a cross beam. Each is formed of a double bow-shaped arm (*gong*), which supports a block of wood (*dou*) on each side. Fixed layer upon layer, the arrangements bear the load of the roof. Owing to hierarchical restrictions in feudal society, the *dougong* structure can be found only in the most magnificent buildings such as palace and temple halls. The number of layers of these bracket structures also depended on the importance of the buildings.

The *dougong* is measured in "piles" which vary greatly in their complexity of structure, from those composed of 106 parts to the most simple made up of five.The number of "tiers" also vary in each "pile". To take the double-eaved Taihedian, the building of the highest grade in the country, as an example. Its lower eaves are supported by *dougong* brackets of 7 tiers, whereas the higher eaves, 9 tiers.The number of tiers, normally 9, 7, 5 or 3, also represents the extent to which the eaves protrude.

From the point of view of structural mechanics, the *dougong* structure is highly resistant to earthquakes. It could hold the wood structure together even though brick walls would collapse in the same earthquake. This helped so many ancient buildings to stand intact for hundreds of years.

Caisson Ceiling
(藻井 *Zaojing*)

Visitors to an ancient Chinese palace hall often have their attention drawn to the centre of the ceiling. The *zaojing* or caisson ceiling is a distinctive feature of classical Chinese architecture, if not unique to it. It is usually in the form of a sunken coffer bordered in a square, a polygon or a circle, decorated with elaborately carved or painted designs. This architectural decoration dates a long way back for it has been found in tombs of the Han Dynasty 2,000 years ago.

One of the most magnificent *zaojing* is that of Taihedian (Hall of Supreme Harmony) in the old palace of Beijing. Carved and built with consummate skills, its splendour has remained undiminished by time. The caisson consists of three parts of different depths. The central or deepest part is the round "well (*jing*)", the middle part is the octagonal "well",and the outermost part, coming down to the same level as the rest of the ceiling, is a square. The whole design symbolizes the ancient Chinese belief that "Heaven is above and the Earth below" and that "Heaven is round and the Earth square." Dominating the centre of the caisson is a coiled dragon looking down into the hall and holding suspended in its mouth a huge silver-white pearl. It vies for glamour with the gilded dragons on the columns, giving the throne hall a colourful yet solemn nobility not to be found elsewhere.

The Chinese name for the caisson ceiling, *zaojing*, means "aquatic plants" (*zao*) and "well" (*jing*), both having to do with water. It was so named because there was constant worry about fire which might destroy the palace buildings. With water from the *zaojing*, so the ancients believed, the threat of fire would be averted.

"Gold Bricks" (金砖 *Jinzhuan*)

Palace halls and courts have been paved with bricks for 2,000 years since the Spring and Autumn Period, and this has become a distinctive feature of classical architecture. Today one can see brick-paved floors and grounds in the Forbidden City, the Summer Palace, the Ming Tombs and similar places elsewhere. The

bricks so used are called *jinzhuan* ("gold bricks").

Naturally not made of real gold, they are so-called because, when knocked, they produce a metallic sound. Another explanation for the name is that they were officially called during the Ming and the Qing dynasties *jingzhuan* (capital bricks) because bricks of this quality were meant only for the imperial house in the capital, In time, *jingzhuan* came to be known as *jinzhuan* or gold bricks. Whatever the reason for the unusual name, they did involve great costs and difficult skills to make and in this sense, the name might not be a great exaggeration.

The area around Suzhou used to be the home of these "gold bricks". Lying close to the Grand Canal, it abounds in a kind of fine clay most suitable as the material for compact bricks. To make those meant for the palace buildings, a strict procedure of manufacture must be adhered to. It included selecting the caly, pugging, setting, moulding, drying in the shade and, finally, firing in the kiln.This last process was the most complicated one. According to *The Illustrated Book on the Selection of Bricks*, a Ming Dynasty (1368-1644) work, (The unburnt bricks) after being put in the kiln, are smoked with smouldering husks for a month, burnt with fire-wood chips for another month, with twigs for a third month and with pine branches for yet another 40 days — totalling 130 days — before they are left to cool down and taken out of the kiln. The cost of a "gold brick" made this way was 0.96 taels of silver,enough to buy in those days one *dan** of rice. Another source says that, during the reign of the Ming emperor Jiajing, three years were spent to produce 50,000 bricks of this quality, averaging only 5 bricks per day. All finished "gold bricks" were shipped to the capital by the Hangzhou-Beijing Grand Canal.

The laying of the bricks, like their manufacture,must follow strict prescriptions. A bricklayer assisted by two helpers could only lay five in a day. Every piece must be ground and polished on site in such a way that, when paved, they fitted perfectly with other pieces, leaving no crevices. The bricks must also be soaked with raw tung oil so that they became lustrously dark like black jade.

Worn by several hundred years of time and trodden during the last decades by millions upon millions of sighteers, these bricks have largely remained intact, thanks to their rock-like hardness. Now they are from time to time mopped with a kind of high-quality vegetable oil to get a new layer of protection.

* *Dan*, a dry measure of grain, holding about 100 litre.

Patterned Footpaths

(花石子路 *Hua Shizi Lu*)

On a stroll through a Chinese garden or park, one often finds oneself walking on footpaths of coloured pebbles arranged in patterns — a feature of Chinese landscape gardening.

These patterned paths are not designed by architects, but made by artisans from beginning to end. The paving of pebbles is a complicated job calling for skill and experience. First, lime mortar is spread out as the foundation layer, then the designs are outlined by means of plain and roofing tiles set in the mortar. On this is spread a special putty made of lime, wheat flour and tung oil, on which again are fixed the pebbles of various natural colours — green ones for plant leaves, black ones for animals' eyes, and so on. And the designs include all the usual subjects of traditional Chinese painting: landscapes, figures, flowers, birds, historical and popular legends.

The best of patterned footpaths in China are found in the Imperial Garden in the rear of the Forbidden City. The coloured pebbles there make up pictures under such familiar titles as "Magpie Announcing the Spring", "Dragon and Phoenix", "Cranes in Clouds", "Guan Gong Felling an Enemy", "Two Greybeards Watching a Game of Chess" and so forth, which symbolize good luck, victory, longevity and the like.

On the whole, patterned paths are found more often in parks and private gardens in the southern provinces than in the north. Prominant in this respect are the gardens in Suzhou, where the designs on pebbled paths display a wide range of subjects. Some are just geometric patterns, for instance a square inside a circle like an ancient copper coin, signifying the old belief that "heaven is round and earth square". Others are in the forms of bats and cranes, Chinese symbols for good fortune and long life. Still others are patterned after the fishing net, expressing perhaps the general wish for affluent abundance.

Zoomorphic Ornaments (吻兽 *Wenshou*)

Chinese palaces, temples and mansions have on their roofs a special kind of ornaments called *wenshou* or zoomorphic ornaments, some on the main ridges and some on the sloping and branch ridges.

The monstrous thing at either end of the main ridge, called *chiwen*, appears roughly like the tail of a fish. Fierce and formidable, it looks as if it were ready to devour the whole ridge; so it is also known as *tunjishou* or the ridge-devouring beast. It is, according to Chinese mythology, one of the sons of the Dragon King who rules the seas. It is said to be able to stir up waves and change them into rains. So ancient Chinese put a *chiwen* at either end of the main ridge for its magic powers to conjure up a downpour to put out any fire that might break out. But for fear that it might gobble up the ridge, they transfixed it on the roof with a sword.

At the end of the sloping and branch ridges there are often a string of smaller animals, their sizes and numbers being decided by the status of the owner of the building in the feudal hierarchy.

The largest number of zoomorphic ornaments is found on the Taihedian Throne Hall or the Hall of Supreme Harmony of the Forbidden City. Leading the flock is a god riding a phoenix, after whom come a dragon, a phoenix, a lion, a heavenly horse, a sea horse and five other mythological animals, all called by unusual names. Quanqinggong (the Palace of Heavenly Purity), which the emperor used as his living quarters and his office for handling daily affairs, being next in status to Taihedian, has a band of nine animal figures. Still next in importance is Kunninggong (the Palace of Female Tranquility), which served as the empress's apartments; it has a group of seven zoomorphic figures. This number is further reduced to five for the twelve halls in side courtyards, that used to house the imperial concubines of different grades.Some of the side halls have only one animal figure each on their roofs.

These small animals were also believed to be capable of putting out fires. While this can be easily dismissed as superstition, they do add to the grandeur and magnificence of the imperial buildings.

The earliest ridge animals so far discovered in the country came to light in 1960 in a suburban area of Shashi, Hubei Province. On the interior wall of a roll tile which served as the body of a ridge animal figure was engraved "first year of Yuanguang", which means the year 134 B.C. It can be seen that installing animal figures on roof-ridges has been an established practice for at least 2,100 years.

Roof Crown

(宝顶 *Baoding*)

One of the structural members of traditional Chinese architecture, the *baoding* (literally, "treasure top") stands at the centre on top of certain types of pavilions, pagodas and towers which have no horizontal main ridges. Normally made of glazed tile, it may be in one of several forms (a gourd-shaped bottle, a vase, a pagoda, etc.), often surrounded by bas-relief carvings of dragons, phoenixes, peonies and the like.

The roof crown is not only an ornament at the top of a building but helps to reinforce the roof itself. Buildings on which *baoding* crowns are found are all constructed according to a traditional method by which the wooden parts of the roof structure go upward and gradually gather together at the top of a king post in the middle. The king post keeps the roof structure securely balanced rather like the stick of a parasol holding the ribs of its frame together. To give additional strength to the structure, ancient Chinese used glazed material for the crown to protect the king post from weathering and erosion. As the top of a building is most vulnerable to lightning, the king post was named in old times *leigongzhu* (post of the God of Thunder) in the hope that thunderbolts might keep away.

Many ancient buildings of this type, thanks to the king posts and roof crowns, have stood innumerable tests including storms and earthquakes over the ages and remained intact down to this day.

Zhonghedian (Hall of Complete Harmony) and *Jiaotaidian* (Hall of Union and Peace) in the Forbidden City (where the Ming and Qing emperors handled state affairs) have roof crowns completely gilded with gold, in harmony with the sumptuous surroundings and setting them apart from the red-or green-glazed crowns of lesser buildings.

Pavilions

(亭 *Ting*)

A common sight in the country, the Chinese pavilion (*ting*, which means also a kiosk) is built normally either of wood or stone or bamboo and may be in any of several plan figures — square, triangle, hexagon, octagon, a five-petal flower, a fan and what not. But all pavilions described as *ting* have this in common: they have columns to support the roof, but no walls. In parks or at scenic spots, pavilions are built on slopes to command the panorama or on lakeside to create intriguing images in the water. They are not only part of the landscape but also belvederes from which to enjoy it.

Pavilions also serve diverse purposes. The wayside pavilion is called *liangting* (cooling kiosk) to provide weary wayfarers with a place for a rest and a shelter in summer from the sun. The "stele pavilion" gives a roof to a stone tablet to protect the engraved record of an important event. Pavilions also stand on some bridges or over water-wells. In the latter case, dormer windows are built to allow the sun to cast its rays into the well, as it has been the belief that water untouched by the sun would cause diseases. Occasionally one finds two pavilions stand side by side like twins. In modern times, kiosks (also called *ting* in Chinese) have been erected in urban areas as postal stalls, newsstands or photographers' sheds for snapshot services.

Rare among pavilions are those built of bronze. The most celebrated of these is *Baoyunge* (Pavilion of Precious Clouds) in Beijing's Summer Palace. The entire structure including its roof and columns is cast in bronze. Metallic blue in colour, it is 7.5 metres tall and weighs 207 tons. Elegant and dignified, it is popularly known as the "Gold Pavilion".

The largest pavilion in China is also in the Summer Palace. The ancient building, named *Kuoruting* (the Pavilion of Expanse), has a floor space of 130 square metres. Its roof, converging in a crown on top and resting on three rings of columns (24 round ones and 16 square ones), is octagonal in form and has two eaves. With all its woodwork colourfully painted, the pavilion looks at once poised and majestic, well in harmony with the surrounding open landscape.

"Flowing-Cup Pavilion"
(流杯亭 *Liubeiting*)

This is a pavilion which used to serve as a place of recreation for men of letters.In the stone floor is cut a winding ditch to which water from a spring is channelled. Participants to the "flowing-cup" game would in turn fill a cup with liquor and set it "sailing" down the mini-canal. The man whose cup reached the end of the ditch without spilling would be a winner. On the other hand, a loser would be made to drink or compose a poem as a forfeit.

The game, according to another source, could be played in a different way. Players took their respective positions along the ditch. He, in front of whom the cup stopped, would be made to drink or chant a poem of his composition.

Emperor Qianlong (1711-1799), it is said, was a great enthusiast for this game. The "flowing-cup pavilion" built for the emperor still stands today in the Imperial Garden of the Forbidden City. Another pavilion of this type in Beijing is found at Tanzhe Temple. Although a poem (praising the pleasures of the game, "especially on a rainy day when there is little else to entertain the visitors with") is still intact on its columns, yet, alas! there is now neither flowing water nor cup. If the pastime should be revived with some modern variations—beer, lemonade or tea instead of spirits, singing or telling a joke as the forfeit if the players are not poets—it would certainly arouse considerable interest.

Another famous "flowing-cup pavilion" is *Lanting* (Orchid Pavilion) in Shaoxing, Zhejiang Province, which was a favourite resort of the great 4th-century calligrapher Wang Xizhi (321-379) and his friends, who used to gather there for the game and poem recitals. The little stream which carried the sailing cup is still there to greet modern admirers.

Terrace

(台 *Tai*)

The *tai* was an ancient architectural structure, a very much elevated terrace with a flat top. Generally built of earth and stone and surfaced with brick, it was used as a belvedere from which to look into the distance. In fact, however, many a well-known ancient *tai* as we know it today is not just a bare platform but has some palatial halls built on top.

A good example in hand is the Round City of the Beihai Park in Beijing. A terrace five metres high, it has, on its top space of 4,500 square metres, a main hall with side corridors.

The *tai* could be built to serve different practical purposes. It could be used as an observatory, as for instance the one near Jianguomen in Beijing which, with its brass astronomical instruments, dates to the Ming and Qing dynasties. It could also be used militarily, like the beacon towers along the Great Wall, to transmit urgent information with smoke by day and fire by night. Also on the Great Wall, there is a square *tai* at intervals of every 300 to 400 metres, from which the garrison troops kept watch. On the track of the ancient Silk Road can still be seen, here and there, ruins of the old defence fortifications in the form of earthen terraces.

Storeyed Building

(楼 Lou)

When the Chinese speak of a *lou*, they refer to any building of two or more storeys with a horizontal main ridge.

The erection of such buildings began a long time ago in the Period of the Warring States(475-221 B.C.), when *chonglou* ("layered houses") was mentioned in historical records.

Ancient buildings with more than one storey were meant for a variety of uses. The smaller two-storeyed buildings of private homes generally has the owner's study or bedroom upstairs. The more magnificent ones built in parks or at scenic spots were belvederes from which to enjoy distant scenery. In this case it is sometimes translated as a "tower". A Tang Dynasty poet upon his visit to a famous riverside tower composed a poem, two lines of which are still very much quoted: "To look far into the distance, Go up yet one more storey".

Ancient cities had bell and drum towers (*zhonglou* and *gulou*), usually palatial buildings with four-sloped, double-eaved, glazed roofs, all-around verandas and coloured and carved *dougong* brackets supporting the overhanging eaves. They housed a big bell or drum which were used to announce time, and the local officials would open the city gates at the toll of the bell early in the morning and close them with the strike of the drum in the evening.

During the Ming and Qing dynasties (14th to 20th century), in front of each city gate of Beijing stood an archery tower, forming a barbican as a defence fortification. Two of them can still be seen today, at Qianmen and Deshengmen gates. Also in Beijing, a "corner tower" still remains relatively intact at the southeastern corner of the old Inner City; it is put under state portection as a cultural relic, being the only one left in the ancient capital.

The art of constructing tall buildings was highly developed in China already in ancient times. Many multiple-storeyed towers of complex structure had wholly wood frameworks fixed together with *dougong* brackets without the use of a single piece of metal. Yueyang Tower in Hunan and *Huanghelou* (Tower of the Yellow Crane) in Wuchang are masterpieces among anicent towers.

Storeyed Pavilion

(阁 *Ge*)

The Chinese *ge* is similar to the *lou* in that both are of two or more storeys, but the *ge* has a door and windows only on the front side, with the other three sides all solid walls, and it is usually enclosed by wood balustrades or decorated boards all around.

Such storeyed pailions were used in ancient times for the storage of important articles and documents. *Wenyuange*, for instance, in the Forbidden City of Beijing was in effect the imperial library. *Kuiwenge* in the Confucius Temple of Qufu, Shandong Province, was devoted to the safekeeping of the books and works of painting and calligraphy bestowed by the courts of various dynasties. Visitors to the city of Ningbo, Zhejiang Province, can still see *Tianyige*, which houses the greatest private collection of books handed down from the past. Monasteries of a large size normally have their own libraries built in the style of a *ge* and *called cangjingge* to keep their collections of Buddhist scriptures. Some of the *ge*, notably those erected in parks, like other pavilions or towers (*ting*, *tai* and *lou*), were used for enjoying the sights.

The name *ge* is also used to describe the towers which shelter the colossal statues one finds in some great monasteries.

A prominant example in the *Guanyinge* of Dulesi Temple in Jixian County, Hebei Province. Twenty-three metres high and housing the huge idol of the Goddess of Mercy (Guanyin), it is the oldest exitsing multiple-storeyed structure of its kind in China. Built in the Liao Dynasty (907-1125 A.D.), it has withstood twenty-eight earthquakes including three of a devastating nature. When all the houses in the area collapsed, it was the only one that survived the disaster. This goes to show how well its wood frame was structured. Other well-known religious buildings housing Buddhist statues, big or small, include *Foxiangge* in Beijing's Summer Palace, *Dashengge* in Chengde's Puningsi Temple and *Zhenwuge* in Ronxian,Guangdong Province. All of them, tall, graceful and dignified, can be listed as representative works of classical Chinese architecture.

Waterside Pavilion
(榭 *Xie*)

One of the structures in traditional Chinese landscape gardening is the *xie*,a special form of pavilion.The earliest *xie* referred to the wood houses built on high terraces, but with the change of taste it became more and more the fashion in later epochs to build the single-storyed *xie* on the shore of lakes or ponds.

It is the special feature of the *shuixie* (waterside pavilion) to be rectangular or near square in plan figure, half erected on land and half over water supported by stone pillars driven into the lake bottom. This structure is walled not with bricks but with wood frames having fancy windows on all sides. The side on the water is bordered with railings and equipped with seats, fixed or movable, to provide visitors with a vantage point to feast their eyes on the scenes of the lake.

A typical example of this structure is the waterside pavilion in Xiequ Garden (Garden of Harmonious Interest) of the Summer Palace, from which Cixi, the all-powerful Empress Dowager of the late Qing Dynasty, is said to have enjoyed herself at fishing.

Other well-known buildings of the same style include *Furongxie* in Zhuozheng Yuan (the Humble Administrator's Garden) of *Suzhou*, Shuixie in the Zhongshan Park of Beijing and *Shuixinxie* in the Mountain Resort of Chengde.

House of Retreat

(斋 *Zhai*)

Certain types of Chinese buildings or rooms that provide or promise a quiet retreat for specific purposes are usually called *zhai*. This is originally a word with religious implication, meaning "purification by ablution and abstinence." From this has been derived the name *zhaigong* (palace of purification), a special housing complex where the mind and body were "purified" in preparation for sacrifice or other solemn ceremonies.

Such a *zhaigong* still stands on the precincts of Beijing's Temple of Heaven, inside its western entrance on the righthand side. The emperors of the Ming and Qing dynasties, before they presented themselves at the annual rites of Heaven worship, used to stay there to bathe themselves and observe abstinence from pleasures. During this period of preparation, there would be no banqueting, no music, no drinking; no criminals would be tried or punishments meted out. This palace attached to the temple is of considerable size. In a compound of more than 40,000 square metres stand the main halls, living quarters for the emperor, a drum tower and a number of supporting buildings, totalling over 60 rooms. The magnificent structures, defended by two moats and bordered by a long corridor of 167 bays, make up the largest palace of its kind in the country.

In private houses, the rooms used as studies or for the keeping of books are called *shuzhai* or "book chambers". All *zhai*, whether devoted to religious activities or intellectual pursuits, were built as a rule in quiet, secluded spots, away from the sightseeing areas, sometimes with enclosure walls of their own. In Beijing's Beihai Park, for instance, there is a "garden within a garden" called *Jingxinzhai* or the Tranquil Heart Studio. Covering an area of 4,700 square metres, this peaceful place with houses of a distinctively graceful style used to be frequented by Emperor Qianlong when he wanted to do some serious reading or pursue quiet pleasures. Other examples par excellence among buildings described as *zhai* are *Juanqinzhai* (Studio of Relaxation) of the Qianlong Garden and *Yangxinzhai* (Studio of Metal Cultivation) of the Imperial Garden, both in the Forbidden City.

Studio

(轩 *Xuan*)

This is usually a simple but elegant structure built in parks or gardens to give an embellishing touch to the landscape. It is called *xuan* after the name of a high-fronted, curtained carriage used in ancient times by people of rank probably because, like the carriage, it is also high in front and airy and spacious inside.

Architecturally, the *xuan* is rather similar to the *ting* (pavilion), and both are used to adorn the scenic views either standing on the side of a lake or nestling on the slope of a mountain. The difference between the two is that the *xuan* is larger in size, more closed and normally rectangular in plan, whereas the smaller *ting* has always a pointed round roof and no walls; the *xuan* is simply furnished with some tables and chairs so that people may sit down for a cup of tea, play a game of *weiqi* or appreciate works of art, whereas the *ting* is as a whole devoid of furniture.

The word *xuan* occasionally appears in the name of a teahouse or a restaurant. A well-known example is *Laijinyuxuan* (Come New Friends Studio) in Beijing's Zhongshan Park. Established in 1914, it operated at the beginning as a teahouse and snackbar. Lu Xun, the great writer used to frequent it to have tea, read newspapers and meet friends. The present Laijinyuxuan is a restaurant specializing in Sichuan and Jiangsu cuisine.

Among other structures repesentative of this style of architecture, imperial or private, one should count *Xieqiuxuan* (Paint Autumn Studio) in Beijing's Summer Palace and *Zhuwaiyizhixuan* (Lone Bamboo Outside the Grove) in Suzhou's *Wangshiyuan* (Master-of-nets Garden).

Covered Corridor
(廊 *Lang*)

The covered corridor represents a typical architectural style in Chinese landscape gardening. A long, belt-like structure, it is a roofed walk with low railings or long side benches. Providing people with shade from the sun and protection from the rain, it not only adds beauty to the general scenery but plays a useful role as well.

Chinese covered corridors fall into many varieties, but roughly they may be divided into *youlang* which links two or more buildings, *qulang* (the zigzag corridor), *huilang* (the winding corridor), *hualang* which is used for the display of potted flowers, and *shuilang* which borders on lakes or goes over ponds.

It is the general consensus that at the top of all classical corridors must be listed by any standards the Long Corridor in Beijing's Summer Palace, a unique treasure in the art of gardening arrangement. An exquisite winding structure of 728 metres, it stretches its 273 bays* between the hill and the lake, broken at intervals by four double-eaved, octagonal pavilions, which represent the four seasons of the

year. All its beams are painted with coloured pictures of landscapes, human figures, flowers, birds and scenes of historical and popular stories. These paintings total more than 40,000 in number,and the visitor would need eight hours just to linger two seconds before each picture.

The Long Corridor, it is said, was built by Emperor Qianlong of the Qing Dynasty in order that his mother might safely enjoy the scenes of rain or snow over the lake. In effect it is a piece of ingenious engineering which at once divides and links up the hill and the lake of the Summer Palace. Whether one looks at the lake from the hill or at the hill from the lake, the Long Corridor is always there, not only a pretty frame border for a nice picture but a colourful belt to bind the two parts together.

Famous private Chinese gardens, located mostly in the southern provinces, likewise, are often ornamented with corridors. In Suzhou's Zhuozhengyuan (The Humble Adminitrator's Garden), part of the winding corridor is erected over a pond and has been described as a "rainbow over water". With its reflection in the water, sometimes ruffled by a breeze, it is a favourite spot for visitors to take snapshots of themselves. In Liuyuan (Garden to Linger In), another well-known garden of Suzhou, the buildings — pavilion, terrace, hall, tower, etc.— break, and at the same time are linked by, a 600-metre-long corridor. Its walls have fancy cut-through windows which reveal scences on the other side, and they are also inset with 300 stone-engravings of calligraphical works and poems by famous masters; both the windows and the engravings are regarded as masterpieces of their respective kinds.Visitors come here either to feast their eyes on the natural views or on the works of art and poetry, all at their choice.

* The bay or the area within four columns was the Chinese traditional unit for measuring floor space.

Altar

(坛 *Tan*)

The Chinese *tan* is an altar where ancient rulers used to offer sacrifices to Heaven or the gods, and architechurally it refers to a special type of terrace-like building. Several ancient *tan* in Beijing, mostly dating from the Ming (1368-1644) and Qing (1644-1911) dynasties, have remained in name if not in fact. A number of Beijing's parks, for instance, still have the word *tan* in their names:

Tiantan (Temple of Heaven),
Yuetan (Altar to the Moon),
Ditan (Altar to the Earth),
Ritan (Altar to the Sun), and
Xiannongtan (Altar to the God of Agriculture).

All five were first built in the Ming Dynasty for the worship of such gods as indicated in their names. On the grounds of what have become parks stood the altars of worship, either round terraces of three tiers (as in the Temple of Heaven) or square ones of one or two tiers.

The most celebrated altar in China is Huanqiutan (or the Circular Mound Altar) in Beijing's Temple of Heaven, religiously the most important temple construction. Built in 1530 under the Ming, the all-marble terrace is five metres high and consists of three tiers, respectively 30, 40 and 70 metres across. The terrace is circular, in keeping with the ancient Chinese belief that Heaven was round. The number of the stones used for the surfaces of the terrace and on the steps and the number of the balusters for each tier are all nine (the highest masculine figure* or its multiples. The terrace is devoid of

any other structure and it was to this bare altar that the Ming or Qing emperor came to offer sacrifices to Heaven. In a ceremony called "open-air rite", obeisance was made to Heaven, unobstructed by anything overhead.

* See article entitled "The Number 'Nine' and Imperial Buildings".

Altar of the Land and Grain
(社稷坛 *Shejitan*)

In the Zhongshan Park in central Beijing lies a terrace filled and surfaced with earth of five different colours. This is Shejitan (the Altar of the Land and Grain), popularly known as *Wusetu* (Five-Coloured Earth).

The classical sense of the word *she* means the God of the Land or Soil, while *ji* refers to the God of Grain. *Shejitan* was the site where ancient emperors held rites of worship and offered sacrifices to the Gods of Land and Grain and prayed for good harvests.

The terrace is an elevated square bordered with three tiers of low walls of white marble. The surface earth shows five patches of different colours with nuclear demarcation — green to the east, red to the south, white to the west, black to the north and yellow in the middle. The arrangement symbolizes the ancient principle that "all earth under the sky belongs to the emperor".

The five colours of the altar, some say, are also intended to represent the five elements (metal, wood, water, fire and earth) which ancient Chinese philosophy held to compose the physical universe.

According to others, the altar could be taken as a rough model showing the distribution of different types of soil in China as the various colours of the earth on the terrace point approximately to the same directions in which soils of similar types actually lie in the country.

What is noteworthy is that the altar gives prominance to the yellow colour by putting yellow earth in the middle. Yellow was held in high esteem in old China because it is the colour of the Yellow River, the once-supposed only cradle of the Chinese civilization. And for the same reason, all Chinese still call themselves the descendants of the Yellow Emperor, a legendary leader in prehistoric China.

Besides, yellow is also the colour of the ripe grain, whose god was the object of worship at Shejitan. The land and the grain, both yellow in colour, made up the material foundation of the imperial power, and therefore yellow became the imperial colour in China. This was another reason for putting yellow earth in the middle.

Originally a square stone column stood at the centre of the altar to symbolize the rock-like solidarity of the empire, It was removed in 1950.

The Altar of the Land and Grain was built in A.D.1421 in the Ming Dynasty (1368-1644). Since then, sacrifices had been offered by the emperors of different generations twice a year in spring and autumn until the fall of the Qing Dynasty in 1911.

Archway

(牌楼 *Pailou*)

The *pailou*, also known as *paifang*, is an archway of a memorial or decorative nature. It could be made of wood, brick or stone, with or without glazed tiles, often carrying some inscriptions on the middle beam. The normal places where such archways stood were thoroughfare crossroads, shrines and temples, government offices, bridges, parks, tombs and mausoleumns, and they generally carried inscriptions to propagate certain moral principles or to extol government achievements. The *pailou* could also serve as the facade of a shop to prettify its entrance and attract customers. Many a *pailou* was erected to praise the "lofty virtues" of certain individuals in the locality. Fettered by the feudal ethical code, many widowed women refrained from remarriage just in the hope to have "pailou of chastity" built for them when they reached a ripe old age.

According to relevant records, there used to be some 57 archways in old Beijing. Among the well-known ones were one each at the crossroads of Dongdan and Xidan, four each at Dongsi and Xisi, one at Qianmen and a couple standing astride Chang'anjie, the main street running east-west in front of Tian'anmen. Nearly all of these have been taken apart or moved elsewhere.

A well-preserved *pailou* is the one in

front of the main entrance to the Summer Palace Park. Built 200 years ago, it is composed of four columns forming three arches and carrying on top seven roofed ornamental units. Inscribed in front and at the back are two Chinese classical characters each, succinctly summing up the beauty of the hill and the lake in the park. Painted on it amidst rich colour are 176 golden dragons and 36 golden phoenixes, giving the visitor a foretaste of the sumptuous splendour that he is going to witness.

Among the *pailou* of imperial mausoleums, the best-known is the great archway standing at the southern end of the grounds of Beijing's Ming Tombs, the first structure that the visitor will see. A *pailou* of 6 columns, 5 arches and 11 superstructures, it is built entirely of white marble, and its stone columns are engraved with dragons, lions, unicorns and other mythical animals to display the power and dignity of the imperial house. Majestic and simple, it measures 28.86 metres wide and stands 14 metres high in the middle, one of the greatest of its kind in the country.

In the city proper of Beijing, a few other ancient archways have survived down to this day. There is a glaze-tiled *pailou* of 3 arches and 7 superstructures in Shenlujie Street, Chaoyang District. Not far from the Lama Temple (Yonghegong), in the side street of the ancient Imperial College (Guozijian), two *pailou* have been renovated recently and are shining with new lustre.

Marble Boat

(石舫 *Shifang*)

An ornamental structure in classical Chinese landscaping, *shifang*(marble boat)is also popularly known as *shichuan* (which means the same thing) or, in southern China, *hanchuan* (land boat). A marble boat usually has its underwater base and its body built of stone and its on-deck cabins of wood in the form of a pavilion (*xuan*, *xie* or *lou* — see previous articles); it may also have a cabin at the bow and at the stern, just like a model of the "official boat" of ancient times. Normally built near the shore, it is accessible by means of a stone bridge. Sightseers go aboard to appreciate the surrounding scenery, feeling as if they were gently water-borne on a real boat.

The largest existing marble boat in China is the one of 36 metres in the Summer Palace of Beijing. Popularly known as the Marble Boat, its official name Qingyanfang has long fallen into oblivion. First built in A.D. 1755 completely of white stones during the reign of Emperor Qianlong, it was meant to be a water-surface belvedere for the imperial family as well as a symbol of the rockfirm solidarity of the imperial power. The original wood cabin-house was burnt down by British and French troops in 1860. The present structure, rebuilt in 1893 during the reign of Guangxu,was supposed to be patterned after the cabin-house on a Western vessel, the windows paned with stained glass and the floor paved with enamelled tiles. It is generally believed that the powerful Empress Dowager Cixi watched from the Marble Boat the exercise of naval units on the lake. It is now one of the tourist attactions in the park.

Similar stone boats but of smaller sizes can be seen in the royal palace of the Taiping Heavenly Kingdom (1851-1864) in Nanjing, in three private gardens of Suzhou and on Lake Shouxihu (Slender West Lake) of Yangzhou.

Scenic Openings (景洞 *Jingdong*)

Jingdong or the "scenic opening" is the general term for fancy gates and windows, another feature of the national art of Chinese architecture. Usually found in parks and private gardens, they make part of the landscape or provide picture frames, as it were, to natural scenes while serving their proper practical purposes.

The fancy gate (*jingmen*) may be of any form — round, square, oval, a polygon, a vase, a crescent, a bay leaf, a lotus petal,a garland and what not. On either side of such a gate are usually planted bamboos, flowering plants and grass and occationally also rockeries. Leading to and through the gate is sometimes a pebbled pathway with flowery patterns. Thus beautiful scenes are created with the fancy gate as the focus.

Fancy windows (*jingchuang*), likwise, may be built in various shapes — round, oval, a drum, a crescent, a polygon, an open book, a bay leaf, a flower... And as a rule they are fixed on fancy or corridor walls in pleasure gardens and, through them as picture frames, sighteers may view scenes on the other side, which change as they walk on.

Noteworthy is the type of scenic windows called *louchuang* or "hollowed windows". They may be constructed of tiles or bricks, wood or stone carvings, leaving openings of geometric patterns and decorated with carved-through human or animal figures. Strollers, through the openings of such windows, will get fragmentary and changing glimpses of the views across the wall. The idea of the *louchuang*, probably an artistic conception unique to Chinese architecture, has recently been extensively adopted for modern buildings such as theatres, art galleries, cultural centres, exhibition halls, art shops and certain high-class residences. They help ventilation and interior lighting, and create pleasing sights as well.

Taihu Rockery

(太湖石 *Taihu Shi*)

Grotesque rockeries are often seen in Chinese parks and gardens. They range from a little over a metre to 5 or 6 metres in height. Some stand on the roadside, others are planted in the middle of ponds. They are as a rule grown with exotic flowers and rare plants, making scenic attractions. More often than not they are made from "Taihu rocks" produced at Lake Taihu in Jiangsu Province.

The said lake area is rich in carbonate limestone rocks and enjoys abundant rainfalls. Constant weathering and rainwater erosion over the ages bore through the rocks, turning them into exquisite nature-wrought pieces of art, characterized by special features of their own. They are slender and elegant in shape, marked with clear veins, riddled with holes, rich in curves and lines on the surface, and porous in substance so that water may be passed up or down for an even distribution of moisture. For these reasons, they are favourite with Chinese painters and landscape architects.

Taihu rocks are not works of nature alone.Since the Song Dynasty (960-1279) masons on the shores of Lake Taihu have been engaged in the quarrying of rocks on the mountains. On the basis of their natural forms and sizes and according to the requirements of landscape gardening, they chisel the rocks and improve on their shapes and then place them in the lake to be washed and sculpted by the moving water. Left thus they become well-polished and smooth in a few years' time. A good example for rockeries made of such rocks can be seen in the Yuyuan Garden of Shanghai under the appropriate Chinese name of "Yulinglong" (literally, "Jade Exquisiteness").

Rocks have been used to make artificial miniature hills in pleasure gardens. Well-known among these one can list the rock hill named Duixiu ("Heaped Elegance") in the Imperial Garden of Beijing's Forbidden City and another hill in Suzhou, named Shizilin ("Forest of Lions") because it is made up of rocks that resemble as many lions in myriad postures. An artificial hill in the Summer Palace, lying to the east of Xijialou Pavilion,is also built of Taihu rocks and in imitation of Suzhou's Forest of Lions just mentioned.

In the old days, to glue the rocks together into rockeries or hills, a cementing material made of lime and glutinous rice gruel was used. Today the work is made easier by the use of cement. Large rockeries and artificial rock hills often contain man-made caves which wind through them left and right, up and down, now lighted through openings, now completely dark, forming labyrinths to provide sightseers with delightful surprises. The hills are normally grown with trees and plants on their slopes and crowned with pavilions on top where visitors may linger to take in the panorama. Such arrangements often engender an illusion of space bigger than the reality, while partitioning a compound into secluded sections, tranquil from the noise of the outside world.

The Chinese Quadrangle
(四合院 *Siheyuan*)

Traditionally most urban Chinese used to live in quadrangles called siheyuan or "four-side enclosed courtyards" . These courts, as the name implies, are formed by inward-facing houses on four sides, closed in by enclosure walls.

A small or medium-sized *siheyuan* usually has its main or only entrance gate built at the southeastern corner of the quadrangle with a screen wall just inside to prevent outsiders from peeping in.

Such a residence offers space, comfort and quiet privacy. It is also good for security as well as protection against dust and storms. Grown with plants and flowers, the court is also a sort of garden.

All the quadrangles, as products of feudal society, were built in accordance with a strict set of rules. From their size and style one could tell whether they belonged to private individuals or the powerful and rich. The simple house of an ordinary person has only one courtyard with the main building on the north facing, across

through pavilion). Behind the main building there would be a lesser house in the rear and,connected with the main quadrangle, small "corner courtyards".

The lord and lady of the house lived in the sunny main building and their children in the side chambers. The southern row on the opposite side, those nearest the court, the southern building with rooms of northern exposure and flanked on the sides by the buildings of eastern and western chambers. The mansion of a titled or very rich family would have two or more courtyards, one behind another, with the main building separated from the view of the southern building by a wall with a fancy gate or by a *guoting* (walk-to the entrance gate, were generally used as the study, the reception room, the manservants' dwelling or for sundry purposes.

Not only residences but ancient palaces, government offices, temples and monasteries were built basically on the pattern of the *siheyuan*, a common feature of traditional Chinese architecture.

Bridges

(桥梁 *Qiaoliang*)

Chinese bridges from ancient times, highly varied in material and form, are an important legacy with national characteristics, occupying an important position in the world history of bridge-building.

China, a country with such a long history, has inherited from her past bridges without number: there are, it is said, four milion of them if one counts the stone arch bridges alone. In the southern regions of rivers and lakes, the landscape is dotted with bridges of various sized and descriptions, which make it all the more picturesque.

1.The Stone Arch Bridge
(石拱桥 *Shigong Qiao*)

The stone arch bridge is the most common type of bridges one sees in China. According to historical records, the first stone arch bridge named *Lurenqiao* (Wayfarers' Bridge) was built in A.D. 282 near the ancient Luoyang Palace.That was more than 1,700 years ago. Then, in a Luoyang tomb dating back to the early Zhou Dynasty, archaeologists found the gate to the burial chamber to be of arch structure, showing that the stone arch existed in China already in about 250 B.C. at the latest.

Anji Bridge is the most famous stone arch bridge in China. It spans the Jiaohe River in Zhaoxian County, Hebei Province,and is better known as Zhaozhou Bridge after the ancient name of the county. Built during the years 591-599 A.D. by the mason Li Chun, it is still being used as a bridge, so is one of the bridges with the longest service life in the world. It is 9 metres wide and stretches all its 50.82 metres on a single arch spanning 37.4 metres of the river. On each of the "shoulder" of the main arch, there are two spandrel or minor arches. They not only improve the general look of the bridge but help to reduce its weight and thus lighten the load on its foundations. In times of flood water, the minor arches join the main one to facilitate the passage of the current, weakening its impact on the body of the bridge. A masterpiece of bridge construction, this old stone structure has been taken in subsequent ages as the model for stone arch bridges.

On wide rivers and lakes, multiple-arch bridges were erected of stone. One of them is *Lugouqiao* (better known to Westerners as Marco Polo Bridge). Built in 1189-1192 in the southern vicinity of Beijing, it is 265 metres long and lies on 11 arches which range in their span from 16 to 20 metres. The tops of the 280 stone balusters flanking the bridge are carved in the form of squatting lions. It is therefore also called popularly as Shiziqiao (Lions Bridge), making it one of the scenic spots around Beijing.

The bridge with the largest number of stone arches is *Baodaiqiao* (Treasure Belt Bridge) on the Grand Canal in Suzhou. Winding 317 metres long, it is formed of 53 arches, three of which are higher than the others to allow the passage of boats sailing on the main channel. The floor of

the bridge is level and smooth, making it easier for the boat-trackers of the old days to trudge on. It is said that the bridge was built with money realized from a precious belt donated by Wang Zhongshu, Governor of Suzhou in the Tang Dynasty (618-907 A.D.), hence its name. It has become one of the local sightseeing attractions.

The stone arch bridge is strong and sturdy but capable of being built in a great variety of shapes. It has long been used as a landscaping structure in China. A splendid example is *Yudaiqiao* (Jade Belt Bridge) in Beijing's Summer Palace. A stone bridge of a single span, it has a high arched back rather like the hump of a camel. Flanked by finely-carved white marble balustrades, it is a picturesque decoration to the lake.

But the typical example of landscape bridges is the Seventeen-arch Bridge in the same palace. Built in 1750, the 150-metre-long bridge has often been compared to a rainbow spanning the lake between the eastern shore and the Nanhu Island. Adorning the stone balustrades on the sides are 554 lively lions exquisitely carved out of marble.

Technical improvements have been made since the founding of New China. In 1966 a single-span stone bridge with minor arches was built at Yixiantian on the Chengdu-Kunming Railways. It is the largest of its kind, being 63.2 metres long, 26 metres high, with the main arch spanning 54 metres. Again in 1971, a stone bridge was constructed at Jiuxigou in Fengdu County, Sichuan Province. Straddling 116 meters on a single span, it is the largest single-arch stone bridge in China up to date.

Stone arch bridges are highly resistant to weathering and can be very beautiful and dignified. Their material is often available locally. For these reasons, they still have a great future even though other bridges are being built with more modern techniques.

2.The Zigzag Bridge (曲折桥 *Quzhe Qiao*)

A landscaping structure, the zigzag bridge is found in some gardens or suburban scenic spots. It is intended to give an interesting feature to the scene on lakes and ponds and enlarge the scope of the sightseers' stroll over the water surface.

Such a bridge may have three, five or more zigzags. *Jiuqu Qiao* (the Nine-bend Bridge) in Yuyuan Garden of Shanghai's old town is typical one. Going over a lake thirty metres across, the bridge winds more than a hundred metres because of its nine twists. Flanked by balustrades with square posts, it has also by its side a mid-lake pavilion in which visitors may have a cup of tea upstairs and enjoy the view all around.

Another well-known zigzag bridge lies at Gulangyu, a beautiful island just off the Fujian city of Xiamen (Amoy). Zigzagging along the islet's southern shore, the bridge lies nestled against a nice garden. Standing on it at intervals are graceful pavilions known under such names as "Watching Anglers", "A Thousand Waves" and "Moon in Water". Ramblers on the bridge draw pleasure from the feeling as if they were walking on the sea, especially when the tide is in.

3.The Cross Bridge (十字形桥 *Shizixing Qiao*)

This is a very rare bridge in China; in fact, probably only one of its type still exists in the country. Named Yuzhaofeiliang (Flying Bridge over Fish Pond), it is situated in front of the Hall of the Goddess in Jinci Temple of Shanxi Province. It is a stone bridge with "wings" so that it looks like a cross. The main bridge floor is 18 by 6 metres, while each wing spreads 6 metres long and 4 metres wide. Erected over a pond, in which fish play about, it also looks like a huge bird about to take off. Sightseers may get on it from any direction and cross the lake anyway they want.

According to recorded history, such cross bridges began to be built as early as the Northern Wei Dynasty (A.D.386-534). The existing one just described is thought to have been built during the Northern Song (960-1127) at the same time as the Hall of the Goddess. Nearly a thousand years old, it is generally regarded as a treasure among ancient Chinese bridges.

4.The Pavilion Bridge (亭桥 Ting Qiao)

A component part of the art of landscape gardening, the pavilion bridge is often built over the surface of a quiet lake, forming a small scenic area and providing sightseers with a place for a rest, sheltered from the sun and rain.

The Five-Pavilion Bridge (*Wuting Qiao*) in Yangzhou, Jiangsu Province, is a fine example of this style. Built in 1757 and like a belt worn on the narrow waist of Shouxihu (Slender West Lake), it bears five pavilions on its 55-metre-long floor. The middle pavilion is higher than the other four, which are spaced two on each side in perfect symmetry. And the middle pavilion is a double-eaved structure while the rest have only single eaves. All pavilions have their four corners upturned, with rows of tiles gathered up in the middle under a *baoding* (roof crown—see a previous article). The pavilions, lined up with short covered corridors, have yellow glazed tiles on the roofs but green ones for the curving ridges, forming a splendid contrast of colour.

Inside the pavilions, the ceilings are decorated with colourful sunk panels and the beams and columns are carved with beautiful patterns.

The body of the stone bridge is formed on 15 arches of varying sizes, all large enough to allow the passage of boats that ply the lake.

In contrast to the exquisiteness of the pavilions, the supporting piers look sturdy and rugged. With its structural complexity, the bridge may claim to be a masterpiece of its kind.

Another well-known pavillion bridge is Chengyang Bridge, also known as *Fengyuqiao* (Wind-and-Rain Bridge), on the Linxi River in the Dong Autonomous County of Sanjiang in the Guangxi Zhuang Autonomous Region.

Built in 1916, the bridge is not so old.

Its wood body, 70 metres long by 10 metres wide, rests on piers built completely of big stone blocks. Standing on it are five tile-roofed and pagoda-like pavilions connected by a long covered corridor. So the bridge may also be described as a covered bridge.

The five-storeyed pavilions have multiple eaves, which are upturned as if about to take wing. The wall panels in the pavilions and corridors are carved with popular Dong motifs, showing marked characteristics of this ethnic minority. All the well-structured woodwork, crisscrossed with thousands of laths, purlins and rafters, were joined together by means of tenons and mortises without the use of a single nail,bearing testimony to the ingenuity of the Dong people.

There are in China a large number of bridges with pavilions and corridors; they can often be seen especially down in the south. The buildings of some bridges are so large that they could be used as meeting halls or trade markets on water.

Underground Irrigation Tunnels
(坎儿井 *Kan'erjing*)

In the Hami and Turpan areas of Xinjiang, there is an unusual kind of irrigation system formed by underground tunnels and wells. A system worked out by the people in the light of local climate and topography, it has a history of over 2,000 years.

These areas are extremely arid. The Turpan area, for instance, has an annual precipitation of 16 mm only but a rate of evaporation of 3,000 mm. Given such conditions, surface irrigation is evidently out of the question. Fortunately Turpan is a basin surrounded by snow-covered mountains, which prove to be sources of abundant underground water. Making use of the land inclination, the local people succeeded in building such *kan'erjing* systems. Though simple in construction, the tunnels and wells represent gigantic engineering work. First many perpendicular wells are sunk at inervals of one or several dozen metres. Then underground tunnels are dug, linking up the bottoms of the wells. The sand and gravel thus excavated are usually piled around the mouths of the wells,making them look like miniature volcano crater.

The depths of the wells vary from those on high ground, which are as deep as 60-70 metres, to those close to the outlet of the water, which are only a few metres.

The underground water, following the sloping tunnels, flows in a steady stream to the oases, where it is guided into open channels and finally farmlands, making an ideal system of irrigation by gravity flow.

The tunnels are generally about three kilometres long, but can be more than ten kilometres in some exceptional cases.

According to a recent count, there are in the Turpan area alone 300 underground irrigation channels. In the whole of Xinjiang, the total length of all kan'er jing is estimated at 3,000 kilometres, forming a great underground canal system. The Xinjiang kan'erjing, also known as "karez", is thought to have been introduced from ancient Persia. Historical sources suggest, however, it may have been developed in China proper. According to *the Book on Rivers and Channels* of Sima Qian's *Historical Record* (completed in about 90 B.C.), Emperor Wu of the Han Dynasty (140-87 B.C.) ordered 10,000 troops to build a canal in what was today's Shaanxi Province. But the earth in these parts was loose, landslides were frequent, so wells were sunk, some as much as 40 *zhang**". deep, and they were linked up from below to allow the water to flow..." It was thus obvious that a *karez* was built in China as early as 2,000 years ago. Wang Guowei (1877-1927), a scholar on the history of Xinjiang, in his *Channel-Building in the Northwest*, offered the theory that it was people from the Han Empire who came to Xinjiang after relations were established and taught the local people how to construct underground tunnels through the soft, sandy and collapsible ground.

Visitors to Turpan as a rule wish to try the local grapes and inspect a *kan'erjing* irrigation system. They are right in menttioning these two things in the same breath, for without underground irrigation how could the "Land of Flames" produce grapes so sweet and tasty?

---

* *zhang*, a linear measure about 3 metres

Stupas and Pagodas

(塔 *Ta*)

Stupas appeared in China with the import of Buddhism and, during a long history of well over a thousand years, have become a valued part of the national Buddhist art.

"Stupa", a word from ancient Sanskrit meaning a square or round tomb or a "soul shrine", was mentioned by old Chinese works under no less than half a dozen varying translations. In modern times, people call all tower-like Buddhist structure *ta*, which includes all types of stupas and pogodas.

At the beginning, the stupa was a reliquary for keeping the relics or ashes of a saintly Buddhist. It is said that bead-like crystals of white or some other colour were often found among the ashes after cremation, and they are called *shelizi* or "holy relics".

Buddhists believe that when Sakyamuni, founder of the faith, was cremated, 84,000 beads of holy relics were found. They were shared among the kings of eight nations, who built stupas to house them for worship. This was generally thought to be the origin of stupas or pogadas. Subsequently they were built not only to bury the relics or ashes of venerable monks but also to safekeep holy scriptures and various ritual implements. They are therefore also called *fota* (Buddha's pagodas) or *baota* (treasure pagodas) and are objects of homage.

A Chinese proverb says, "To save a life is a holier deed than to build a stupa of seven storeys." Pagodas are mostly of seven or thirteen storeys. This is because odd numbers were supposed to be masculine and auspicious in China, but this has nothing to do with the teachings of

Buddhism.

Architecturally speaking,Chinese pagodas have special features of their own. A pagoda may be built of any of a number of materials—stone, brick, wood, glazed tile, iron or gold. In plan figure, it may be round, square, hexagonal or octagonal. In architectural style, it may be in one of a variety of forms, which will be discussed in the following pages.

Chinese pagodas, in short, are a significant part of the country's cultural heritage. With their beautiful shapes,bas-relief carvings, *dougong* brackets and upturned eaves, they no longer serve religious purposes alone but are exquisite tourist attractions as well.

1. The Close-Eaved Pagoda (密檐塔 *Miyan Ta*)

This is an earliest style of Chinese pagodas, typified by the Pagoda of Chongyuesi Temple in Dengfeng County, Henan Province. Built in A.D. 523 in the Northern Wei Dynasty, it is also one of the oldest existing pagodas in the country.

The twelve-sided, 41-metre-tall pagoda is built entirely of blue bricks. The body is girdled round by 15 closely-arranged eaves, which get smaller in beautiful proportions towards the tapering top. The inside of the pagoda is a structure of 10 floors, its octagonal rooms linked up by wooden stairs.

The Chongyuesi Pagoda is of great value in the history of Chinese architecture. Constructed in an age long before the reinforecd concrete was dreamed of, the all-brick structure, despite the ravages of wind and rain over 1,400 years, is still standing erect in testimony to the high level of skills at the command of the unknown ancient builders.

2. The Tower Pagoda (楼阁塔 *Louge Ta*)

This is the most common type of pagodas seen in China, which visitors may climb up for a brid'seye view of the surrounding country.

The world-famous Wooden Pagoda in Yingxian County, Shanxi Province, is a typical tower-like pagoda. Built in 1056 during the Liao Dynasty, it is the tallest and oldest of its kind in the country. Stand-

ing on a two-tiered stone terrace and true to its name, the structure, 67.13metres tall and 30 metres across at the bottom, is all wood. The ground storey has double eaves, so the 5-storeyed octagonal building has altogether 6 eaves. The interior of the pagoda consists of nine floors, with four of them hidden from outside view.

Structurally, the pagoda was erected by stages with separate sets of columns, beams and purlins in between every two storeys. Joining these together are *dougong* brackets of 50-60 kinds, which hold the huge wooden structure together in an integral piece, strong and magnificent, without the help of a single piece of metal. Visitors can scale the pagoda by the wooden stairs inside, which lead up to the top floor.

It is estimated that more than 3,500 cubic metres (or about 3,000 tons) of timber must have been used to build the pagoda.

The 900-year-old Wooden Pagoda, during its long life, has been weathered by the elements, shelled on by warlords' firearms, and shaken by strong earthquakes. Though slightly tilted, it still stands majestic today — an architectural marvel not only for China but for the whole world.

3. The Diamond-Throne Pagodas (金刚宝座塔 *Jingang Baozuo Ta*)

This type of religious architecture has its origin in India and is not often seen in China. Prominent examples are the group of pagodas in Beijing's Zhenjuesi Temple, popularly known as Wutasi (the Five-Pagoda Temple) because of them, and another group of Sarira-Stupas on a diamond-throne in Huhhot, Inner Mongolia. This type of pagodas have the common feature: five smaller pagodas being built on a high and solid square base called the "diamond-throne". The arrangement of the five pagodas, as for instance those in Beijing, is one at the centre and one each at the four corners of the base, dedicated to the Buddhas of all quarters. The lower parts of the pagodas and the sides of the diamond-throne are carved with bas-relief images of Buddha, considered to be of high

artistic value.

Recorded history tells us that, early in the Yongle reign (1403-1423) of the Ming Dynasty, a venerable monk named Bandida came from India to Beijing and presented to the Emperor five gold statues of Buddha and a plan for a diamond-throne. The emperor bestowed on him the title of "National Master" and ordered a temple with pagodas to be built according to his plan. The resultant structure was basically after the Indian design, with some Chinese modifications. The base was enlarged to be 1.78 metres high, while the five pagodas were reduced to about 6 metres tall. Furthermore, a Chinese pavilion of glazed tiles with a round roof and double eaves was erected in the midst of the pagodas on the platform base. It became an Indian religious structure with pronounced Chinese features—an early example of the happy integration of Chinese and Indian art.

4. The Dagoba

(喇嘛塔 *Lama Ta*)

The dagoba is a pagoda of Tibetan style and its most remarkable example is the White Dagoba in Beijing's Miaoyingsi (Temple).

The Mongolians of China were believers of the Lamaist school of Buddhism, which originated in Tibet. When Kublai Khan (Emperor Shizu) of the Yuan Dynasty united the country in 1260 he set about rebuilding a large Liao Dynasty dagoba in Beijing into the symbol of the Mongolian regime blessed with divine power to keep the capital's inhabitants and the nation in peaceful submission.

The project took eight years and was completed in 1271. The 731-year-old dagoba is like a nectar vessel or divine vase rising 50 metres towards the clouds, towering and dignified.

The dagoba consists of three parts: the base, the body and the crown. The base, covering 1,422 square metres, is a huge platform of brick representing the "throne of Mt.Sumeru". The main part of the body is in the shape of an upturned alms-bowl more than 18 metres across. Higher up is the part like a truncated tapering column bearing the sign of the Buddhist wheel. It carries on its top a canopy 9.7 metres across like a huge, opened umbrella. Hung from the edge of the canopy are a ring of 36 bronze bells, which tinkle in the wind. The crown of the dagoba, on the plate of the canopy, is a smaller pagoda of 4 metres, glistening with its gold plate in sunlight.

Chinese dagobas were patterned after Nepalese prototypes. The Beijing dagoba just described was designed by a Nepalese engineer known in Chinese as Anigo. So it shows in its appearance an obvious foreign artistic style. It remains an eloquent symbol of the enduring friendhip between China and her Himalayan neighbour.

5. Mother-and-Children Pagodas (母子塔 *Muzi Ta*)

The "mother-and-children pagodas" are an architectural complex rarely seen in China. The best-known example is the Manfeilong White Pagodas at Damenglong in Jinghong County, a district populated by the Dai nationality in Xishuang Banna, Yunnan Province.

They were built in the year 565 of the Dai calendar (A.D.1204) as a group arrangement of nine pagodas. The one in the middle is the "mother", erect and elegant with her height of 16.29 metres. Standing around her at what would be the corners of a regular octagon are her "children"—eight smaller pagodas 9.1 metres high.The bottoms of the pagodas consist of niches containing statues of Buddha. Viewed from above, the group resembles a lotus blossom with its petals open. The pagodas have snow-white bodies and golden tips and, seen through the green foliage of trees,also look like new bamboo shoots after a rain, a familiar sight to the local people, so the Dai also call them by the pet name "bamboo-shoot pagodas".

Legend has it that Sakyamuni,founder of Buddhism, once came to sermonize at Damenglong and left a huge footprint, 58 cm by 85 cm, on a blue rock. In commemoration of this important event, local followers built the group of nine pagodas on the same rock where he had stood. For this association, they are held in high esteem by Buddhist circles and many pilgrims come here from different quarters to pay homage.

The Manfeilong Pagodas are noted for their peculiar shape and beautiful style, and also for the pronounced Dai flavour shown by the bas-relief carving and sculpture. They are therefore a cultural marvel in the southwestern region of the country.

6. Forest of Pagodas
(塔林 *Talin*)

As a pagoda is the burial place of monks, a "forest of pagodas" may be said to be the graveyard of Buddhists.

One of such forests belongs to the famous Shaolin Monastery in Dengfeng County, Henan Province. With its 220 brick pagodas, it is the resting place of the abbots and senior monks of the monastery who lived at various times under several dynasties, from the Tang to the Qing, spanning a thousand years. It is the forest of pagodas of the largest scale and built over the longest stretch of time.

The pagodas, mostly decorated with carvings and inscriptions, are generally of three to seven storeys and of varying heights up to 15 metres. They are of different forms: square or hexagon in cross-section, a column, a cone or a vase in shape, with straight or curving lines.

Another rare "forest of pagodas" lies in the vicinity of Lingyansi (Temple) in Shandong Province. It compirses 176 pagodas of a variety of attractive forms, also built at different times since the Tang Dynasty.

These pagodas, in Henan, Shandong and elsewhere, are a valuable storehouse of information about various sects of Chinese Buddhism, and about the arts of sculpture and architecture of different ages.

Beijing City Gates
(北京城门 *Beijing Chengmen*)

In times of yore Beijing consisted of an outer city and an inner city, with the imperial city (otherwise known as Forbidden City, or the Former Imperial Palace) contained in the inner city. Altogether there were 20 city gates. Entering or exiting these gates by carts and horses was governed by hard-and-fast

regulations. The following is a brief introduction of it.

There are nine gates for the inner city which used to be on what is today's Second Ring Road.

First, Zhengyang (South-Facing) Gate. The Zhengyang Gate is for the exclusive use of royal sedan chairs and carts to show the supremacy of the feudal monarchs. The gate stands to the south of Tian'anmen Square; during the Ming and Qing it was the front gate of the inner city of Beijing. Built in 1419 or the 17th year of the Yongle reign of the Ming, it is by far the only well-preserved city gate tower in Beijing.

Second, Xuanwu Gate, or Gate of Military Virtue. Known in old days as Gate of Complaisant Rule, it was the gate for prison vans. Felons sentenced to death by decapitation were escorted through this gate to the executioner's ground at Caishikou south of the city.

Thirdly, Fucheng Gate or Mound-Formed Gate. It was the gateway for coal transportation in ancient times. In ancient times Beijing got its coal supplied from Mentougou on the western outskirts, and the Fucheng Gate was the only gateway for coal-shipping carts.

Fourth, Xizhi Gate or Straight West Gate. Known in the past as Gate of Peaceful Righteousness, the Xizhi Gate was for tanks transporting water from Yuquan Hill to the imperial city. At the time the emperors drank water only from the Yuquan Hill.

Fifth, Desheng Gate, or Gate of Moral Triumph. It was the gate through which the imperial army returned to the capital from an expedition.

Sixth, the Anding Gate, or Gate of Peace and Stability. The Anding Gate was for carts transporting night soil out of the city. There is something symbolic about the name of this gate, which means Gate of Stability.

Seventh, Dongzhi Gate, or Gate of Worship of Benevolence, was opened exclusively for timber transportation. For this reason it is also known as Gateway of Firewood.

Eighth, Chaoyang Gate or Sun-Facing Gate, also known as Gate of Homogeneous Civilization. It was the city's passageway for grain transportation. That is why there were quite a few imperial granaries inside the gate. These included the Lumi Granary, the Nanmen Granary, and the Qianliang

Granary.

Ninth, Chongwen Gate or the Gate of Literary Virtue. Known otherwise as Hade (or Hada) Gate, it was the gateway through which liquor and wine were brought into the city.

There were seven gates for the outer city: Guangqu, Guang'an, Zuo'an, You'an, Dongbian, Xibian and Yongding. During the Ming, to protect south Beijing as a commercial and handicraft centre, the imperial court had planned for the construction of an outer city wall around the imperial city, but due to financial difficulties only part of the wall was erected in southern Beijing. Seven gates were opened into this wall for the convenient of local residents.

Access to the imperial city was by four gates, Tian'an, Di'an, Dong'an and Xi'an, which were for the exclusive use of officials and generals going to and from the imperial court. These gates were off limits to commoners.

Few of these gates exist now, as most of them have been torn down, but their names have remained.

Passes

(关隘 *Guan'ai*)

Passes were defence fortifications in ancient China. Born of war, they were built at points of strategic importance.

In the early days passes were built of rammed earth and masonry at places easily defended and hard to be conquered. Later, cities were developed around the passes. Countless passes were built in ancient China. The nine best known ones are Shanhai Pass, Jurong Pass, Zijing Pass, Niangzi Pass, Pingxing Pass, Yanmen Pass, Jiayu Pass, Wusheng Pass and Youyi Pass.

The passes fall roughly in two types: those on the Great Wall and those on postal routes.

The passes built on the Great Wall

were regarded as national defence facilities. At the eastern terminus of the Great Wall to the northeast of Qinhuangdao stands Sanhai Pass, which holds vital access between northeast and central China. Reputedly the most important pass on the eastern section of the Ming-dynasty Great Wall, Sanhai Pass is therefore billed as "No. 1 Pass on the Great Wall". On the western terminus of the Great Wall stands Jiayu Pass, an imposing citadel with the *gobi* desert to the north and the Qilian Mountain to the south. For its vital strategic importance as a major transportation hub on the celebrated Silk Road for economic and cultural exchange between China and the West in ancient times, Jiayu Pass is billed as "First Formidable Pass under Heaven". Other major passes on the Great Wall that played a major role in resisting foreign invaders and defending the national territory include Juyong Pass of Beijing and Niangzi Pass of Shanxi Province. Many of the passes on the Great Wall have been placed under government protection as key cultural heritage sites.

The passes on postal roads may be regarded as regional fortresses. A common feature about these passes is that virtually all of them were on provincial or county boundaries. Though not as large as those on the Great Wall, they were also strategically located for defence purposes. In warring periods they were often bones of contention between rivalling strategists. Major postal road passes in existence today are Loushan Pass of Guizhou, Jianmen Pass of Sichuan, Yanmin Pass of Shanxi, Tiemen Pass of Xinjiang, and Guimen Pass of Guangxi, which have all become popular scenic spots today.

Lingxing Gate

(棂星门 *Lingxingmen*)

The Lingxing Gate, also known as Heavenly Gate or Gate of Dragon and Phoenix, was a kind of ancient structure built in different places with different meanings. More often than not they stood in front of mausoleums, altars and temples dedicated to emperors. The Lingxing Gate comprises baluster columns and decorated

tie-beams. The space between the columns has three to nine partitions which are either blocked with walls or left open with gates to symbolize access to heaven - meaning that the deceased could ascend the sky once through this gate.

The Lingxing Gate is also found in front of Confucian temples to symbolize the Confucian school's willingness to accept people with talent and virtue.

Hakka Castle-Like Dwellings

(客家土楼 *Kejia Tulou*)

The Hakka people inhabiting southeast China are known for the distinctive style of their dwellings in a variety of castle-like designs. They are round or square, and there are also those in the style of big mansions or in the shape of the Eight Diagrams.

These castle-like dwellings go back a long way in history. The Hakkas, who had moved from central China and settled in the south after the Western Jin Dynasty, developed this unique style of house construction, but it was not until after the Qing that their dwellings began to grow in

height and size to function as fortifications. A mixture of clay, ash and bran was the major construction material for these dwellings, which are reinforced with bamboo and timber. A typical Hakka dwelling is a 10-metre-high structure with three to five floors, and the walls, more than one metre in thickness, were built of earth repeated rammed until they became sturdy enough against earthquake and intruders. Each dwelling covers an area of over 1,000 square metres, with 30 or so houses on each floor. Thus a dwelling with more than 100 rooms is large enough to accommodate 100-300 people. Access to such a dwelling is by a single gate, and a well was dug inside it to supply drinking water. Some Hakka dwellings are fashioned in the shape of a palace richly decorated with carved beams and lacquered pillars. Most phenomenal of all the Hakka dwellings are a kind of round castle, in which houses are arranged in three mutually containing circles. In some places a single castle-like Hakka dwelling is seen atop a mountain, or several or a dozen such dwellings are clustered in a tiny basin. They are evocative of ancient Roman castles, yet each looks distinctive in its Hakka architectural style.

The term "Hakka" means "outsiders" — the Hakka people were settlers from north. That is why elements of central Chinese architecture, such as symmetry and a clear distinction between the centrepiece and the ancillary structures, are palpable in their dwellings. As newcomers small in number and meagre in strength, they were in dire need of a kind of dwelling that could ward them off invaders and allow them to live in a compact community and rally their strength against any possible invasion.

The castle-like dwellings in Yongding, Fujian Province, are definitely the finest examples of Hakka architecture, which attract a constant stream of visitors from at home and abroad.

Eaves Tiles

(瓦当 *Wadang*)

Eaves tiles are small accessories in classical Chinese architecture fixed at the end of rafters for decoration and for shielding the eaves from wind and rain.

Eaves tiles emerged as a culture in their own light during the Zhou (c. 11th century-771 B.C.) and reached their zenith during the Qin and Han (221B.C.-220 A.D.). In the intervening years they underwent the transition from a half-round design to a cylindrical design, and from plain surface to decorative patterns, from intaglio to bas-relief carvings, from lifelike imagery to abstraction, and from patterns to inscriptions, until they became an art that involved language, literature, aesthetics, calligraphy, carving, decoration and architecture, with themes that ran the gamut from nature and ecology to mythology, totems, history, palaces, yamens, mausoleums, place names, auspicious phrases, folklore, and family names. Together the eaves tiles form a history book that reflects vividly the natural scenery, humanities and political science and economics. The Beijing Museum of Ancient Ceramic Civilization is billed as the nation's first exhibition centre of ancient eaves tiles: its collection of more than 400 eaves tiles has no lack of rare and valuable pieces of art.

Cave Dwellings

(窑洞 *Yaodong*)

Many labouring people on the Loess Plateau in northwest China live in caves dug into the mountains. The caves are laid out in rows one atop the other, looking like buildings of multiple floors in the distance.

These cave dwellings were either tunnelled into the face of a stupendous cliff or scooped into a cross-section of the Loess Plateau. A cave dwelling is usually six metres deep and four metres wide. Stone slabs are piled up to form a semicircle at the entrance, which is decorated with exquisite latticed windows in a variety of styles. There are also arched cave dwellings of masonry that are covered with earth, which is definitely a variation between stone and loess structures.

The beauty about the cave dwellings

is that they help maintain local topography and save on farmlands by making use of space that would have been otherwise left unused. They are warm in winter and cool in summer. The temperature inside is usually 13 degrees Celsius higher than in the open in winter and 10 degrees Celsius lower in summer. Moreover, the cave dwellings are sequestered in peace and quiet as they are shut from the noise of the outside world. There are drawbacks as well. For example, daylighting is poor, humidity high in summer, and ventilation leaves much to be desired.

Statistics show that 40 million live in cave dwellings that are scattered over an area of 600,000 square km in the middle and upper reaches of the Yellow River. In recent years curious visitors and scholars are arriving in droves to study the loess cave dwellings.

Embrasured Watchtower and Barbican Entrance (箭楼与瓮圈 *Jianlou yu Wengquan*)

Standing opposite every city gate of old Beijing was an embrasured watchtower, an imposing and distinctive structure that added tremendously to the landscape of the city in old days. Today, only two of them are still there: the Zhengyang Gate and the Desheng Gate.

In days of yore the watchtower was a defence fortification whose tall and sturdy structure, vast vistas and impregnability had won the favour of many an emperor in this country. A typical embrasured watchtower is found in the southeast corner of Beijing. Scooped into its walls are 144 embrasures in four rows.

A barbican entrance was built between a city gate and a watchtower, with a gateway built into either side of the barbican wall to facilitate the traffic of pedestrians, carts and horses. The barbican entrance was an ancillary defence facility that con-

tained a tiny temple and a store selling pots and basins of varying sizes. When the city was under siege, a heavy sluice gate was lowered to close down the city gate, soldiers hidden in the watchtower shot arrows at the enemy, and on the city walls the defenders filled pots and basins with boiling water and poured it at the enemy troops attempting to gain the top of the city wall by scaling ladders. Thus the store selling pots and basins was actually an integral part of the defence system of the city gates.

Aobao (Mongolian Stone Heaps for Worship) (敖包 *Aobao*)

Travellers to Inner Mongolia are impressed by pillbox-shaped heaps that stand singularly or in clusters on the grassland. The local people call them "*aobao*", and they are built of stone in areas where stone abounds, and sand and earth and encircled with willow branches where there is no stone. Buried inside an *aobao* is a Buddhist statue or a metal weapon, and the top of it and the area around it are decorated with streamers and what resemble totem poles. In the beginning they were used as road signs or boundary marks; later, local herdsmen began to worship them as dwellings of a certain divine protector. Legend has it that every time Gengghis Khan launched an expedition, the first thing he did was to offer sacrifices and libation to an *aobao* and pray for victory. Later, the *aobao* sacrificial ceremony also included the citation of soldiers who had performed meritorious deeds or who had died a hero's death. *Aobao* worship can be organized by individuals or local governments. When passing by an *aobao*, the Mongols make it a point to dismount from whatever they are riding. He may also pick up a few stones or lumps of earth and place them on it, or offer sacrifices and kowtow to it to ask for blessings for safety, a rich harvest and national stability.

Latticed Windows
(漏窗 *Louchuang*)

The latticed windows, as the name suggests, are opened for ventilation purposes. They are graced with artistically appealing patterns. According to historical data, latticed windows were widely used in palaces, gardens and dwellings during the Five Dynasties of the 10th century

The latticed windows are fashioned out of brick, tile, masonry or wood carving, and they come in a variety of shapes — square, hexagonal, knife, fan, leaf, or vase, etc. Highly decorative and artistically appealing, the latticed windows are fine works of art that serve to enhance the visual beauty of the walls; and render depth to the scenery by "framing" it into so many lovely pictures.

The latticed window as a favourite means of architecture engineering was widely used by architects in old days. They have remained an integral part of modern architecture.

Hutongs of Beijing
(北京胡同 *Beijing Hutong*)

The alleyways in Beijing are known as "*hutong*", the transliteration of a Mongolian word because most of the hutongs were a heritage of the Yuan Dynasty which established its capital city in Beijing in 1283. Thus the hutongs are 800 years old. There are so many of them in Beijing, as the saying goes, "There are 360 large hutongs and countless smaller ones." Statistics indicate that there used to be 4,550 hutongs in urban Beijing that were laid out in a Ming-dynasty pattern, and they were

from their own breasts. Many are named after famous people, such as Yongkang Hutong (the location of the residence of Xu Zhong, who was Marquis Yongkang), and Maojiawan Hutong (where the mansion of Mao Wenjian of the Ming Dynasty was situated). There is no lack of hutongs named after craftsmen or peddlers; these include Liulansu (Sculptor Liu Lan) Hutong, Mudao'r (Knife Sharpening) Hutong, Fengfangliu (Bean Noodle Maker Liu) Hutong, and Doufuchen (Beancurd Master Chen) Hutong. Some hutongs derived their names from their shapes, such as Chaoshou (Folded Arms) Hutong, Lesser Biandan (Carrying Pole) Hutong, Guaibang (Walking Stick) Hutong, Erduoyanr (External Auditory Canal) Hutong, and Gouweiba (Dog's Tail) Hutong. The hutongs in south Beijing are mostly related to commodities, such as Xianyukou (Fresh Fish) Hutong, Luomashi (Horse Market), Zhubaoshi (Jewellery Market), Guozishi (Fruit Market), Shuazishi (Brush Market) and Roushi (Meat Market) Hutong. Some are named after trees, including Huaishu (Scholar Tree), Songshu (Pine Tree), Sigengbo (Four Cypresses), Shuangliu (Twin Willows), Zongshu (Palm Tree) and Yingtao (Cherry Tree) hutongs. Ten hutongs are named after *chunshu*, the

as wide as four metres and as narrow as 62 cm. These alleyways are a magnum opus in their own right, recorded as they do numerous cultural artefacts, places of historical and cultural interests, fascinating tales of dignitaries and anecdotes about the city and its people.

The hutongs were named in a variety of ways. Some are named after government departments, such as Xingbu (Bureau of Punishment) Hutong, Cayuan (Investigation Bureau) Hutong, Silijian (Directorate of Ceremonial) Hutong, and Huoyaoju (Gunpowder Bureau) Hutong. The Lumicang, Nanxincang, Beixincang and Haiyuncang hutongs were named after the major imperial granaries in East District. Xishiku and Houku hutongs in West District got their names from warehouses in the service of the imperial family. Naizifu (Department of Nursing Ladies) Hutong was so named because in old days it was inhabited by women whose job was to supply the imperial family with milk

Chinese toon tree. Some have names that do not sound good, such as Fenchang (Night Soil Field), Kudang (Crotch) and Kushuijing (Bitter Water Well) hutongs, and most of these names have been changed.

The hutongs are a truthful reflection of the fact that the east district of Beijing was rich, the west district noble, the south district poor, and the north district dilapidated. As a legacy of history, the hutongs are rich in historical and cultural connotations.

A tour of the hutongs has become a major tourist program Beijing has to offer.

Yellow Tiles and Vermillion Walls

(黄瓦红墙 *Huangwa Hongqiang*)

The imperial palaces in Beijing are graced with yellow-glazed tiles and vermilion walls because they looked pleasant and reflected the wealth, dignity and authority of the emperors.

The tiles are generally glazed yellow, green, blue and black. Yellow-glazed tiles were for the exclusive use of roofs of palaces, mausoleums, gardens, temples and other imperial structures. Yellow was chosen as the royal colour and a symbol of dignity because in the "five elements" theory (gold, wood, water, fire and earth), yellow earth is in the centre of universe. In the imperial garden, such as the Summer Palace, however, roofs are covered with tiles of different colours. Only the houses in which the emperor lived or administered state affairs are covered with yellow-glazed roofs, while the houses for officials feature green-glazed roofs, and scenic buildings and commoners' dwellings are covered with black-glazed tiles. However, non-imperial buildings some-

times also featured yellow-glazed roofs, such as the Confucian Temple and the Lord Guan's Temple, because of the fact that the Chinese emperors had worshiped Confucius as Duke for the Propagation of Culture and the Qing emperors decorated Lord Guan as "Emperor Guan". All the buildings in the Imperial Palace are supposed to have their roofs covered with yellow-glazed tiles. The exception, however, is the national library (Chamber of Literary Profundity), whose roof is decorated with black-glazed tiles because black is the colour of water. As the library is prone to fire hazard, the use of black tiles was meant to subdue fire with water. The Hall of Prayer for Good Harvests in the Temple of Heaven is covered with a blue-tiled roof to symbolize the colour of the sky. It is clear that the colours adopted for the Chinese ancient structures have symbolic meanings.

The appeal of the yellow-glazed roofs is supplemented with the vermilion (darkish red) colour of the walls. By Chinese tradition red is the colour for festivities, and that is why even today the lanterns and streamers used during holidays and festivals are mostly red in colour. The imperial buildings are decorated with yellow tiles and vermilion walls to imply the emperor's wish for happiness. Many Buddhist temples in this country also featured yellow-glazed roofs and vermilion walls with the mandate of the royal family. During the Ming and Qing, yellow-glazed tiles could be used for imperial palaces, the mausoleums for emperors and those temples and altars built in compliance with the order of the emperors. Those who violated the rule could be sentenced to death.

The Great Wall
(长城 *Changcheng*)

The ancient and imposing Great Wall extends 6,350 kilometres through nine provinces, municipalities and autonomous regions. Passes have been built through this artificial barrier at a number of strategic posts. The Juyong Pass is one among them. Badaling is an outpost north to Juyong.

Construction of the Wall started in the 7th century B.C. After he unified the whole country by force, the First Emperor of Qin Dynasty had the northern defensive walls of the former Qin, Zhao and Yan states repaired and linked together. The present version of the Great Wall was built under order of Emperor Tai Zu of the Ming

Dynasty. Work started in 1368, the first year of his reign, and continued for over 200 years.

The Juyong Pass is strategically posed to the northwest of Beijing. It used to be the gateway to the ancient capital. Badaling rises high to over 1,000 metres above sea level. The section of the Great Wall between the Juyong Pass and Badaling is a typical Ming product. The mean height of its body is 7.8 metres, the maximum height being 8.4 metres. The average width of its base is some 6.5 metres; and that of its top is 5.8 metres, wide enough for five horses or ten soldiers passing abreast. The top is evenly paved with square bricks. Steps are built at places where the Wall rises abruptly into the clouds. The magnificent Great Wall is one of the seven great ancient engineering wonders of the world. Astronauts have confirmed that the Great Wall is the only artificial project perceivable from the moon.

Grand Canal of China

(大运河 *Da Yunhe*)

The Grand Canal, which cuts a 2,700-kilometre-long course from Beijing in the north to Hangzhou in the south, is extolled as a great water conservancy project of ancient China. It is also one of the longest of its kind in the world. It took three major engineering campaigns to bring the canal to its present shape:

First, the predecessor to the canal was the 150-kilometre-long Hangou Ditch dug near present-day Yangzhou in 485 B.C. (towards the end of the Spring and Autumn Period) in the State of Wu to link the Yangtze with the Huai River.

Second, during 1st-6th year (605-610 A.D.) of the Dayi reign of the Sui Dynasty, a canal 2,700 kilometres in length and 30-70 metres in width — known as the "Sui Emperor Yangdi's South-North Grand Canal"—was dug with the capital city of Luoyang in the middle to connect the Haihe, Yellow, Huai, Yangtze, and Qiantang rivers into a unified water shipping network.

Third, during the Yuan Dynasty (1206-1368), Beijing became the northern terminal of a 1,794-kilometre-long canal that flows all the way to Hangzhou in Zhejiang Province by way of Hebei, Shandong and Jiangsu provinces. This canal, known in history as the "Beijing-Hangzhou Grand Canal", was actually 900 kilometres shorter than its Sui-dynasty counterpart. Hence the difference between the South-North Grand Canal and the Beijing-Hangzhou Grand Canal.

In 1949 the Chinese government conducted a large-scale refurbishment of the Grand Canal. Some of the sections were widened or deepened, some of the zigzagging sections were straightened out, and a number of water conservancy and ship locks were added. Today, quite a few sections of this canal are large enough to accommodate large shipping fleets over 1,000 tons in capacity. The canal has also provided ample irrigation water for the farmlands on both sides. Cruise tours have been opened along the section that connects Hangzhou, Suzhou and Wuxi, to the delight of travellers from at home and abroad.

THINGS CHINESE 中国风物

Calligraphy and Painting

书画

Origin of the Chinese Script
(汉字的起源 *Hanzi de Qiyuan*)

There have been various stories about the origin of the Chinese script, with nearly all ancient writers attributing it to a man named Cangjie.

Cangjie, according to one legend, saw a divine being whose face had unusual features which looked like a picture of writings. In imitation of his image, Cangjie created the earliest written characters. After that, certain ancient accounts go on to say, millet rained from heaven and the spirits howled every night to lament the leakage of the divine secret of writing.

Another story says that Cangjie saw the footprints of birds and beasts, which inspired him to create written characters.

Evidently these stories cannot be accepted as the truth, for any script can only be a creation developed by the masses of the people to meet the needs of scocial life over a long period of trial and experiment. Cangjie, if there ever was such a man,must have been a prehistoric wise man who sorted out and standardized the characters that had already been in use.

A group of ancient tombs have been discovered in recent years at Yanghe in Lüxian County, Shandong Province. They date back 4,500 years and belong to a late period of the Dawenkou Culture. Among the large numbers of relics unearthed are about a dozen pottery wine vessels (called *zun*), which bear a character each. These characters are found to be stylized pictures of some physical objects. They are therefore called pictographs and, in style and structure, are already quite clsoe to the inscriptions on the oracle bones and shells, though they antedate the latter by more than a thousand years.

The pictographs, the earliest forms of Chinese written characters, already possessed the characteristics of a script.

As is well-known, written Chinese is not an alphebatic language, but a script of ideograms. Their formation follows three

principles:

1) Hieroglyphics or the drawing of pictographs — As explained before, this was the earliest method by which Chinese characters were designed and from which the other methods were subsequently developed. For instance, the sun was written as ⊙, the moon as ☽, water as ≀≀≀, the cow as ψ and so on. These picture-words underwent a gradual evolution over the centuries until the pictographs changed into "square characters", some simplified by losing certain strokes and others made more complicated but, as a whole, from irregular drawings they became stylized forms.

2) Associative compounds — The principle of forming characters by drawing pictures is easy to understand, but pictographs cannot express abstract ideas. So the ancients invented the "associative compounds", i.e., characters formed by combining two or more elements, each with a meaning of its own, to express new ideas. Thus, the sun and the moon written together became the character ⊙☽ (ming), which means "bright"; the sun placed over a line representing the horizon formed the ideogram ⊙ (dan) which means "sunrise" or ìmorningî.

3) Pictophonetics — Though pictographs and associative compounds indicate the meanings of characters by their forms, yet neither of the two categories gives any hint as to pronunciation. The pictophoneitc method was developed to create new characters by combining one element indicating meaning and the other sound. For instance, 爸 (*ba*) the Chinese character for "papa" is formed by the element 巴 (*ba*) which represents the sound and the element 父 (*fu*) which represents the meaning (father). Likewise the character 芭 (*ba*) is formed by 巴 (the sound) and 艹, indicating a plant. In this way, more and more characters were made until such pictophonetics constitute today about 90 percent of all Chinese characters.

Oracle Inscriptions (甲骨文 *Jiaguwen*)

These refer to the scripts carved by the ancients of the Shang Dynasty (c.17th to 11th century B.C.) on tortoise shells and ox scapulas (shoulder blades), which are considered to be the earliest written language of China.

Their discovery was by accident.

In 1899, Wang Yirong, an official un-

der the Qing Dynasty, fell ill. One of the medicaments prescribed by the physician was called "longgu" (dragon bones). They turned out to be fragments of tortoise shells which were found to bear strange carved-on patterns. He kept the "dragon bones" and showed them to scholars who, after careful study, came to the conclusion that the carvings were written records from 3,000 years before and were of great historical significance. Further enquiries revealed that the "dragon bones" had been unearthed at Xiaotun Village, Anyang County, Henan Province, site of the remains of the Shang Dynasty capital.

Further digs made at the site in later years brought to light a total of more than 100,000 pieces of bones and shells all carved with words. About 4,500 different characters have been counted, and 1,700 of them deciphered.

Three thousand five hundred years ago, Anyang was a marshy area teeming with tortoises, a favourite food of the local inhabitants. And the Shangs were a very superstitious people. Their rulers would resort to divination and ask the gods for revelation whenever there was a gale, downpour, thunderstorm, famine or epidemic. Before going on a war or a big hunt, they would still more want to divine the outcome.

The method of divination then was to drill a hole on the interior side of the tortoise shell and put the shell on a fire to see what cracks would appear on the obverse side. By interpreting the cracks the soothsayer predicted the outcome of an event. After each divination, the dates, the events and the results would be written down and carved on tortoise shells or bones. And the collection of these became the earliest

recorded historical material in China, from which modern scholars have divined "how things were in the Shang society".

In the oracle inscriptions,one finds many pictographs in their primitive picture forms, for example, ⊙ for the sun, 𩵋 for a fish, and so on. Together they show that a well-structured script with a complete system of written signs was already formed in that early age.

Later on, the area around Anyang became dry, and tortoises grew scarce, so people began to use bamboo strips instead for divination. From this grew the practice of asking the gods about the future by drawing bamboo sticks, as one may see today at certain temples—a practice that has its remote root in the superstition of the Shang people.

Inscriptions on Bronze Objects (金文或钟鼎文 *Jinwen huo Zhongdingwen*)

Another type of early Chinese script in its long history of development is represented by the inscriptions cast or carved on ancient bronze objects of the Shang and Zhou dynasties. It is called *Jinwen* (literally, script on metal) and, as ancient bronzes are generally referred to as *zhongding* (bells and tripods), it is also called *zhongdingwen*.

The *ding*, originally a big cooking pot with three (rarely four) legs, became a ritual object and a sign of power, and the owning of such tripods, as well as their sizes and numbers, was a status symbol of the Shang slave-owning aristocrats. At the beginning only the names of the owners were cast or engraved on the tripods. Later the tripods (and other bronzes) began to carry longer inscriptions stating the uses they were put to and the dates they were cast. Towards the end of the Warring States Period (475-221B.C.), the ducal states of Zheng and Jin had their statutes promulgated and cast on tripods.

Thus the inscriptions on the bronzes grew longer, from a few characters to a few hundred, from simple phrases to detailed accounts.

Many bronze objects bearing inscriptions have been unearthed in China and can be seen in a large number of museums.

A priceless tripod is the Dayuding (Large Tripod Bestowed upon Yu) dating from the early Zhou Dynasty (c.11th century to 256 B.C.), now kept at the Museum of Chinese History in Beijing. About one metre high and weighing 153.5 kilograms, it has on its interior wall an inscription of 291 characters in 19 lines, by which King Kang summed up the experience in founding a new nation and drew lessons from the failure of the preceding Shang Dynasty. The inscription also mentions that the King awarded his aristocrat follower Yu 1,722 slaves of various grades and large numbers of carriages and horses.

Another important bronze called Maogongding, now kept in Taiwan Province, belongs to the late Western Zhou. It bears an inscription of 497 characters, the longest ever discovered on any bronze hitherto unearthed. It is an account of how King Xuan admonished, commended and awarded Maogong Yin; it also reveals the instability of the Western Zhou regime at the time.

Both tripods furnish rare and valuable information to throw light on the slave society under the Western Zhou.

The ancient bronzes reflect not only the high level that Chinese metallurgy attained in their time. The inscriptions they bear may well be regarded as "books in bronze" which fill important gaps left by the scanty written history of that remote age.

Bamboo and Wood Slips
(竹简与木简 *Zhujian yu Mujian*)

In museums of ancient history one often sees bamboo or wood strips written with characters by the writing brush. These slips are called *jian*, the earliest form of books in China.

The practice of writting on slips began probably during the Shang Dynasty (c.17th-11th century B.C.) and lasted till the Eastern Han (A.D. 25-220), extending over a period of 1,600-1,700 years. *The Historical Records*, the first monumental general history written by the great historian Sima Qian (c.145 B.C.-?), consisting of 520,000 characters in 130 chapters and covering a period of 3,000 years from the legendary Yellow Emperor to Emperor Wudi of the Han, was written on slips. So were other well-known works of ancient China, including *the Book of Songs* (the earliest Chinese anthology of poems and songs from 11th century to about 600 B. C.) and *Jiuzhang Suanshu* (*Mathematics*

in Nine Chapters completed in the 1st century A.D., the earliest book on mathematics in the country).

Excavations in 1972 in an ancient tomb of the Western Han Dynasty (206 B.C.-A.D.25) at Yinque Mountain, Linyi, Shandong Province, brought to light 4,924 bamboo slips. They turned out to be handwritten, though incomplete, copies of two of China's earliest books on military strategy and tactics: *The Art of War by Sun Zi* and *The Art of War by Sun Bin*. The latter had been missing for at least 1,400 years.

To write on bamboo or wood slips was no easy task. Take bamboo slips for example. Bamboos were first cut into sections and then into strips. These were dried by fire to be drained of the moisture of the natural plant to prevent rotting and wormeating in future. The finished bamboo slips run from 20 to 70 cm in length. Judging from those unearthed from ancient tombs, royal decrees and statutes were written on slips 68 cm long, texts of the classics on 56-cm-long slips, and private letters on 23-cm ones. The brush was used in writing and, in case of mistakes, the wrong characters would be scraped off by means of a small knife to allow the correct ones to be filled in. The knife played the same role as the rubber eraser today.

Writing on bamboo or wood slips was done from top to bottom, with each line comprising from 10 to at most 40 characters. To write a work of some length, one would need thousands of slips. The written slips would then be bound together with strips into a book. Some books were so heavy that they had to be carried in carts. In some cases the blank slips were first bound into books before they were written on.

An unofficial story tells about Dongfang Shuo (154-93B.C.), a courtier and humorist, who wrote a 30,000-character memorial to the Western Han Emperor Wudi, using more than 3,000 slips. These had to be carried by two men to the audience hall.

Legend also extols the hard work of the First Emperor of the Qin of 2,200 years ago by telling that he had to peruse and comment on 60 kilograms of official documents every day. This may not be so astonishing as at first hearing, when one recalls that the passages were written on wood or bamboo slips.

Heavy and clumsy as they were, an-

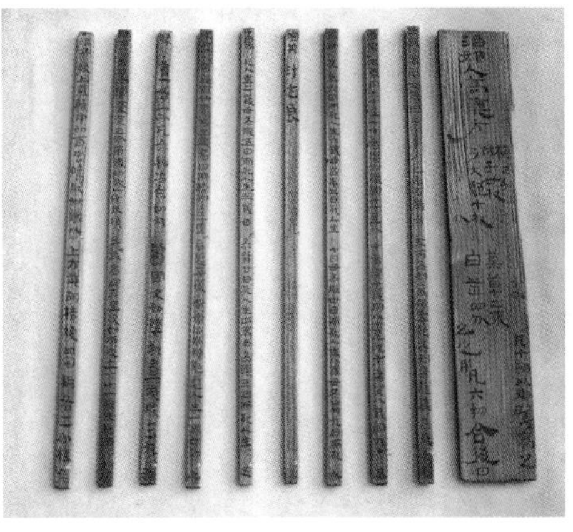

cient books of bamboo and wood played an important part in the dissemination of knowledges in various fields. They were in circulation over a long period until gradually replaced by paper which was invented in the Eastern Han Dynasty (A.D. 25-220).

Inscriptions on Drum-Shaped Stone Blocks (石鼓文 *Shiguwen*)

Shiguwen, the earliest Chinese script cut on stone, is kept in the Palace Museum (Forbidden City) of Beijing. It is in the form of inscriptions, on 10 drum-shaped stone blocks, of 10 poems of 4-character lines, depicting the ruler of a state on a big hunt. The characters are written in a style called *dazhuan* (big seal character) and have been taken as the "earliest model of *zhuan*-style writing", important to the development and studies of Chinese calligraphy.

The "stone drums" were discovered in the Tang Dynasty (A.D. 618-907) at Tianxing (present-day Baoji in Shaanxi Province) and caused a stir among men of letters and calligrahpers. Celebrated poets like Du Fu, Han Yu and Su Dongpo sang of the discovery in verse. It was only after the end of World War Ⅱ that the "stone drums" were moved to Beijing for safekeeping. But age, rough handling and long-distance transport have told on the valuable relics. Many of the characters have disappeared or eroded by weathering, and one of the "drums" has even become completely devoid of any engraving.

Before the invention of paper and printing, the best way in China to keep outstanding writings and calligraphic works was to carve them on stone. Those cut on drum-shaped blocks are called *shiguwen* (stone-drum inscriptions); and those cut on steles and tablets are called *beiwen*.

The former, being much earlier and rarer, are greatly treasured.

The dating of the set of stone drums under discussion was a subject of controversy over the ages. Careful research made by archaeologists in recent years has led to the conclusion that they were engraved in the state of Qin during the Warring States Period (475-221 B.C.) and are therefore well over 2,000 years old.

Inscriptions on Stone Tablets
(碑文 *Beiwen*)

Before the invention of the art of printing, how did ancient Chinese preserve and disseminate their culture and art? As mentioned before, they relied to a great extent upon inscriptions on stone tablets.

These inscriptions are known as *beiwen* (writings on stelae) or, less common, *shishu* ("stone books"). The earliest examples so far discovered are a set of 46 stelae engraved with the Confucian classics after the handwriting of the great Eastern Han calligrapher Cai Yong, carved in A.D. 175 or the fourth year in the reign of Xiping.They are called "Xiping Shijing"(Xiping Classics on Stone). They were stood in front of the lecture halls of the then Imperial College in old Luoyang (the site of the 3rd-century town, a little to the east of today's Luoyang) as standard versions of the classics for the students to read or to copy from.

To engrave a voluminous work or series of works would require thousands of stone tablets and generations of perseverance and painstaking work. By far the greatest work engraved on stone is the *Dazangjing* (Great Buddhist Scriptures), which comprises more than 14,000 tablets. The carving of the stupendous collection began in the Sui Dynasty (581-618) and concluded about 1644, when the Ming Dynasty was replaced by the Qing, extending over a thousand years! This rare collection of books on stone is kept in 9 rocky caves on Shijingshan (Stone Scripture Mountain) in Fangshan, southwest of Beijing.

In order to preserve the "stone books"of various periods, scholars in China started as early as 1090 (5th year of the Yuanyou Period under the Song

Dynasty) to collect the stelae scattered around the country and keep them together at Xi'an.Today in the halls of the "Forest of Stelae" are 1,700 tablets of many dynasties from the Han down to the Qing—the greatest collection in China.

The engravings on these stones cover a wide range of subjects—from the classics to works of calligraphy, from linear drawings to pictures in low relief. They include *the Thirteen Classics* (*Book of Changes, Book of History, Book of Songs, the Analects*, etc.), the basic readings required of Confucian scholars of past ages. These, totalling 650,252 characters, were cut on both sides of 114 stelae in A.D. 837 of the Tang Dynasty. The stelae stand side by side like walls of stone, a veritable library of stone books.

The Forest of Stelae at Xi'an is not only a treasure house of Chinese literature and history but represents, a galaxy of the best calligraphers of different ages and schools, including all the different scripts-*zhuan* seal character, *li* (official script), *cao* (cursive) and *kai* (regular) — each with its representative works. Visitors here may feast their eyes on the whole gamut of Chinese calligraphy.

Writings and Paintings on Silk

(帛书与帛画 *Boshu yu Bohua*)

From sometime in the Warring States Period (475-221 B.C.) and over a long priod of time in ancient China, plain silk of various descriptions joined bamboo and wood slips as the material for writing or painting on. Silk had advantages over the slips in that it was much lighter and could be cut in desired shapes and sizes and folded, the better to be kept and carried. But owing to its much greater cost, silk was never so popularly used as the slips.

The most valuable find of ancient silk writings was made in 1973 from an ancient tomb known as the No.3 Han Tomb at Mawangdui, Changsha, Hunan

Province. It is in the form of 30-odd pieces of silk, bearing more than 120,000 characters. They consist largely of ancient works that had long been lost. For instance, *Wuxingzhan* describes the orbits of five planets (Venus, Jupiter, Mercury, Mars and Saturn) and gives the cycles of their alignment, all with a precision far more remarkable than similar works which appeared later. Also found were three maps drawn on silk, showing the topograpghy, the stationing of troops and the cities and towns of certain regions of China. They are the earliest maps in China, and in the world as well, that have been made on the basis of field surveys. Contrary to their modern counterparts, they show south on top and north at the bottom.The topographic map is at a scale of 1:180,000, and the troop distribution map at about 1:80,000/100,000. Their historical value may be easily imagined when one remembers that they are at least 2,100 years old.

Silk was considered in old China an exquisite material for writing on; some were pre-marked with lines in vermilion. During the Tang Dynasty (618-907), it was the fashion to weave the lines into plain white silk to be used exclusively for writing.

Many artists of today have carried on the ancient practice of painting and writing on silk.

Calligraphy

(书法 *Shufa*)

Calligraphy is understood in China as the art of writing a good hand with the brush or the study of the rules and techniques of this art. As such it is peculiar to China and the few countries influenced by ancient Chinese culture.

In the history of Chinese art, calligraphy has always been held in equal importance to painting. Great attention is also paid today to its development by holding exhibitions of ancient and contemporary works and by organizing competitions among youngsters and people from various walks of life. Sharing of experience in this field often makes a feature in Sino-Japanese cultural exchange.

Chinese calligraphy, like the script itself, began with the hieroglyphs and, over the long ages of evolution, has developed various styles and schools, constituting an important part of the heritage of national culture.

Chinese scripts are generally divided into five categories: the seal character

the state of Qin) had long been lost, yet it is generally agreed that the inscriptions on the drum-shaped Qin stone blocks were basically of the same style as the old *zhuan* script.

When, in 221 B.C., Emperior Qin Shi Huang unified the whole of China under one central government, he ordered his Prime Minister Li Si to collect and sort out all the different systems of writing hitherto prevalent in different parts of the country in a great effort to unify the written language under one system. What Li did, in effect, was to simplify the ancient *zhuan* (small seal) script.

Today we have a most valuable relic of this ancient writing in the creator Li Siís own hand engraved on a stele standing in the Temple to the God of Taishan Mountain in Shandong Province. The 2,200-year-old stele, worn by age and weather, has only nine and a half characters left on it.

2) The *lishu* (official script) came in the wake of the *xiaozhuan* in the same short-lived Qin Dynasty(221-206B.C.). This was because the *xiaozhuan*, though a simplified form of script, was still too complicated for the scribers in the various government offices who had to copy an increasing amount of documents. Cheng Miao, a prison warden, made a further simplification of the *xiaozhuan*, changing the curly strokes into straight and angular ones

(*zhuan*), the official or clerical script (*li*), the regular script (*kai*), the running hand (*xing*) and the cursive hand (*cao*).

1) The *zhuan* script or seal character was the earliest form of writing after the oracle inscriptions, which must have caused great inconvenience because they lacked uniformity and many characters were written in variant forms. The first effort for the unification of writing, it is said, took place during the reign of King Xuan (827-782 B.C.) of the Western Zhou Dynasty, when his *taishi* (grand historian) Shi Zhou compiled a lexicon of 15 chapters, standardizing Chinese writing under script called *zhuan*. It is also known as *zhouwen* after the name of the author. This script, often used in seals, is translated into English as the seal character, or as the "curly script" after the shape of its strokes.

Shi Zhou's lexicon (which some thought was written by a later author of and thus making writing much easier. A further step away from the pictographs, it was named *lishu* because *li* in classical Chinese meant "clerk" or "scriber". Another version says that Cheng Miao, because of certain offence, became a prisoner and slave himself; as the ancients also called bound slaves "*li*", so the script was named lishu or the "script of a slave".

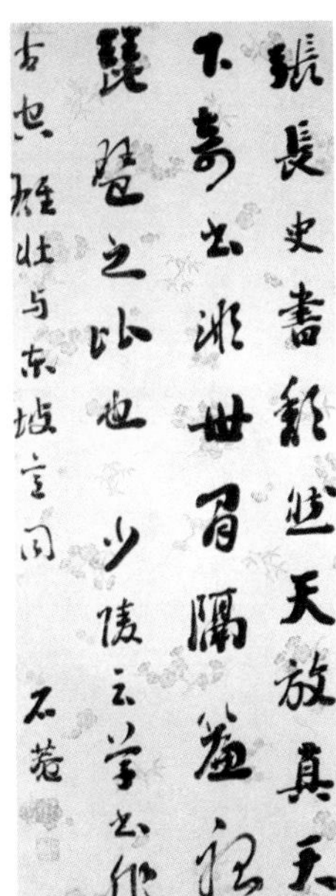

3) The *lishu* was already very close to, and led to the adoption of, *kaishu*, regular script. The oldest existing example of this dates from the Wei (220-265), and the script developed under the Jin (265-420).The standard writing today is square in form, non-cursive and architectural in style.The characters are composed of a number of strokes out of a total of eight kinds—the dot, the horizontal, the vertical, the hook, the rising, the left-falling(short and long) and the right-falling strokes. Any aspirant for the status of calligrapher must start by learning to write a good hand in *kaishu*.

4) On the basis of *lishu* also evolved *caoshu* (grass writing or cursive hand), which is rapid and used for making quick but rough copies. This style is subdivided into two schools: *zhangcao* and *jincao*.

The first of these emerged at the time the Qin was replaced by the Han Dynasty between the 3rd and 2nd centuries B.C. The characters, though written rapidly, still stand separate one from another and the dots are not linked up with other strokes.

Jincao or the modern cursive hand is said to have been developed by Zhang Zhi(?-c. 192 A.D.) of the Eastern Han Dynasty,flourished in the Jin and Tang dynasties and is still widely popular today.

It is the essence of the *caoshu*, especially *jincao*, that the characters are executed swiftly with the strokes running together. The characters are often joined up, with the last stroke of the first merging into the initial stroke of the next. They also vary in size in the same piece of writing, all seemingly dictated by the whims of the writer.

A great master at *caoshu* was Zhang Xu(early 8th century) of the Tang Dynasty, noted for the complete abandon with which he applied the brush. It is said that he would not set about writing until he had got drunk. This he did, allowing the brush to "gallop" across the paper, curling, twisting or meandering in one unbroken stroke, thus creating an original style. Today one may still see fragments of a stele carved with characters in his handwriting, kept in the

Provincial Museum of Shaanxi.

5) The *xingshu* or running hand is something between the regular and the cursive scripts. When carefully written with distinguishable strokes, the *xingshu* characters will be very close to the regular style; when swiftly executed, they will approach the *caoshu* or cursive hand. Chinese masters have always compared with vivid aptness the three styles of writing — *kaishu*, *xingshu* and *caoshu* — to people standing, walking and running.

The best example and model for *xingshu*, all Chinese calligraphers will agree, is *the Inscription on Lanting Pavilion* in the hand of Wang Xizhi (321-379) of the Eastern Jin Dynasty.

To learn to write a nice hand in Chinese calligraphy, assiduous and persevering practice is necessary. This has been borne out by the many great masters China has produced. Wang Xizhi, the great artist just mentioned, who has exerted a profound influence on, and has been held in high esteem by, calligraphers and scholars throughout history, is said to have blackened in his childhood all the water of a pond in front of his house by washing the writing implements in it after his daily exercises. Another master, Monk Zhiyong of the Sui Dynasty (581-618) was so industrious in learning calligraphy that he filled many jars with worn-out writing brushes, which he buried in a "tomb of brushes".

Renewed interest in brush-writing has been kindled today among the pupils in China, some of whom already show promises as worthy successors to the ancient masters.

Rubbings

(拓本 *Taben*)

To make rubbings from carved inscriptions was the earliest method of making copies in China before printing was invented. In ancient times, engravings were often made on stone of important imperial decrees, texts of Confucian classics, Buddhist scriptures, proved medical recipes as well as poems, pictures and calligraphic works by noted men of letters so that they may be appreciated and preserved for posterity.

To make rubbings is to make copies from these cut inscriptions or pictures. The method followed is rather simple in principle: paste a wetted piece of soft but firm paper (*xuan* paper is normally used) closely over the stone tablet or bronze and beat it lightly all over with the cush-

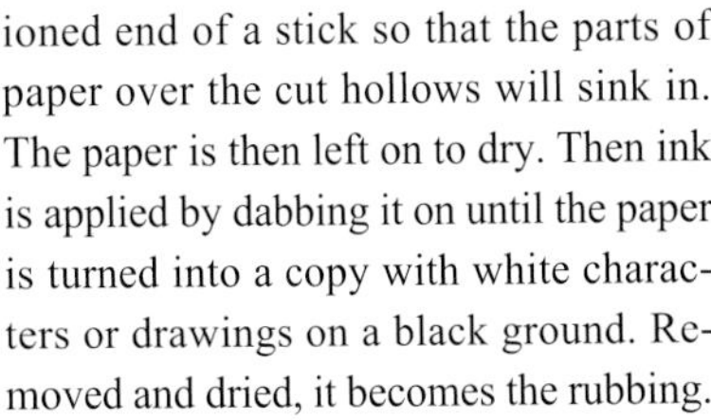

ioned end of a stick so that the parts of paper over the cut hollows will sink in. The paper is then left on to dry. Then ink is applied by dabbing it on until the paper is turned into a copy with white characters or drawings on a black ground. Removed and dried, it becomes the rubbing.

Rubbings vary and are called by different names according to the ink used. *Wujinta* (black gold rubbings) are made with very black ink; *chanyita* (cicada wing rubbings) are made with very light ink; *zhuta* (vermilion rubbings) with vermilion ink. Bound book form, the rubbings become *beitie* (stele rubbings), which may be used either as models for calligraphy or kept in a collection for appreciation or research.

As inscriptions on bronze, stone or wood wear out with time, early rubbings made from famous pieces of work are more valued and cherished than the ones made later.

Rubbings are convenient and meaningful mementoes for foreign tourists to remind them of their China tours. They are especially liked by Japanese visitors who share the same written character.

The Four Treasures of the Study (文房四宝 *Wenfang Sibao*)

The writing brush, ink stick, paper and inkslab are the traditional implements and materials for writing and painting and have always been named collectively as the "four treasures of the study".

Each of these items is represented by its "best": the *xuan* paper, *hui* ink stick, *hu* brush and *duan* inkslab are highly valued in the country and known abroad as well.

1. Xuan Paper (宣纸 *Xuanzhi*)

This paper is mainly used for writing or painting on with a brush. It has a history of over 1,000 years, being a "tribute paper" for the court as early as the Tang Dynasty (618-907). What we know today as Chinese painting is, for the over-

whelming part, executed on *xuan* paper, without which one might say there would be no Chinese painting as it is.

Xuan paper is known to some Westerners as "rice paper", which is a misnomer. In fact, it is made from the bark of the wingceltis (*Pteroceltis tatarinowii*) mixed with rice straw. Its home is Jingxian County, Anhui Province. As the county belonged in ancient times to the prefecture of Xuanzhou and the trading centre of the paper was at Xuancheng, so it has always been called *xuan* paper.

The making of *xuan* paper is a painstaking procedure involving 18 processes and nearly 100 operations and lasting over 300 days from the selection of materials to the finished product.

The *xuan* paper is praised as the "king of all papers" and is supposed to "last a thousand years". This is because it is white as alabaster, soft and firm, resistant to ageing and worms. It absorbs but does not spread the ink from the brush, which goes over it with a feel neither too smooth nor too rough. For these qualities, the *xuan* paper is not only used for painting and calligraphy, it is increasingly used nowadays for diplomatic notes, important archives and other documents. In addition, it may also be used for blotting, filtering and moisture-proof purposes.

2. The *Hu* Writing Brush
(湖笔 *Hubi*)

The writing brush is a functional handicraft article peculiar to China, an instrument still used by its pupils in calligraphy and painting exercises.

The first writing brush, according to

legend, was made by Meng Tian, a general under the First Emperor of Qin (259-210 B.C.), long time in command of the troops stationed along the Great Wall.

Once he happened to see a tuft of sheep's wool stuck on the wall. Taking it down and tying it on a stick, he made the first writing brush. Archaeological finds, however, have given the lie to this story. Traces on the painted pottery unearthed at the ruins of the neolithic site of Banpo Village near Xi'an show that the brush in its crude, primitive form was used 6,000 years ago. But people still called Meng Tian—who may have improved upon the brush—the originator of the writing tool. Shanlian Township in Wuxing County, Zhejiang Province — dubbed the "metropolis of the writing brush" — is also known as Mengxi (Meng's Stream) in memory of Meng Tian. The brushes produced at the township, which used to be under the Huzhou Prefecture in the old days, are called *Hubi* (Huzhou brushes) and supposed to be the best in the country.

The *hu* brush is made of the hairs of the goat, hare and yellow weasel, all marked by a quality which is at once soft and resilients. Dipped in the black Chinese ink, the *hu* brush may follow the manoeuvres of the writer's hand to produce a variety of strokes — dark or light, wet and solid or half dry and hollow — for different effects in the writing or painting.

First-grade *hu* brushes must meet four requirements: a sharp tip, neat hair arrangement, rounded shape and great resilience. Their making involves more than 70 steps of careful work. For instance, the preparation of the material alone means that the hairs of a goat or hare must be sorted out into dozens of bunches according to thickness, length, and softness or stiffness. Then hairs of different specifications are used to make different brushes meant for different uses. Now *hu* brushes are produced in more than 200 varieties.

The sticks for the brushes, made from local bamboo of high quality, are often decorated with ivory, horn or redwood; some are mounted at the top with horn or bone for the purposes of inscription.

Hu brushes, renowned as "king of writing brushes", used to be supplied to the imperial court. They were also a necessary item on the desks of men of letters or of means.

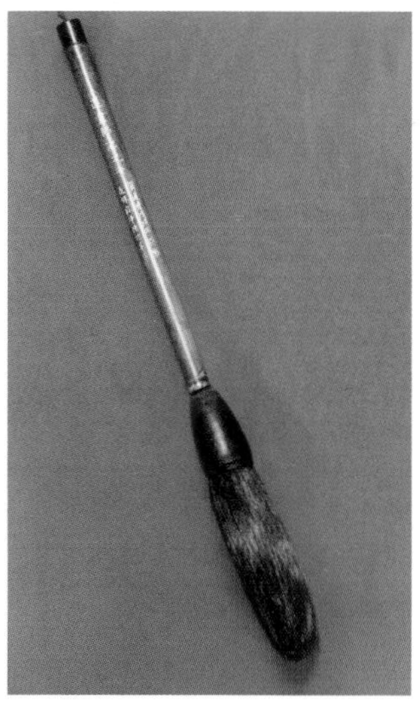

3. The *Hui* Ink Stick (徽墨 *Huimo*)

The Chinese "solid ink" or ink stick is used to produce ink, when needed; it can also be a work of art.

The way to make Chinese ink is to put a little water on an inkslab and then rub the ink stick on it round and round. When the liquid becomes thick and black enough, it is ready for writing with a brush.

Before the ink stick was developed, graphite was used for writing.When the country became more developed,it was felt during the Han Dynasty (206 B.C-220 A.D.) that graphite could not meet the growing demand. It was then that ink sticks began to be produced with pine or *tung* soot. The art was perfected during the Ming Dynasty (1368-1644), when high-quality ink sticks were made of the soot of pine resin, pork lard and vegetable oil.

The best Chinese ink sticks were first made in Shexian County, Anhui Province, and they are generally called *hui* sticks because Shexian was named Huizhou in the Song Dynasty.

This type of ink sticks was developed by ink artisan Xi Chao and his son Xi Tinggui of the Tang Dynasty, and then the art spread to the whole prefecture of Huizhou.

Hui ink sticks of the best quality contain musk, borneol and other precious aromatics normally used in Chinese medicine. These preserve the black colour for a long period of time.

Ordinary ink sticks are sold by the piece, but costly ones are more often than not sold in pairs. They are as a rule decorated with pictures and poems, gilded and coloured by the hand of well-known artists. Arranged in pairs in a satin-finished box, they are too good to be used but are kept by collectors as postage stamps are kept by philatelists.

Accomplished Chinese artists and calligraphers have always attached great importance to the selection of ink sticks. During the Qing Dynasty, a first-rate piece could be literally worth its weight in gold.

4.The *Duan* Inkslab (端砚 *Duanyan*)

To write with a brush, one must prepare one's own ink. Chinese ancestors developed the inkslab or inkstone for this purpose.

The earliest Chinese inkslabs unearthed so far date from the Han Dynasty (206 B.C.-220 A.D.), showing that this utensil for ink-making has been in use in the country for at least 2,000 years.

In a nutshell,the inkstone (*yan* or *yantai*) is a sort of millstone on which water is turned into ink by the rubbing of an ink stick. It is generally made of stone of a smooth and fine-grained variety.

To the fastidious calligrapher, a good inkslab should be made of the stone produced at *Duanxi*, a suburb east of the city of Zhaoqing(formerly Duanzhou), Guangdong Province. Named after the home of the stone, the *duan* inkslab has a history of over 1,500 years and has always been regarded as a valuable item in the scholar's study.

The stone must go through several painstaking processes before it is turned into the finished slab. These include quarrying, selecting, cutting, polishing and making of the containing box. The most difficult part is the digging-out of the stone, which lies under the Keshan Mountain near Zhaoqing. Quarrymen have to make tunnels at the foot of the mountain, drain them of water and creep in to dig out the right kind of stoneóall carried out under exacting circumstances.

Duan inkslabs are valued for their fine and smooth surfaces which look as if glossy with moisture. They make ink fairly fast and wet the hair of the writing brush evenly; they are also good for keeping leftover ink. A well-chosen piece of stone may also bear fine veins, indistinct but pretty to look at.

Seals

(印章 *Yinzhang*)

Seal-cutting is traditionally listed along with painting, calligraphy and poetry as one of the "four arts" expected of the accomplished scholar and a unique part of the Chinese cultural heritage. A seal stamp in red is not only the signature on a work of calligraphy or painting but an indispensable touch to liven it up.

The art dates back about 3,700 years to the Yin Dynasty and has its origin in the cutting of oracle inscriptions on tortoise shells. It flourished in the Qin Dynasty of 22 centuries ago, when people engraved their names on utensils and documents (of bamboo and wood) to show ownership or authorship. Out of this grew the cutting of personal names on small blocks of horn, jade or wood, namely the seals as we know them today.

As in other countries, seals may be used by official departments as well as private individuals. From as early as the Warring States Period (475-221B.C.) an official seal would be bestowed as token of authorization by the head of a state to a subject whom he appointed to a high office. The seal, in other words, stood for the office and corresponding power. Private seals are likewise used to stamp personal names on various papers for purposes of authentication or as tokens of good faith.

Seals reflect the development of written Chinese. The earliest ones, those of the Qin and Han dynasties, bear the *zhuan* or curly script, which explains why the art of seal-cutting is still called *zhuanke* and also why the *zhuan* script is also known in English as "seal characters". As time went on, the other script styles appeared one after another on Chinese seals, which may now be cut in any style except the cursive at the option of the artist.

Characters on seals may be cut in relief or in intaglio. The materials for seals vary with different types of owners. Average persons normally have wood, stone or horn seals, whereas noted public figures would probably prefer seals made of red-stained Changhua stone, jade, agate, crystal, ivory and other more valuable materials. Monarchs in the old days used gold or the most precious stones to make their imperial or royal seals. Today Chinese government offices at the central level have brass seals as a rule, while offices at lower levels wood ones.

Seals cut as works of art should excel in three aspects — calligraphy, composition and the graver's handwork. The artist must be good at writing various styles of the Chinese script. He should know how to arrange within a limited space a number of characters—some compact with many strokes and others sketchy with very few —to achieve a vigorous or graceful effect. He should also be familiar with the various materials — stone, brass or ivory — so that he may apply the cutting knife with the right exertion, technique and even rhythm. For the initiated to watch a master engraver at work is like seeing a delightful stage performance.

Image Seals (肖形印 *Xiaoxingyin*)

Seals carved with images (*xiaoxingyin*) developed as an off-shoot from the art of character-cutting on seals. They bear likenesses of scenes in life or things in nature. The cutting of these images come close in technique and skill to the art of engraving in general; only it is done on the limited space of a small seal, hence it is also called "miniature engraving".

The images that went on these seals were already many and varied in the Han Dynasty. Old image seals are found to cover a wide range of subjects, including the imaginary dragon and phoenix, the tiger, crane and other animals which are supposed to bring luck and good fortune. Other images are of the more familiar animals: chicken, duck, sheep, goose and fish. Still others portray activities such as dancing, music playing, hunting and livestock-raising. Every seal is a piece of art reflecting something in the life of the artist's age and showing distinctive local and national features. A great deal is contained in a space rarely exceeding the size of a postage stamp.

Image-bearing seals, like seals in general, may be cut in relief or in intaglio.

With the development of the tourist industry in China, shops at certain scenic sites have introduced souvenir seals with images of the Great Wall, the Tang Dynasty Tri-coloured pottery horse, etc. to be stamped on the albums of the tourists — a traditional art put to practical use, which is very well received.

Red-Stained Stone
(鸡血石 *Jixueshi*)

Jixueshi (literally, chicken-blood stone) is a precious stone found in China and is particularly good for making seals. A piece of this red-stained stone, greatly valued because it is rare, is worth up to 10,000 *yuan*.

Produced at Yuyan Mountain in Changhua County, Zhejiang Province, the stone is a mineral intergrowth of cinnabar and pyrophyllite. It derives its name because cinnabar is brilliantly red, like chicken blood. Pyrophyllite, on the other hand, may be in any of a variety of colours — white, yellow, grey, green or black —

which, stained with the red, presents at its best a glittering and translucent splendour never to be matched by human creations. The market value of such a piece of stone is assessed by the amount of red in it, the brillance of its colours, its translucence and purity.

First discovered during the Ming Dynasty (1368-1644), the stone was carved at the time into art objects used by the nobility as gifts to one another. Down to the Qing Dynasty (1616-1911), the imperial family and the aristocrats chose the best of the stone to make seals, buying it at high prices for their collection. Today it is occasionally available at antiquarian shops and Friendship Stores.

Ink Paste for Seals

(印泥 *Yinni*)

The ink paste used for the imprinting of seals is called *yinni* in Chinese, which means literally "seal clay". It stems from the clay that was used in ancient times to seal official documents and which, like the modern sealing wax, was stamped by a seal. Later on the word *yinni* began to refer to the traditional equivalent of the inking pad — the paste, usually red — which gives the seal its colour before it is stamped on paper.

High-quality inking paste is made of eight ingredients, some very precious: cinnabar, pearl, musk, coral, ruby, moxa, castor oil and a red pigment. Called the "paste of eight treasures", it produces brilliantly red prints. Paste of a still higher grade may contain pure gold and other rare materials and is so finely made that it may remain unchanged in hundreds of years. It also emits a faint perfume, and its oil neither oozes in summer nor congeals in winter. Ink paste of this description is greatly valued by painters and collectors.

To make a seal imprint, let the cut face of the seal touch lightly the inking pad several times, take a look and see that it is evenly coloured, place the paper to be stamped on a desk, cushioned beneath with some other paper, and then use the seal

lightly on it, holding it for a little while and increasing the pressure of the hand toward the end. An impression made this way, whether of characters or patterns, will be clear, well-defined and nice-looking.

Traditional Chinese Painting
(中国画 *Zhongguo Hua*)

An important part of the country's cultural heritage, the traditional Chinese painting is distinguished from Western art in that it is executed on *xuan* paper (or silk) with the Chinese brush, Chinese ink and mineral and vegetable pigments.

To attain proficiency in this branch of art calls for assiduous exercise, a good control of the brush, and a feel and knowledge of the qualities of *xuan* paper and Chinese ink.

Before setting a brush to paper, the painter must conceive a well-composed draft in his mind, drawing on his imagination and store of experience. Once he starts to paint, he will normally have to complete the work at one go, denied the possibility of any alteration of wrong strokes.

Xuan paper, as discussed in a previous article, is most suitable for Chinese painting. It is of the right texture to allow the writing brush, wet with Chinese ink and held in a trained hand, to move freely on it, making strokes varying from dark to light, from solid to hollow. These soon turn out to be human figures, plants and flowers, birds, fish and insects, full of interest and life.

Many a Chinese painter is at the same time a poet and calligrapher. He will often add a poem in his own hand on the painting, which invariably carries an impression of his seal. The resulting piece of work is usually an integrated whole of four branches of Chinese art—poetry, calligraphy, painting and seal-cutting.

Chinese paintings are divided into two major categories: free hand brushwork (*xieyi*) and detailed brushwork (*gongbi*). The former is characterized by simple and bold strokes intended to represent the exaggerated likenesses of the objects, while the latter by fine brushwork and close attention to detail. Employing different techniques, the two schools try to achieve the same end, the creation of beauty.

It is difficult to tell how long the art of painting has existed in China. Pots of 5,000-6,000 years ago were painted in colour with patterns of plants, fabrics, and animals, reflecting various aspects of the life of primitive clan communities. These may be considered the beginnings of Chinese painting.

China entered the slave society about 2,000 B.C. Though no paintings of that period have ever come to light, that society witnessed the emergence of a magnificent bronze culture, and bronzes can only be taken as a composite art of painting and sculpture.

In 1949 from a tomb of the Warring States Period (475-221 B.C.) was unearthed a painting on silk of human figures, dragons and phoenixes. The earliest work on silk ever discovered in China, it measures about 30 cm long by 20 cm wide.

From this and other early paintings on silk it may be easily seen that the ancients were already familiar with the art of the writing or painting brush, for the strokes show vigour or elegance whichever was desired. Paintings of this period are strongly religious or mythological in themes.

Paintings on paper appeared much later than those on silk for the simple reason that the invention of silk preceded that of paper by a long historical period.

In 1964, when a tomb dating to the Jin Dynasty (265-420 A.D.) was excavated at Astana in Turpan, Xinjiang, a coloured painting on paper was discovered. It shows, on top, the sun, the moon and the Big Dipper and, below, the owner of the tomb sitting cross-legged on a couch and leisurely holding a fan in his hand. A portrayal in vivid lines of the life of a feudal land-owner, measuring 106.5 cm long by 47 cm high, it is the only known painting on paper of such antiquity in China.

Water Colour Block Printing
(木版水印 *Muban Shuiyin*)

Water colour block printing, a type of block printing, is employed to reproduce famous works of painting and calligraphy.

The art has a long history in China. In 1900, the world's oldest known book printed by engraved blocks came to light from the Dunhuang Grottoes in the form of the 1,100-year-old version of *the Prajnaparamita* (or *Diamond*) *Sutra* produced in A.D. 868 under the Tang Dynasty, now kept in the British Museum, London.During the reign of Tianqi (1621-1627) of the Ming Dynasty, a colour printing process called *douban* was perfected for the first time to produce coloured pictures by means of separate blocks, each printing a different colour.

The art of water colour block printing currently employed is developed on the basis of the Ming Dynasty *douban* and consists of four major operations: tracing on separate blocks, carving, printing and mounting. The method excels modern printing in two major respects: 1) the materials used, including paper or silk, ink and colours, are the same as those of the original works, so much so that the reproductions look almost authentic; 2) the reproductions, made of materials that are fast in colour and decay-resistant, are highly durable.

Leading in the field of water colour block printing is Rongbaozhai, a famous art shop in Beijing, with rich experience and superb craftsmanship. It has reproduced works of many noted artists. A prominant example produced by the shop in recent years is the celebrated horizontal scroll "Han Xizai's Evening Party" by the 10th-century artist Gu Hongzhong. The original, measuring over 4 metres long, is noted for its refined portrayal of characters and intricate combination of tones. But, owing to age, the colours on this 1,000-year-old work have become dim and vague. If copied by hand, the imitation would be too brilliant to look genuine. When reproduced by the veteran workers of Rongbaozhai, the original picture was broken down into component parts for which 1,667 tracings were drawn and as many blocks were carved. It took eight years to produce some three dozen copies, which look hardly distinguishable from the original. Reproductions of this calibre are highly valued by artists and collectors, almost as much as their ancient model.

Picture Mounting (装裱 *Zhuangbiao*)

A Chinese painting or piece of calligraphic work cannot be properly hung up for appreciation unless it is mounted. So, with the development of Chinese art in general came the special Chinese art of picture mounting, specially suited to *xuan* paper.

The process of mounting, put in a nutshell, consists in pasting a sheet of unrefined *xuan* paper at the back of the picture; this serves not only to reinforce it but also give it a smooth appearance. Then, damask silk of a matching colour is pasted all round the painting to form a border. Finally, another sheet of paper is mounted at the back of the whole.

If the mounted work is to be in the form of a vertical scroll, a wooden roller is normally fixed at the bottom. This serves as the weight to hold the picture in place when hung up, and also helps to roll it up, when put away. The roller is sometimes decorated at both ends. Another horizontal stick is mounted inside on top, attached with silk ribbons for hanging.

Good mounting enhances the work of art whereas shoddy workmanship would make it less presentable. The saying that a finished painting depends for its excellence "30% on art itself but 70% on mounting" may be an exaggeration, but it does bring home the importance of mounting.

Chinese picture-mounters not only add charm to new paintings, but the veterans among them can repair and remount old works that were mounted but have deteriorated. This obviously requires superb craftsmanship involving more than a dozen painstaking steps. The old mounting must be taken apart, the antique colour has to be preserved, the damaged or missing parts have to be mended — all that with paper which must be identical with the original in texture. One can imagine how difficult the whole job is.

New Year Pictures

(年画 *Nianhua*)

The expression explains itself. The Chinese people have the custom of sticking up pictures to celebrate the traditional New Year — now called the Spring Festival. This was recorded in historical works of the Song Dynasty (960-1279). The custom is particularly popular in the vast countryside, where just before the festival day every household will be busy spring cleaning and pasting colourful pictures or paper cuttings on their doors, windows, walls, even wardrobes and stoves.

Traditional New Year pictures, usually made by the blockprinting method, are characterized by simple, clear lines, brilliant colours and scenes of prosperity. The method consists of several steps: drawing and tracing, block engraving, printing, colouring and, in some cases, mounting. The finished pictures, therefore, have the features of both woodcut prints and Chinese paintings, making a special branch in traditional folk art.

The themes expressed in New Year pictures cover a wide range, from plump babies to the Old God of Longevity, from landscapes to birds and flowers, from

the ploughing cattle in spring to rich harvests in autumn. Human figures often show artistic exaggeration, but the message in all pictures is always good luck, festivity or other nice things in the wish of the people.Usual objects in the pictures include the crane or the peach which symbolizes a long life, the plum or peony which is a mark of good fortune and happiness. The colours most favoured are red, green, purple, yellow and black — which are not only bright but contrast well with one another — intended to give fresh, vivid, pleasant and inspiring impressions.

To meet the specific needs of the vast rural population, New Year pictures are produced in all regions in China with different local characteristics. But the leading producers are at three localities: Yangliuqing Village near Tianjin, Taohuawu near Suzhou and Weifang in Shandong.

The Iron Picture

(铁画 *Tiehua*)

A cross between painting and sculpture, the iron picture is an art probably unique to China.

Reportedly it was first created by Tang Peng (*alias* Tang Tianchi), a blacksmith who lived in Wuhu, Anhui Province, in the mid-17th century when the Ming was replaced by the Qing Dynasty. Using the anvil as his inkstone and the hammer as his brush, he forged, filed and shaped iron (or low-carbon steel) strips and wires into pictures by following the principles of composition of the Chinese painting.

This art developed by the smith-artist has been handed down and cultivated for three hundred years. The picture in iron is normally painted black, with or without lustre, which forms a clear contrast with the light-coloured wall on which it is hung. The landscapes, flowers and plants represented in iron appeal to viewers with a three-dimensional effect of simplicity and boldness rarely found elsewhere.

A popular story tells how Tang Tianchi hit upon the idea of "drawing in iron". A close neighbour to Xiao Yun, a painter of some renown at the time, the blacksmith with an artistic penchant used to go and watch Xiao at work, only to be sneered at as "stupid" by the latter. Infuriated, he managed making pictures with iron, pioneering a new genre.

Interior Painting in Snuff Bottles
(鼻烟壶内画 *Biyanhu Neihua*)

Snuff bottles are not native to China but were reportedly introduced from the West by Fr. Matteo Ricci, an Italian Jesuit father who worked in Beijing in the early 17th century. Yet the art of interior painting in snuff bottles was born and developed in China and unique to the country.

A popular story tells how the art originated. In the Qing Dynasty, an official addicted to snuff stopped on his way at a small temple for a rest. When he took out his crystal snuff bottle to take a sniff, he found it was already empty. He then scraped off a little of the powder that had stuck on the interior wall of the bottle by means of a slender bamboo stick, thus leaving lines on the inside, visible through the transparent wall. A young monk saw him at this and hit upon the idea of making pictures inside the bottle. Thus a new art was born.

The "painting brush" of the snuff bottle artist today is not very different from what the official in the story used at the beginning. It is a slender bamboo stick, not much thicker but much longer than a match, with the tip shaped like a fine-pointed hook. Dipped in coloured ink and thrust inside the bottle, the hooked tip is employed to paint on the interior surfaces of the walls, following the will of the painter.

The art became perfected and flourished towards the end of the Qing Dynasty at the turn of the century. Curio dealers began to offer good prices to collect them for a profit.

Snuff bottles are small in size, no more than 6-7cm high and 4-5 cm wide, yet the accomplished artist can produce, on the limited space of the internal surfaces, any subject on the whole gamut of traditional Chinese painting — human portraits, landscapes, flowers and birds — and calligraphy. Liu Shouben, a celebrated contemporary master in this field, succeeded in painting all the 108 heroes and heroines of the classical novel *Water Margin*, each with his or her characteristic expression, all inside one single bottle!

Calligraphic Copybooks (帖 *Tie*)

Before paper was invented our ancients were writing on bamboo or wooden slips, cloth and silk fabrics. Books written on bamboo or wooden slips are known as *jian* (slips), and those written on cloth or silk are books or *tie* (copybook). Copybooks are collections of rubbings of stone inscriptions in the handwriting of famous calligraphers; they are made for people to learn calligraphy by imitation. For this reason the copybook is also known as "model calligraphy".

A model calligraphy copybook contains the works of either a single artist or several artists in different styles.

One-man copybooks came in vogue during the Wei and Jin dynasties (220-420 A.D.) some 1,500 years ago, and the better known of them are Wang Xizhi's *Kaihuang Orchid Pavilion* and Wang Xianzhi's *On the Goddess of the Luo River in Thirteen Lines*.

The best ancient copybooks of multiple calligraphic styles is the *Three-Rarity Hall Model Copybook*. In 1746, or the 11th year of the reign of Emperor Qianlong of the Qing, the emperor had what he regarded as the nation's three foremost calligraphic works collected and enshrined in the "Hall of Three Rarities", which was actually the western wing of the Hall for Mental Cultivation in the Imperial Palace. The rarities, worshiped by calligraphers through the ages, refer to the *Copybook of a Sunny Day after Pleasant Snow* by Wang Xizhi of the Jin Dynasty, the *Mid-Autumn Copybook* by Wang Xianzhi, and the *Boyuan Copybook* by Wang Xun.

The invention of photocopying and modern printing technology has made it possible for the works of celebrated Chinese calligraphers to be photo-printed. This, however, can in no way eclipse the value of hand-made model calligraphic copybooks as cultural artefacts and collector's items.

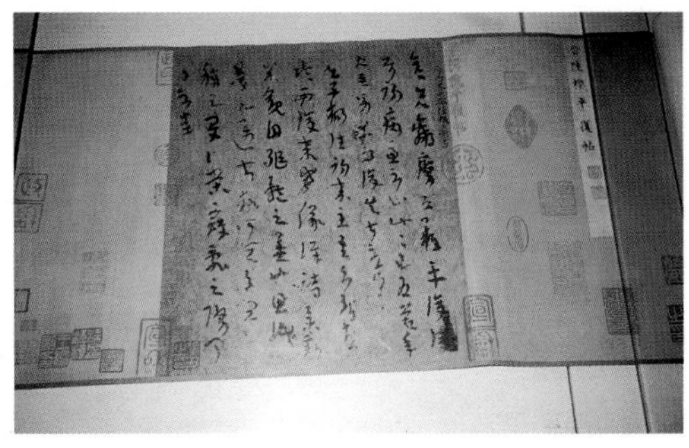

Tianhuang Stone Carvings
(田黄 *Tianhuang*)

"*Tianhuang*" is the name of a kind of stone regarded as the most valuable of all stone sculpture materials in China. For this reason there are suggestions that *tianhuang* be designated as the "king of stones" of China. In bygone days one ounce of *tianhuang* was worth one ounce of gold; today it has become even more precious. In autumn 1996, the Beijing Hanhai Company put a mid-Qing 460-gram *tianhuang* seal carved with a dragon-shaped top for auction at an offering price of 300,000-50,000 *yuan*, but the deal was clinched at a whopping 1.4 million yuan, an all-time high worldwide concerning the *tianhuan* stone.

Tianhuang is produced in the mountains by the Shoushan Stream in the northern suburbs of Fuzhou, capital of Fujian Province. In remote antiquity, cracked stone fell off the mountain and settled in a layer of sand that lay below paddy fields by the Shoushan Stream, and was gradually turned into a kind of sedimental sandy ore that is called *tianhuang* (which literally means "field and yellow") because of its yellowish colour and because it was mined from underneath paddy fields. Mixed with *tianhuang* are also stones red, white, black and grey in colour, which are consequently known as *hongtian*, *baitian*, *heitian* and *huitian*. After many centuries of constant mining, these stones are virtually in non-existence. With a crystal and moist texture, *tianhuang* is regarded as the best material available for the carving of seals, a Chinese obsession.

Tangkha Paintings

(唐卡 *Tangka*)

Tangkha, a transliteration of a Tibetan word, refers to a kind of painting scroll mounted on dyed brocade. The *tangkha* painting is one of two splendid gems of Tibetan art along with Tibetan-style murals. A *tangkha* is usually one metre long, but the largest could extend for several dozen metres. For their distinct ethnic flavour, heady religious aura, and unique art style, *tangkha* has been cherished among the Tibetans as treasures. These paintings cover a wide range of themes, which fall into the following categories:

Mahasanghika school of *tangkha*

painting. This school of *tangkha* painting is devoted to Sakyamuni, Maitreya and the Eighteen Arhats who are the main characters of the Mahasanghika sect of Buddhism. Paintings devoted to this sect are found in various temples in Tibet.

Esoteric School of tangkha painting. The figures portrayed by this school of *tangkha* painting are mostly in grotesque and ferocious images. Quite a few of the paintings feature two figures that have their bodies intertwined.

Indian Adaptations of *tangkha* painting. In this school of *tangkha* painting Buddhist sages are portrayed with their torso naked and their body twisted, with slender waists and fat hips. The facial expressions of the subjects are as a rule calm and gentle.

Goddess school of *tangkha* painting. In start contrast with the Han tradition of Buddhism which is virtually devoid of female deities, Tibetan Buddhism abounds in them. This give rise to a school of *tangkha* painting devoted exclusively to goddesses.

Apart from these four categories, there are also *tangkha* paintings that are devoted to folklore, local habits and customs, Tibetan medicine and historical tales.

The *tangkha* paintings can be hung up on walls, and thus they are easy to be collected and stored. Such paintings can be done on a variety of media, such as cloth, embroidery, tapestry woven in fine silk and gold thread, and mosaic fashioned out of pearls. Padded embroidery, however, is the most artistic of all, as this school of *tangkha* painting is made by patching up hundreds or even thousands of pieces of brocade, which is a combination of Han and Tibetan art. Pearl mosaic tangkhas are a rarity anywhere in this world.

THINGS CHINESE 中国风物

Articles of Everyday Use 日用品

Chopsticks

(筷子 *Kuaizi*)

When the Chinese began to use chopsticks as an eating instrument is anybody's guess. They were first mentioned in writing in *Liji* (*The Book of Rites*), a work compiled some 2,000 years ago, but certainly they had their initial form in the twigs which the primitive Chinese must have used to pick up a roast after they began to use fire. The twigs then evolved into the wooden, tapering sticks as we know them today.

Chopsticks may be made of any of several materials:bamboo, wood, gold, siler, ivory, pewter, and plastics. In cross-section, they may be either round or square. Some of them are engraved with coloured pictures or calligraphy for decoration. Ordinary chopsticks used in Chinese homes are of wood or bamboo, those for banquets are often ivory, whereas gold ones belonged only to the royalty and aristocracy.

The correct way to use chopsticks is to hold the pair in the hollow between the thumb and forefinger of your fork hand. The one closest to your body should rest on the first joint of the ring finger and stay relatively immobile. Hold the other one with the forefinger and middle finger, which manipulate it like pincers to pick up the food. The strength applied by the fingers should vary with the things to be taken hold of. The skill to pick up, with speed and dexterity, small things like beans and peanuts and slippery things like slices of preserved eggs can only come from practice and coordinated action of the fingers.

Incidentally, using chopsticks has a great deal in common with wielding a brush to write Chinese characters. Those who write a good hand, some scholars have observed, are invariably those who handle the chopsticks correctly. One holds the writing brush basically in the same way as one would the moving chopsticks and, while writing, one must achieve a coordination in the movement of the shoulder, arm, wrist and fingers in order to write well.

Westerners are often impressed with the cleverness of the Chinese hand that makes embroideries and clay sculptures with such consummate skill. Could not this also be attributed, at least partly, to the constant use of chopsticks?

Earthen Pot

(沙锅 *Shaguo*)

The earthen pot is commonly used in China both as a cooking utensil and a table vessel. Various soups made in such a pot with vegetables and meatballs and/or soya bean curd are inexpensive, tasty and therefore highly popular.

The Chinese earthen pot is made of a special white pottery clay which, with its stable chemical property, is impregnable to acid, alkaline or salt. It is superior in several ways to cooking vessels of iron or aluminium. Food cooked or stored away in the clay casserole will not easily deteriorate in the heat of summer.

Clay pots of a smaller size are also used by the Chinese to boil medicinal herbs, as they do not add any extraneous substance to the resultant decoction.

Most of the earthen pots come from two sources—Foshan area in Guangzhou and Yixing area in Jiangsu Province. The sandy clay in these places makes an ideal material for the pottery industry. "*Shiwan sanbao*" produced at Shiwan in Foshan city, Guangdong Province, are sold to Hongkong, Macao and Southeast Asia. It is a cooker (*bao*) that can be used for triple (*san*) purposes — to cook rice, to make gruel and to boil tea.

Being made of burnt clay, the earthen pot is easily breakable and must be handled with care. It must not be heated on the fire when it contains no liquid inside; otherwise, it will crack and become leaky. A new pot, before being used, should be soaked in cold water for three to four hours and then heated over a fire to bring the water to a boil two or three times; this will "temper" the clay and give it a higher degree of hardness.

The clay pot is a slow heat-conductor, and that is why it keeps the food warm for a long time on the table in winter. When used in cooking, however, it should be heated first by a slow fire before intense heat is applied. When it is removed from the fire, it should be placed on a mat or wooden board, not direct on something damp and cold, for sudden contact with a cold surface may cause the hot pot to crack.

Stoves and Warmers

(火炉 *Huolu*)

Stoves are the Chinese people's traditional tools for heating in winter. According to the purposes they serve, they may be classified into heating stoves, fire pans, hand warmers and foot stoves. They are in most cases fueled by charcoal.

In the northern parts of China, winter is rather severe, with the temperature generally below freezing point, and few of the old houses there are installed with central heating. So, since ancient times, coal burning stoves have been used to keep the rooms warm and a kettle of water boiling. To prevent carbon monoxide poisoning, tinplate pipes are fixed to channel the coal gas outdoors. Still, owing to faulty installation or bad ventilation, cases of gas poisoning are occasionally reported.

Winter in the middle parts of China is comparatively mild, but the mercury may also drop below zero at times. When this happens, a simple fire pan is used in schools, hospitals and offices. Such a pan or brazier, using charcoal as the fuel, is made of brass or iron, sometimes put under a protecting cage for safety.

The handwarmer and footwarmer made of brass, which first appeared during the Tang Dynasty (618-907), are still used by some people. Charcoal is burned slowly amidst ashes in the handwarmer which, protected by an outer frame, may

be carried inside the loose sleeves of a traditional dress. Recently, Beijing has developed a mini-handwarmer made of aluminium. It is a small oval box lined with asbestos and burns a specially treated charcoal. The small size makes it much easier to carry about.

The footwarmer is larger than the handwarmer and is more often made of brass than iron. Its cover is perforated with many holes to allow the heat to come up to warm the feet which rest on it.

Also counted in the category of warmers are various types of hotwater bottles. The rubber bottle is not indigenous to China where, traditionally, such bottles are made of brass, iron or porcelain. Filled with hot water, they may be used during the day or put under quilts for the night as welcome bedfellows for the elderly.

In the apartment houses newly built in the north, modern heating facilities are installed as a rule, a small number even using solar energy. The various stoves and warmers are being replaced gradually by electric or infrared radiation heaters.

Food Steamers

(蒸笼 *Zhenglong*)

Food steamers are a kind of kitchen utensils most commonly used in China. Generally made of bamboo strips, they vary in size from more than a metre in diameter, as those used in public canteens and restaurant kitchens, to only about 30 centimetres, as those used in private homes. Mini-steamers, measuring only about a dozen centimeters in diameter, are used by certain restaurants to make and serve dainty snacks in.

Food to be cooked by steaming (e.g. *mantou*, stuffed buns or *jiaozi*) is arranged on racks, which are piled up one on top of another, and steamed under cover over a boiling pot. The steam from the water heats and cooks the food. *Mantou*, as explained in a preceding article, is made this way and that is why Westerners call it

"steamed bread".

Wheaten food cooked in bamboo steamers is free from excessive moisture, and it carries a faint fragrance of the bamboo. Rustless steel has been used to make steamers in the belief that they can be mass-produced and last infinitely longer than bamboo steamers. In practice, however, steam condensed by the metal surface gives the food a moist coat and makes it less appealing to the palate. Steel, furthermore, proves to be less heat-insulating and does not keep the food warm. In comparison, bamboo steamers have many advantages over those made of other materials. No wonder most Chinese families still cling to the former.

Fans

(扇子 *Shanzi*)

Hand-held fans are still a necessity in summer in most parts of China. They fall in two major categories: the folding and the unfolding. They may be made in several forms (round, square, oval, hexagonal, sunflower and so on) and of different materials (paper, feathers, silk, coarse and very fine bamboo strips, palm leaves, wheat straw, sandalwood and ivory). According to their material, fans may be pasted, woven, or carved; as for finish, they may be burnt with drawings of bear paintings and writings.

Fans for everyday use in the house are usually made of bamboo or palm leaves. They are so popular-priced that, apart from cooling the holders, they may also be used to fan the kitchen fire. Outside of the house, people prefer folding ones. Womenfolk, however, take to the round silk fans. A folding fan, hand-painted by a celebrated artist, becomes a valuable work of art and a status symbol of its owner. Fans of this description are never used but can only be found in a small number of antiquity shops and old families.

Sandalwood joined the family of fans only in modern times. The sandalwood fan is made entirely of the wood, beautifully shaped and with the ribs and leaves carved through with typical Chinese designs. It makes an ornament rather than an article of practical use. Even in an air-conditioned room, such a fan held in hand will add some sophistication to the charm of a woman, to say nothing of the fragrance it gives out. It is received with growing appreciation from customers at home and abroad.

Fans are an indispensable part of the traditional stage. Male characaters waving their fans in different ways are supposed to reveal different inner feelings in different situations. A young maid in a costume play, meeting her first love, will often use the fan to cover her face and also her bashfulness.

At certain tourist resorts, fans are printed with visitors' itineraries and pictures of sights, serving as a travel guide and thus having an additional role to play.

Needless to say, fans are used to dispel the summer heat, yet in ancient times they were employed rather to give shade from the sun and the wind and served as a symbol of status. As early as three thousand years ago, long-shafted fans made of bird feathers were held by attendants standing on either side of an emperor or prince. These may still be seen on the traditional stage, in the Forbidden City and the Summer Palace; they were part of the imperial guard of honour. It is said that fans began to be used for cooling from the Han Dynasty (founded in 206 B.C.).

A speical fan called "Ten Thousand Characters of Tang Poems" was made in 1982 at Wangxingji Fan Factory. On a normal covering of 30 centimetres (12 inches) high, 254 poems of the Tang Dynasty (618-907), when Chinese poetry flourished, were written with real gold powder. The poems total 11,199 characters, each only about a millimetre square, wtitten with clear, distinctive strokes. It was done in a month by Zhu Nianci, a veteran craftsman when he was 63. It certainly is a gem among Chinese folding fans.

Umbrellas

(伞 *San*)

China is believed to be the home of umbrellas, which are still universally used in the country. The earliest umbrellas are known to have existed at least two thousand years ago and were made of silk.

At present, umbrellas in China are made of various materials: oilpaper, cotton, silk, plastic film and nylon. As in other countries, they are used either against the rain or as parasols to give shade from the sun. Some are built on straight frames while others are collapsible.

The best oilpaper umbrellas are generally thought to be those from Fujian and Hunan provinces. Their bamboo frames are treated against mould and worms. The paper covers are hand-painted with flowers, birds, figures and landscapes and then coated with oil so that they are not only practical but pretty and lasting. They may be used either in rain or sunshine.

The prettiest Chinese umbrellas, however, are those covered with silk, and the silk parasols of Hangzhou are veritable works of art which also serve a practical purpose. The silk, as thin as cicada's wing and printed with landscapes, is also fixed on a bamboo frame. A parasol of Hangzhou, usually 53 centimetres or 20 inches long, weighs only 250 grams or 8.8 ounces, is very handy and makes a welcome souvenir for tourists. Local girls, to protect themselves against the sun, like to carry parasols with them, which have long become part of the female attire.

Umbrellas or parasols,apart from their practical uses, have also become part of the paraphernalia of the stage artist. A notable example is the wirewalker who uses a parasol as a balancer to keep herself on the wire.

Abacus

(算盘 *Suanpan*)

The abacus was a great invention in ancient China and has been called by some Western writers "the earliest calculating machine in the world".

The abacus has a long history behind it. It was already mentioned in a book of the Eastern Han Dynasty, namely *Supplementary Notes on the Art of Figures* written by Xu Yue about the year A.D.190. Its popularization occurred at the latest during the Song Dynasty (960-1279), when Zhang Zeduan painted his *Riverside Scenes at Qingming Festival*. In this famous long scroll, an abacus is clearly seen lying beside an account book and doctor's prescriptions on the counter of an apothecary's. During the Ming Dynasty (1368-1644), the abacus was introduced into Japan.

Abacuses are easy to make, handy to carry around and quick to give the answers provided one knows how to move the beads. They have been in use, therefore, down to this day. They are made in different sizes, and the largest known abacus, measuring 26 centimetres high by 306 centimetres long with 117 rods (for as many digits), is over a hundred years old and is kept at Darentang, a well-known traditional pharmacy in Tianjin.

The beads on an abacus may be round or rhombus in shape. Traditionally, there are two beads above the horizontal bar and five below. Simplified modern versions have one bead above and four or five below. The methods of calculation remain unchanged.

At a time when the world has entered the age of electronics, the abacus still enjoys undiminished vitality in China. Tests have shown that, for operations of addition and substraction, the abacus is still faster than the electronic calculator. China developed in 1980 an "electronic abacus" which combines the speed of traditional addition and substraction methods with those of the modern calculator at multiplication and division. It is a happy example of the integration between the East and West, the native and the modern.

Steelyard

(杆秤 *Gancheng*)

The steelyard is a Chinese invention. As early as 200 B.C., China began to make a scale of this type big enough to weigh several hundred pounds. The steelyard consisted of the following parts: an arm, a hook, lifting cords and a weigh. The arm or beam measured about 1.5 metres long, graduated with the weight units-*jin* and *liang**. The hook, hanging from one end of the arm, was used to lift up the object to be weighed. Hanging from the other part of the arm was the free-moving weight, attached on a looped string. On the arm was fixed one, two or three lifting cords, placed much closer to the hook than to the other end. Anything to be weighed should be picked up by the hook, whild the weigher lifted up the whole steelyard, holding one of the cords. He then slided the weight left or right until he found a perfect balance of the beam. He then read the weight from the graduation mark on which the weight-string rested.

This kind of steelyards is still in widespread use at market gatherings in China. They may be made in varying sizes working by the same principle, with the large ones to weigh foodgrain in bulk, pigs or sheep or their carcasses, and medium-sized ones for smaller transactions. There is also a miniature steelyard only about one third of a metre (about 1 foot) long, graduated with *liang* and *qian***. Used to weigh medicinal herbs and silver or gold, it first appeared about 1,000 years ago.

The steelyard is more convenient than the platform scale. Not only can it be carried around easily, but there is also no need for a whole set of weights. Corresponding to the lifting cords are different sets of graduation marks on the arm for different measuring ranges.

It is perhaps worthwhile to mention that the equal-armed platform scale appeared in China earlier than the steelyard with a sliding weight. A scale of the former description with a complete set of weights was discovered lately from a tomb near Changsha, Hunan Province, which dates back to the Period of the Warring States (475-221 B.C.). It is in size similar to those in use today and its component parts are found to be in good proportions.

---

* One *Jin* equals 500 grams or about 1.1 pounds; it used to be divided into 16 *liang*, but now 10 *liang*.
** A *qian* is one-tenth of a *liang*.

Bambooware

(竹器 *Zhuqi*)

China, home of bamboo, makes extensive use of the plant as a material for articles of daily use and interior decoration.

In many southern provinces like Hunan and Sichuan which abound in bamboo groves, the local people build houses, suspension bridges and fishing rafts with bamboo. In their spare time, rural women weave its strips into baskets of various sizes and different descriptions to be sold at fairs and markets.

No part of bamboo is wasted. The

leaves make broadbrimmed country hats and rain capes, or are used for the roofing of small boats. Southern households, needless to say, use bamboo chopsticks for eating, many of which are burnt with patterns and pictures.

Furniture made of the plant may look very distinctive, elegant and even classic in taste. Beds, couches, chairs, sofas, tables, desks and baby carriages can all be made of bamboo.

Bamboo can also be the material for a long list of other handicraft articles — screens, paintings, animal figures, fruit boxes, smoking sets, tea boxes, etc. — which are either interior decorations or articles of practical use or serve both purposes at the same time. Their exquisite appearance, together with their moderate price and light weight, puts them in high favour with Chinese and foreign buyers.

Some sculptors like to split sections of thick bamboo sticks lengthwise in two and engrave on the surfaces a couplet of Chinese poetry or a set of pictures for hanging on the walls of studies or studios. They make interior decorations of pastoral simplicity and refinement.

Bamboo is also an important raw material; the branches can be processed into fibres for the manufacture of high-quality paper and artificial silk.

The tender shoots of bamboo are a delicacy often found at a Chinese banquet. They may be used fresh or canned, or dried for longer storage. Dried bamboo shoots should be soaked in water for a few days before use.

A well-known Chinese drink called *zhuyeqing* (bamboo-leat-green) is made of bamboo leaves mixed with other materials.

Jiaoyi —Ancient Folding Chair

(交椅 *Jiaoyi*)

It is not uncommon for someone to ask an official the oft-repeated question: "Which *jiaoyi* are you in?" The question is meant to clarify the man's exact position in the leadership of his institution. In the eyes of most people, *jiaoyi* is synonymous to power.

But what is a *jiaoyi*? The word refers to a folding chair in use in ancient China. Being collapsible, the *jiaoyi* came in handy for those going outdoors. The predecessor of *jiaoyi* was the folding stools of the northern Huns. Images of such stools can be seen in the frescos in the Thousand-Buddha Grottoes in the Tuyu Gully of Turpan.

Jiaoyi fall roughly into three categories:

Armchair with a round back. This belongs to the highest grade of *jiaoyi* and was for the exclusive use of members of the imperial family. When folded, such chairs could be carried on a journey, and this is why they were also known as "travelling chairs". When the emperor went on a hunting excursion, his bodyguard would follow in tow with the folding chairs on their shoulders. Thus *jiaoyi* was also known as "Hunter's chair".

Armchair with a straight back. This type of *jiaoyi* features arms that are longer than usual, and is mostly made from hardwood. A tiny number of them were made of *Onmosia henryi*, a precious hardwood. Such a *jiaoyi* was usually for the enjoyment of the learned and moneyed gentry in their studies or courtyards.

Chair with a straight back but no arms. This type of *jiaoyi* is relatively simpler in structure and usually made from run-of-the-mill materials. Many of them are still in use in the rural areas of north China.

High-grade *jiaoyi* could be found in museums at home and abroad; there are few of them in the hands of private users. By far there are only about 100 folding *Onmosia henryi* armchairs with a round back that date back to the Ming and Qing dynasties.

Walking Sticks

(手杖 *Shouzhang*)

When a senior citizen sets off on a mountain-climbing journey, he inevitably carries a walking stick with him. That is why the walking stick was known as *fulao* ("companion to the elderly") in ancient China. In old days the walking stick was a status symbol for the man who carried it. A man who has lived to be 50 earns the respect of his clan; at 60 he wins the respect of fellow provincials. In ancient time

60-year-olds were called by the respectful name "Man with a Walking Stick". A 70-year-old man commanded the respect of the entire kingdom; at 80 he was allowed to walk into the imperial court with a walking stick; at 90 even the emperor had to pay him a home visit. Those who could still work at 70 were entitled to a gift from the emperor: a walking stick known as "imperial-mandated stick". This old custom of respecting the elderly people later evolved into a system in which old people were held in high esteem.

Boat with Black Awning (乌篷船 *Wupeng Chuan*)

The boat, covered with an awning that is woven with thin bamboo strips and painted shiny black, is a traditional means of water transportation peculiar to Shaoxing, a water-bound place in south China. It is small of capacity, four metres long and one metre wide, and divided into three cabins. The floor of the passenger cabin is paved with red-lacquered wooden planks. What is interesting about this tiny boat is that the oarsman may sit down and lean his back against a tiny cushion while manoeuvring a pair of oars with his feet. On a cold winter day oarsmen are often seen with hands tucked in the warmth of the sleeves of their coats while their feet keep pedalling the oars to keep their boats sailing smooth and fast.

Old Ration Coupons
(老票证 *Laopiaozheng*)

In the early years of New China commodities were in such short supply under central planning that the government had to ration the supply in order to provide for the world's largest population. Thus coupon tickets were issued. Here we call them "old coupon" because that period has long been history. The old coupons roughly fall into the following categories.

Coupons for food: grain and edible oil, meat, sugar, eggs, pastry, and vegetables;

Coupons for clothing: cloth, cloth supply for army men, garments, cloth shoes and cotton.

Coupons for articles for daily use: coal, soap, detergent, kerosene oil, matches, bicycles, sewing machines, wristwatches, manufactured goods, purchasing coupons for peasants, and purchasing certificates for prisoners.

Coupons for special purposes: those issued for Spring Festival supplies, coupons issued during certain festivals, coupons that allow senior citizens to buy certain things, coupons to ensure the supply for women who had just given birth, coupons for patients, foreign exchange certificates for family members of overseas Chinese, coupons for the relief of flood victims, purchasing certificates for peasants and for prisoners.

Everybody kept these old coupons in the old days but few are keeping them nowadays. Those who have collected these coupons with foresight are happy to see their value soaring. To own some of the old tickets means possession of a piece of Chinese history. Today, the country is thriving and commodity supply is plentiful, and coupons are not needed any more. The younger generation has no idea what a coupon is meant for, still less do they understand why rice should be bought only with a ticket. For the younger generation to learn something about these coupons help them know something about the hard old days of the People's Republic; for the older generation to take a look at these coupons enables them to treasure today's hard-won prosperity of the country.

THINGS CHINESE 中国风物

Clothing

服饰

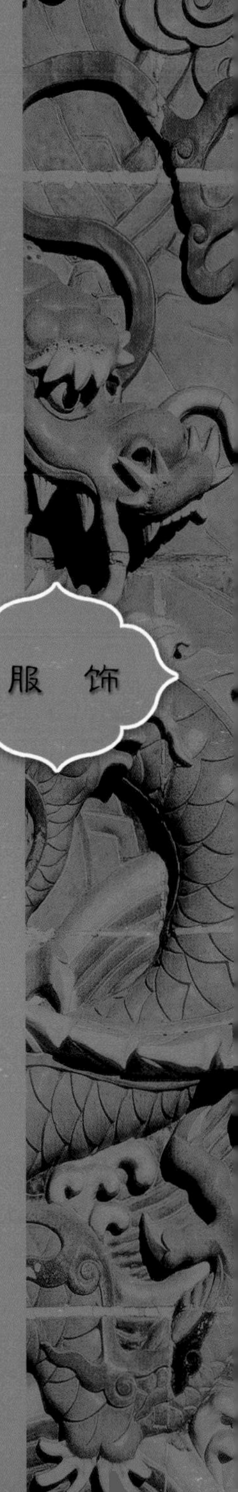

Chinese Tunic Suit
(中山装 *Zhongshan Zhuang*)

The tunic suit has dominated Chinese fashion for many years and is known to Westerners as the "Mao tunic" or "Mao suit". It is a mistake, however, to associate the style with Mao Zedong.

For it is called by the Chinese themselves "Zhongshan Zhuang" or "Zhongshan suit" as it was a uniform that Dr. Sun Yat-sen (better known among the Chinese as Sun Zhongshan) liked to wear and recommended to the people of the country.

It was customary in ancient times to change the styles of the people's clothes whenever a new dynasty replaced an old one. The 1911 Revolution led by Dr. Sun Yat-sen overthrew the Qing Dynasty and founded the Republic of China. Members of his Nationalist Party proposed to change the national costume. During the discussions, Dr. Sun favoured the casual dress prevalent in Guangdong Province but proposed certain modifications. A designer worked on his ideas and produced the tunic with four pockets and a turned-down collar, closed all down the middle with five buttons. It looked simple and tasteful and gave an air of sedateness. From then on Dr. Sun set a personal example by wearing the tunic suit on various occasions. It did not take long before the style became fashionable all over the country.

Cheongsam

(旗袍 *Qipao*)

The cheongsam is a female dress with distinctive Chinese features and enjoys a growing popularity in the international world of high fashion.

The name "cheongsam", meaning simply "long dress", entered the English vocabulary from the dialect of China's Guangdong Province (Cantonese). In other parts of the country including Beijing, however, it is known as "*qipao*", which has a history behind it.

When the early Manchu rulers came to China proper, they organized certain people, mainly Manchus, into "banners" (*qi*) and called them "banner people" (*qiren*), which then became loosely the name of all Manchus. The Manchu women wore normally a one-piece dress which, likewise, came to be called "*qipao*" or "banner dress". Although the 1911 Revolution toppled the rule of the Qing (Manchu) Dynasty, the female dress survived the political change and, with later improvements, has become the traditional dress for Chinese women.

Easy to slip on and comfortable to wear, the cheongsam fits well the female Chinese figure.Its neck is high, collar closed, and its sleeves may be either short, medium or full-length, depending on season and taste. The dress is buttoned on the right side, with a loose chest, a fitting waist, and slits up from the sides, all of which combine to set off the beauty of the female shape.

The cheongsam is not too complicated to make. Nor does it call for too much material, for there are no accessories like belts, scarves, sashes or frills to go with it.

Another beauty of the cheongsam is that, made of different materials and to varying lengths, they can be worn either on casual or formal occasions. In either case, it creates an impression of simple and quiet charm, elegance and neatness. No wonder it is so much liked by women not only of China but of foreign countries as well.

Dragon Robe

(龙袍 *Longpao*)

The robe embroidered with dragon patterns was made for the exclusive use of an emperor during the Qing dynasty. The ritual of embroidering dragon patterns on the emperor's robe, however, dates back to as early as the Zhou Dynasty (11th century-256 B.C.). During the Yuan and Ming, the emperors were already wearing robes graced with dragon patterns, but it was not until the Qing that they were named "dragon robes" and became part of the official attire system. A dragon robe is either yellow or apricot-yellow in colour, and embroidered with nine yellow dragons and five-hued auspicious cloud patterns. The clouds are interlaced with twelve other patterns — the sun, the moon and stars (representing the light of the throne), mountains (synonymous to stability), dragon (symbolizing adaptability to changes) auspicious bird (denoting elegance and beauty) water reeds (which represent purity and cleanness), and fire (meaning light). According to imperial Qing rituals, the emperor's dragon robe was a kind of auspicious attire for lower-grade celebrations and ceremonies — it was by no means the highest grade of imperial attire. The dragon robe that was passed down from one emperor to another is embroidered with a dragon on the front and the back, before or behind the knees, on the shoulders, and on the lining of the chest. Thus a total of nine dragons are embroidered on a dragon robe. Observed from the front or behind it, five dragons could be seen at a glance, because in Chinese tradition the figures nine and five tallied with the dignity of the throne.

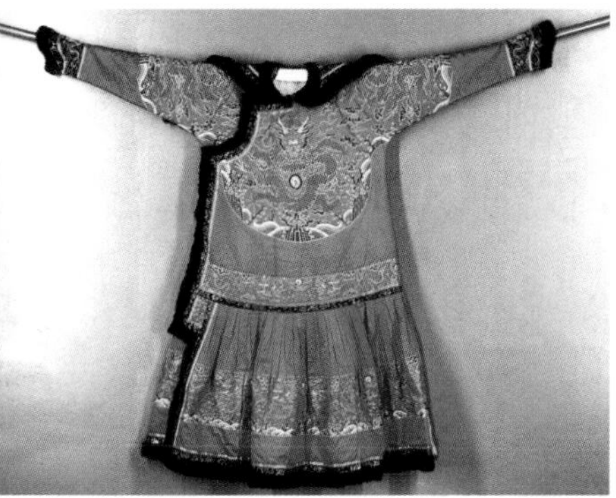

Tibetan Robe

(藏袍 *Zangpao*)

The Tibetans call it *zhuba.* It is their favourite attire, and the most distinctive hallmark that tells the Tibetans from people of other ethnic backgrounds. The Tibetan robe is loose-fitting, with long sleeves and a wider-than-usual waist, and its front is opened from the right side. The Tibetan robe is made from leather among herdsmen, and woollen fabrics among farmers. Virtually every Tibetan man wears such a robe, which is also pocketless. Instead of buttons, it is held together with a waist band, with the front puffing up so as to hold wooden bowls, roast barley flour bag, butter container and even an infant in the bosom. When a Tibetan man puts on his robe, he tends to wear only one sleeve and pull the other sleeve around his back to the front of it — a habit that has much to do with the weather. On the Qinghai-Tibet Plateau there is a glaring difference in temperature between day and night, and the weather changes unpredictably. "A mountain experiences four seasons in a single day, and the weather changes every ten miles," as the local saying goes. In summer it could be chilly in the morning and hot at noon. That is why a local herdsman has to keep warm with the Tibetan robe when he goes outdoors in the morning, but by noontime it becomes so hot that he has to wear only one sleeve or leave both sleeves alone by tying them around his waist. When dusk sets in he has to put on both sleeves because it's become cold once again. The loose-fitting robe also makes an excellent quilt when the wearer stops for the night. Obviously the Tibetan robe with its multiple functions is indispensable for the Tibetans.

Miao-Style Silver Jewellery

(苗族银饰 *Miaozu Yinshi*)

When a girl was born in a Miao family, her parents make it a point to save on food and expenses for a complete set of silver jewellery for her. The set, 15 kg in total weight, includes crown, horns, earrings, neckband, chest plaque, clothing ornament, waistband, and bracelets. It takes more than one hour for a young woman to put the entire kit on and finish her makeup. The Miao people's penchant for silver jewellery stems from their love of beauty, wealth and dignity. The colour of silver symbolizes the Miao people's character of fearing no tyranny and being impervious to temptation of wealth and position. It is also said that wearing silver jewellery helps keep evil at bay. Silver jewellery can also be used as a symbol of a person's marital status or as a betrothal gift.

Patches of Embroidery on Official Robes (补子 *Buzi*)

Buzi is a term referring to animal patterns embroidered with silk thread in yellow and other colours on the front and back of robes worn by officials during the Ming and Qing. In Chinese feudal hierarchy such animal patterns were status symbols for government officials.

In 1393, or the 26th year of the Hongwu reign of the Ming, the imperial court set strict rules on the robes the officials wore: Civil officials and army officers alike should have *buzi* embroidered on either the front or the back of the robes they wore. The *buzi* for civil officials features a flying bird to symbolize literary grace; and that for army officers was a beast to symbolize valour. The crane was for a top-rank civil official; yellow pheasant, second rank; peacock, third rank; mail wild goose, fourth rank; white silver pheasant, fifth rank; egret, sixth rank; mandarin duck, seventh rank; quail, eighth rank; and long-tailed fly-catcher, ninth rank. For army officers, kylin (or unicorn, an auspicious legendary animal with a horn and scales all over its body) was for the first rank; lion for second rank; leopard for third rank; tiger for fourth rank; bear for fifth rank; young tiger for sixth and seventh rank; rhinoceros for eighth rank; and sea horse for ninth rank. The Censor-in-chef and the Surveillance Commissioner were required to wear robes with the pattern of a *xiezhi* (legendary animal credited with the ability to distinguish between right and wrong).

The Qing Dynasty inherited the *buzi* system of the Ming, but there were some differences between the two dynasties. Firstly, the patch of embroidery was made for robes during the Ming but it was for mandarin jackets during the Qing; secondly, during the Ming the *buzi* on the front of an official robe was a whole patch of embroidery, whereas during the Qing, the patch on the front of a mandarin jacket was cut in two because the jacket was buttoned down the middle; third, during the Ming *buzi* appeared either on the front or

the back of a robe, while during the Qing it also appeared on the shoulders. Moreover, during the Qing, *buzi* was round in shape for members of the imperial clan and square for officials in various ranks.

Historical documents indicate that prior to the Tang (618-907), the rank of the official robes in China was marked by colour and the quantity of ornaments an official was supposed to wear. It was not until Empress Wu of the Tang that animal and bird patterns were adopted to distinguish the ranks of court officials and generals. This innovation rendered graphic images to a hierarchical system whose complicated symbolism made it mind-boggling to tell the rank of a court official. The patterns of embroidery on the costumes of the Chinese opera are mostly derived from the *buzi* ornamentation.

THINGS CHINESE 中国风物

Drinks and Snacks

饮食

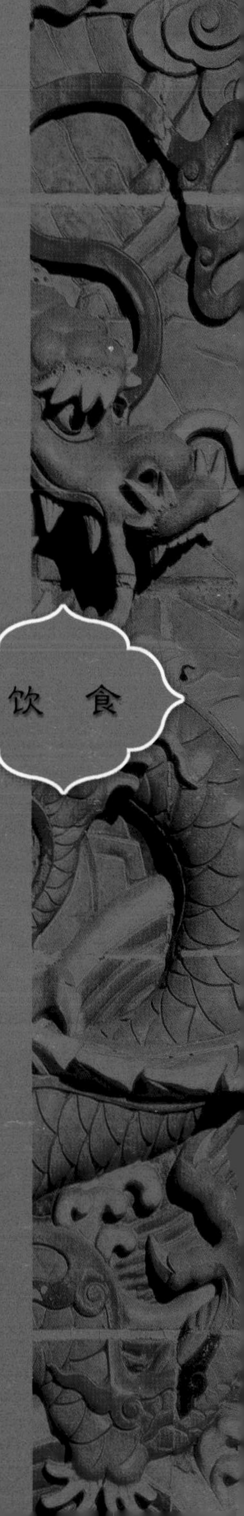

Tea

(茶 *Cha*)

1. China, the Homeland of Tea

Of the three major beverages of the world — tea, coffee and cocoa — tea is consumed by the largest number of people.

China is the homeland of tea. It is believed that China has tea-shrubs as early as five to six thousand years ago, and human cultivation of teaplants dates back two thousand years. Tea from China, along with her silk and porcelain, began to be known the world over more than a thousand years ago and has since always been an important Chinese export. At present more than forty countries in the world grow tea with Asian countries producing 90% of the world's total output. All tea trees in other countries have their origin directly or indirectly in China. The word for tea leaves or tea as a drink in many countries are derivatives from the Chinese character "*cha*". The Russians call it

"cha'i", which sounds like "*chaye*" (tea leaves) as it is pronounced in northern China, and the English word "tea" sounds similar to the pronunciation of its counterpart in Xiamen (Amoy). The Japanese character for tea is written exactly the same as it is in Chinese, though pronounced with a slight difference. The habit of tea drinking spread to Japan in the 6th century, but it was not introduced to Europe and America till the 17th and 18th centuries. Now the number of tea drinkers in the world is legion and is still on the increase.

2. The Categories of Tea

Chinese tea may be classified into five categories according to the different methods by which it is processed.

1) *Green tea:* Green tea is the variety which keeps the original colour of the tea leaves without fermentation during processing. This category consists mainly of *Longjing* tea of Zhejiang Province, *Maofeng* of Huangshan Mountain in Anhui Province and *Biluochun* produced in Jiangsu.

2) *Black tea*: Black tea, known as "red tea" (*hong cha*) in China, is the category which is fermented before baking; it is a later variety developed on the basis of the green tea. The best brands of black tea are *Qihong* of Anhui, *Dianhong* of Yunnan, *Suhong* of Jiangsu, *Chuanhong* of Sichuan and *Huhong* of Hunan.

3) *Wulong tea*: This represents a variety half way between the green and the black teas, being made after partial fermentation. It is a specialty from the provinces on China's southeast coast: Fujian, Guangdong and Taiwan.

4) *Compressed tea*: This is the kind of tea which is compressed and hardened into a certain shape. It is good for transport and storage and is mainly supplied to the ethnic minorities living in the border areas of the country. As compressed tea is black in colour in its commercial form, so it is also known in China as "black tea". Most of the compressed tea is in the form of bricks; it is, therefore, generally called "brick tea", though it is sometimes also in the form of cakes and bowls. It is mainly produced in Hubei, Hunan, Sichuan and Yunnan provinces.

5)*Scented tea*: This kind of tea is

made by mixing fragrant flowers in the tea leaves in the course of processing. The flowers commonly used for this purpose are jasmine and magnolia among others. Jasmine tea is a well-known favourite with the northerners of China and with a growing number of foreigners.

3. Tea Production

A new tea-plant must grow for five years before its leaves can be picked and, at 30 years of age, it will be too old to be productive. The trunk of the old plant must then be cut off to force new stems to grow out of the roots in the coming year. By repeated rehabilitations in this way, a plant may serve for about 100 years.

For the fertilization of tea gardens, soya-bean cakes or other varieties of organic manure are generally used, and seldom chemical fertilizers. When pests are discovered, the affected plants will be removed to prevent their spread, and also to avoid the use of pesticides.

The season of tea-picking depends on local climate and varies from area to area. On the shores of West Lake in Hangzhou, where the famous green tea *Longjing* (Dragon Well) comes from, picking starts from the end of March and lasts through October, altogether 20-30 times from the same plants at intervals of seven to ten days. With a longer interval, the quality of the tea will deteriorate.

A skilled woman picker can only gather 600 grams (a little over a pound) of green tea leaves in a day.

The new leaves must be parched in tea cauldrons. This work, which used to be done manually, has been largely mechanized. Top-grade *Dragon Well* tea, however, still has to be stir-parched by hand, doing only 250 grams every half hour. The tea-cauldrons are heated electrically to a temperature of about 25℃ or 74℃. It takes four pounds of fresh leaves to produce one pound of parched tea.

The best Dragon Well tea is gathered several days before Qingming (Pure

Brightness, 5th solar term) when new twigs have just begun to grow and carry "one leaf and a bud". To make one kilogram (2.2 lbs) of finished tea, 60,000 tender leaves have to be plucked. In the old days *Dragon Well tea* of this grade was meant solely for the imperial household; it was, therefore, known as "tribute tea".

For the processes of grinding, parching, rolling, shaping and drying other grades of tea various machines have been developed and built, turning out about 100 kilograms of finished tea an hour and relieving the workers from much of their drudgery.

4. Advantages of Tea-Drinking

Tea has been one of the daily necessities in China since time immemorial. Countless numbers of people like to have their aftermeal cup of tea.

In summer or warm climate, tea seems to dispel the heat and bring on instant cool together with a feeling of relaxation. For this reason, tea-houses abound in towns and market villages in South China and provide elderly retirees with the locales to meet and chat over a cup of tea.

Medically, the tea leaf contains a number of chemicals, of which 20-30% is tannic acid, known for its anti-inflammatory and germicidal properties. It also contains an alkaloid (5%, mainly caffeine), a stimulant for the nerve centre and the process of metabolism. Tea with the aromatics in it may help resolve meat and fat and thus promote digestion. It is, therefore, of spe-

cial importance to people who live mainly on meat, like many of the ethnic minorities in China. A popular proverb among them says, "Rather go without salt for three days than without tea for a single day."

Tea is also rich in various vitamins and, for smokers, it helps to discharge nicotine out of the system. After wining, strong tea may prove to be a sobering pick-me-up.

The above, however, does not go to say that the stronger the tea, the more advantages it will yield. Too much tannic acid will affect the secretion of the gastric juice, irritate the membrane of the stomach and cause indigestion or constipation. Strong tea taken just before bedtime will give rise to occasional insomnia. Constant drinking of over-strong tea may induce heart and blood-pressure disorders in some people, reduce the milk of a breast-feeding mother, and put a brown colour on the teeth of young people. But it is not difficult to ward off these undesirable effects: just don't make your tea too strong.

Alcoholic Drinks

(酒 *Jiu*)

1. The Invention of Alcohol

China is one of the first countries to have invented alcohol as a drink. A large number of pottery wine vessels were discovered in Shandong at the runis of the Dawenkou culture which dates back 5,000 years. Recorded history tells about wine-making techniques of more than 4,000 years ago.

The earliest wines were made from food grains, mainly various kinds of rice, broomcorn and millet. As a result of improvements in brewing skills, the yellow wine made its appearance probably in the Warring States Period (475-221 B.C.).

From an ancient tomb of the Warring States in Pingshan County of Hebei Province, large numbers of wine-storing and drinking vessels were excavated in the 1970s. Two of them contain an alcoholic drink made from wheat 2,280 years ago. It is probably the oldest liquor ever brought to light in the world.

2. Well-Known Drinks in China

Chinese wines and liquors were assessed by a national panel of wine-tasting experts on three occassions, in 1953, 1963 and 1979.

The 1979 honour roll lists eighteen drinks, namely: *Maotai*, *Fenjiu*, *Wuliangye*, *Jianchunjiu* of Sichuan, *Gujing* Tribute Liquor, *Yanghe Daqu* of Jiangsu, *Dongjiu*, *Luzhou Tequ*, *Shaoxing Jiafan*, *Longyan Chengangjiu*, Tsingtao Beer, Yantai Red Wine, China Red Wine of Beijing, Great Wall White Wine of Shacheng, Hebei, Minquan White Wine, Yantai Vermouth, Yantai Gold Stars Brandy, and *Zhuyeqing* of Shanxi.

Maotai has always been at the top of

any listing of China's famouns drinks. It is named after the small town of *Maotai* in Guizhou Province where it is produced.

Being almost indispensable at state banquets held in Beijing or official receptions given by Chinese envoys abroad, *Maotai* used to be the "national drink" or "diplomatic drink" of the country. It is the most valued drink when friends and relatives gather on holidays or other festive occasions. But owing to the big gap between supply and demand, its price has gone up greatly in recent years.

Maotai is made from a high-quality *gaoliang* (Chinese sorghum) as its main material. The distiller's yeast is prepared from wheat, and the water, which is important to its taste, is from local springs. Unique, too, is its process of manufacture, which consists of eight times of distillation after as many periods of fermentation, each lasting more than a month following the addition of yeast. So the whole process takes more than eight months. It is then stored away for ageing for three years before it is allowed to appear on the market.

Maotai looks crystal clear. Though a potent drink, it is never burning to the mouth or throat, nor does it go to the head or upset the stomach. Since ancient times it has been a favourite drink with poets and other people of artistic penchant. They believe that when setting their writing or painting brushes to paper, they find inspiration from a cup of *Maotai* more than anything else.

The yellow wine is a specialty of China, known to the ancient people as early as 4,000 years ago. Made of glutinous rice or broomcorn millet by a special process, it has an alcohol content of 15-20%. It is called "yellow wine" because it is amber in colour.

Traditionally, yellow wine is to be drunk warm. It is heated in a metal (usually, brass or pewter) wine pot, half immersed in a bowl of hot water before it is served. It is believed that warm wine is appetizing and good for the stomach and builds up general health.

The best yellow wine is made in Shaoxing, Zhejiang Province, and is generally known as *Shaoxing laojiu* after the name of the place. A local custom handed down from ages is to make or buy a few jars of yellow wine at the birth of a baby and store them away sealed with mud in the family cellar till the child's wedding when it will be served to the guest. Matured in the jars during some twenty years, the wine is particularly satisfying because it is unsurpassed in colour, smell and taste.

The yellow wine is also an important condiment in Chinese cooking. A spoon or two of yellow wine in the preparation of a dish will enhance the taste of meat and fish, adding a subtlety to its deliciousness.

Chinese Cuisine
(中餐 *Zhongcan*)

China is a world-renowned "epicurean kingdom". Few visitors leave this country without being smitten by the Chinese culinary art, and quite a few of them regard Chinese dishes as the best in the world. Chinese restaurants are a dime a dozen nowadays around the world, but for a taste of the authentic fare, China is definitely the place to be.

Chinese cuisine by and large falls into six schools:

1. Imperial Dishes

These dishes originated in the kitchen of the imperial palace for the exclusive enjoyment of the emperor and empress in bygone days. Graceful names that give wings to imagination, impeccable selection of ingredients, and state-of-the-art cooking techniques designed to preserve natural hue, aroma and taste are the major hallmarks of these imperial dishes. Peking Duck is one of such dishes.

2. Mansion Kitchen Fare

High officials and famous personages who cared so much for what they ate in bygone days went out of their way to hire famous chefs with handsome pay. With superb culinary skills, these chefs become a school of their own behind the walls of the mansions of the rich and powerful, and eventually their styles of cooking found their way to the public. The Confucian Mansion and the Tan Family are representative of the mansion-style of Chinese cuisine. The Confucian fare is being dished out in the Confucian Restaurant at Beijing's Liulichang, and the Tan Family Kitchen has opened shop in Beijing Hotel.

3. Local Cuisine

Regional differences in resources, climate and folklore have given rise to a variety of cooking schools in China. The Shandong, Sichuan, Yangzhou and Canton are the four major schools. Another theory puts the number at eight, with the addition of Hunan, Fukien, Anhui and Zhejiang. A third theory includes Beijing and Shanghai so that the nation has ten major schools of Chinese cooking. Shandong, Sichuan, Yangzhou and Cantonese cooking, however, are generally regarded as the most influential of all schools of Chinese cuisine — the others are simply regarded as branches.

4. Ethnic Dishes

These dishes were first invented by minority peoples and later spread to other parts of the country. These include the mutton hot pot of Inner Mongolia and the roast whole lamb and shish kebab of Xinjiang.

5. Monastic Dishes

Otherwise known as vegetarian's dishes, monastic dishes had their origin in Buddhist temples around the country. This school of cooking are understandably dominated by vegetables, and it is flourishing because the rising standard of living has prompted many people to become more health-conscious and stick to vegetarian's dishes. Some of these dishes are prepared to resemble the flavour and shape of meat dishes. Apart from their special flavours, the monastic dishes are stomach-friendly and help protect people's health.

6. Therapeutic Dishes

Therapeutic dishes, which go back a long way in this country, can be found only in Chinese cuisine. Since ancient times the Chinese have been incorporating traditional medicinal materials in their dishes. These medicines may taste salty, sour, bitter, sweet or pungent, but if they are properly handled, the dishes can guarantee an unforgettable gourmandising expe-

rience for those who also wish to benefit from the therapeutical effects of what they eat.

Once you have sampled the above-mentioned dishes, you can feel it safe to say that you have obtained a relatively complete idea about Chinese cuisine.

Steamed Bread

(馒头 *Mantou*)

The Chinese people are sometimes thought to be rice-eaters, but most northerners prefer food made of wheat flour, and *mantou* is the most popular form of such food. It is made by steaming the dough and is therefore described in English as "steamed bread".

The first step in the traditional method of making *mantou* is fermenting the dough. Normally a small piece of leaven is kept from the previous time. This is well mixed in flour and water to make a new piece of dough, which is left for a few hours to swell. The leavening dough, when ready for steaming, contains a high degree of acid, so a suitable amount of soda solution must be mixed and well kneaded in it. The dough is then divided into smaller pieces, either round or square, which are arranged well spaced on a rack, and steamed under cover.

A kind of active yeast has been developed in recent years, making the steaming of bread easier. All one has to do is to solve the yeast in cold or lukewarm water and mix it well in dough. The dough is then kneaded, divided and shaped into pieces of a suitable size. Leave them in a temperature of 20℃ to 30℃ for half an hour at most, and they are ready for steaming. This method cuts short the period of leavening and improves the taste of the steamed bread.

An interesting story tells about the origin of *mantou*. It was first made, so the legend goes, by order of Zhuge Liang, a famous statesman and chief minister of the State of Shu during the Period of Three Kingdoms (220-280 A.D.). On an expedition to conquer the cave-dwelling southern *Man* barbarians who had often marauded his state, he came to the side of the Lushui River at the head of a big army. Someone told him that the river was poisonous and treacherous and that human lives would be lost in crossing unless the tyrannical River God was appeased. The way to do this, the man said, was to offer him *mantou* (heads of the captured barbarians) as human sacrifice. Now Zhuge Liang was a kind-hearted man. He accepted the suggestion but ordered to use "heads" (*tou*) made of dough instead of real human ones, thus saving a number of lives.

Since then the story goes on to say, *mantou* (barbarians' heads) has become a popular food and spread to the north of China.

Noodles

(面条 *Miantiao*)

Noodles are a form of staple food very popular among the Chinese. They can be made either by hand or by machine and, by the way they are made, are divided into "cut noodles" or "dried noodles". Made in whatever way, they may be of different widths, varying from ribbons to threads. As a prepared dish, they can be served warm or cold, dressed with chilli oil or not, eaten with fried bean sauce, pork or chicken sauce, duck chops, soup of any concoction and what not.

There is also a variety of "instant noodles", which are precooked, dried and commercially packed. Before eating, all one has to do is to soak them in hot, boiled water for a few minutes. They are very handy for a quick lunch in the office or on a journey.

As noodles are always in the form of long strings, they are symbolic of longevity and are therefore indispensable at Chinese birthday parties.

Two types of noodles stand out

among the rest and require professional skill. The "hand-pulled noodles" are probably unique to China and can be made only by a trained cook. He prepares the paste by stretching it in his hands and, holding it stretched and shaking it gently up and down four or five times, lets down the middle of the long paste and swings it in such a way that it twists around itself. He repeats the stretching, shaking and twisting many times until he feels the paste is firm enough. Then, on a work board he starts pulling the paste with his arms stretched. He folds the thick string of paste into two, pulling again. This he repeats many times over and the strings of paste become longer, more numerous, thinner and thinner, turning finally into very fine noodles. The whole process of making "hand-pulled noodles" is done with such magical dexterity that to watch an experienced cook at it is like enjoying a juggler's show.

Another speciality that one cannot make at home is *longxumian* (dragon beard noodles). Commercially they are available fried, so they are golden in colour, crisp to the bite and with a distinctive flavour. "Dragon beards" are also hand-pulled but are made extraordinarily fine. It has been calculated that a piece of paste prepared with 1.5 kilogrammes of wheat flour can make 144,000 hair-thin noodles, each 0.17 metres long, which means a total length of 2 kilometres.

At the beginning "dragon beards" were simply called ìbeardsî, but since they caught the fancy of an emperor and as the dragon was the symbol of all emperors, they have come to be known as "dragon beards".

Dumplings (1)

(饺子 *Jiaozi*)

Several Chinese snacks have been known in English as "dumplings". Of these, *jiaozi* is taken by the northern Chinese as a symbol of festivity and served as the main dish for the Spring Festival or traditional New Year's Day.

The annals of a northern country have this record from the early Qing Dynasty: "On New Year's Day the family share a sumptuous dinner at which various types of dumplings are served. They are called *jiaozi* because they are eaten at a time when the New Year is ushered in and the old sent off." In the vast areas of North China, especially in the countryside, *Jiaozi* is not only eaten at the New Year but served on ordinary days when there are guests for dinner. In provincial towns and market villages, many eating-places specialize in this dish.

Jiaozi dumplings are made of a paste wrapper with seasoned mincemeat as the filling. They are usually in the shape of a crescent moon. Cooked in boiling water for a few minutes, they become "boiled dumpling" and are ready to serve. If steamed under cover, they are called "steamed dumplings".

A great range of food may be used as the principal material for *jiaozi* fill: minced pork, mutton or beef, minced prawn or shrimp, vegetables and dried mushrooms. The usual seasonings are soya sauce, salt, sugar, minced scallion and ginger root, peanut and sesame oils. Dumplings are particularly tasty because in the process of boiling or steaming the steam generated inside the wrapper does not escape, keeping the flavour inside and the fillings tender.

From a Tang Dynasty (618-907 A. D.) tomb excavated in 1968 in Xinjiang, a wooden bowl was unearthed, containing a number of dumplings which look exactly the same as today's *jiaozi*. This testifies that dumplings had been introduced to the northwestern region of ethnic minorities by the Tang Dynasty at the latest.

Dumplings (2)

(馄饨 *Huntun*)

Another type of Chinese dumplings is called *huntun* (or wonton). It is made in a similar way as *jiaozi*, but the wrapper is thinner and contains less filling, folded in such a way that it leaves a loose flap.

Huntun is always boiled and served about a dozen in a bowl of instant soup seasoned by sesame oil, soya sauce, a pinch of shredded parsley or some other dried vegetable.

Huntun is popular not only in the north but also in many southern parts of China. It was customary in old Beijing for people to eat *huntun* at the winter solstice.

The origin of *huntun* has remained obscure. A Song Dynasty (960-1279) work suggested: "It is called *huntun* because it was first made by the *Hun* and *Tun* clans of the northern parts outside of the Great Wall". There are, however, others who would not endorse this opinion.

Deep-Fried Dough Sticks and Dough Cakes (油条与油饼 *Youtiao yu Youbing*)

These are popular snacks which the Chinese like for breakfast, with the southerners preferring the sticks and the northerners the cakes.

Their preparation is rather simple. A suitable amount of soda, salt and alum is mixed with water and flour to make dough, which is left to ferment for about half an hour. The dough is then cut into finger-sized lengths. Every two pieces are picked up together, stretched with the hands into 20-cm sticks and, by the same movement, twisted around each other. The twisted sticks, when deep-fried in boiling oil, swell into the finished snack.

The cakes are cooked in a similar way except that the dough is not cut into long pieces but into cubes, which are pinrolled into thin cakes before deep-frying.

The deep-fried dough cake dates back to the Tang Dynasty (618-907 A.D.), earlier than the twisted sticks,which made their first appearance in the region of today's Jiangsu and Zhejiang provinces in the Southern Song Dynasty (1127-1279). The following legend tells about their origin. In 1142, Yue Fei, the famous national hero, was framed up by the traitorous prime minister Qin Hui, and executed at Fengbo Pavilion. The people in a nearby eating house were making fried rice balls when

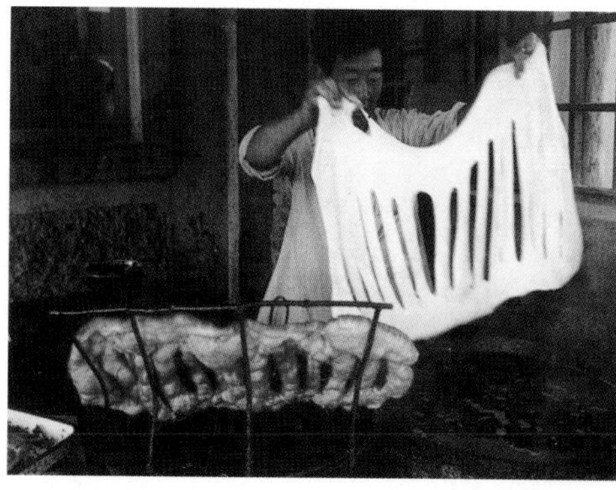

they heard the sad news. In their indignation they picked up some dough,shaped it into figures representing Qin Hui and his wife and,twisting the two together,fried them in deep oil to give vent to their anger.

Thus started the deep-fried sticks, which have become a highly popular snack.

Not everybody knows its origin, though some still call it "*youzha gui*" (oil-fried *Gui*, a variant of *Hui*).

Steamed Corn Bread

(窝头 *Wotou*)

Wotou is a form of staple food in many northern regions of China. Made of corn flour, it is in the shape of a cone hollow from the base, rather like an inverted *wo* (bird's nest), hence its name.

It used to be the cheap coarse food for the poor, but a kind of miniature *wotou* is served by Fangshan (imitation royal kitchen) Restaurant in Beijing as a specialty of the imperial cuisine. This may seem hard to understand but it is explained by the following anecdote.

When China was invaded by the troops of the eight imperialist powers in 1900, Empress Dowager Cixi fled Beijing with Emperor Guangxu for Xi'an. On the way, Cixi was offered a piece of corn bread which, in her hunger, she ate with great relish. Back in Beijing amidst the luxuries of the palace, she told the imperial kitchen to make *wotou* for her which she had found so tasty. The chef dared not contradict her but used the best and most refined corn flour he could find and mixed in it chestnut butter, sugar and sweetened osmanthus flowers. With these ingredients he made dainty pieces of *wotou* which he steamed under cover over a strong fire. The resultant *wotou* looked golden and tasted good. It became one of the delicacies on the imperial menu.

Pyramid-Shaped Glutinous Rice Dumplings （粽子 *Zongzi*）

Pyramid-shaped dumplings made of glutinous rice wrapped in bamboo or reed leaves are a traditional Chinese food for the Dragon Boat Festival which falls on the 5th of the 5th lunar month. The festival, popular among the Han people by tradition, was first established during the Warring States Period (475-221 B.C.) in memory of Qu Yuan, a celebrated poet who was a high official of the state of Chu. A passionate reformist, he courted the wrath of conservatives, who talked the King of Chu into sending him into exile. Dismayed by his failure to salvage his country, Qu Yuan drowned himself in the miluo River on the 5th of the 5th lunar month in 278 B.C. His fellow countrymen made it a point to honour the memory of this great patriotic poet by sailing dragon boats down the miluo River and throwing pyramid-shaped rice dumplings into the water to feed his soul.

Such is the origin of the Chinese tradition of holding dragon boat races and eating pyramid-shaped rice dumplings on the 5th of the 5th lunar month.

Eight-Treasure Rice Pudding （八宝饭 *Babaofan*）

The Eight-treasure Rice Pudding is made from glutinous rice supplemented with red jujubes, lotus seeds, lily, seeds of Job's tears, gingko, dried longan pulp, and finely cut green and red plums. These ingredients may also be substituted with walnut meat, haw jelly, raisin, peanut and cherry. The Eight-treasure Rice Pudding is used as a banquet course for its pleasant colour, fragrance, taste and shape. In some places, brown sugar is melted with burning liquor and as the icing for the Eight-treasure Rice Pudding in some places.

This practice of burning liquor to melt brown sugar originated in the story of the eight scholars recruited by King Wen of the Western Zhou Dynasty in present-day Shaanxi Province to conquer the tyrannical King Zhou of the Shang Dynasty. These scholars, who included Bo Da, Bo Shi, Zhong Tu, Shu Ye, and Shu Xia, indeed played a positive role in toppling the Shang Dynasty. When the triumph over King Zhou was celebrated in the Zhou capital city of Hao, the chefs of the imperial kitchen concocted a kind of pudding made from eight treasured ingredients, and topped it with fiery-coloured haw juice to symbolize the "eight Zhou scholars burning King Zhou of Shang to death". The Eight-treasure Rice Pudding thus came down through the generations as a favoured course of the Chinese banquet.

According to Chinese tradition, the Eight-treasure Rice Pudding is served and eaten on the 7th of the 1st lunar month to mark the end of Spring Festival and the beginning of New Year.

Dumplings (3)

(元宵 *Yuanxiao*)

Yuanxiao is a special dumpling in China for the Lantern Festival (the 15th night of the 1st lunar month). It is a "ball" made of glutinous rice flour.

Yuanxiao, it is said,made its debut in the Eastern Jin Dynasty (317-420 A.D.) and became popular during the Tang and Song periods (7th to 13th century), but not under its present name. *The Notes of the Year in Hubei*, a book by a 10th century scholar, mentioned "bean-paste-filled cakes" which were made on the 15th day

of the 1st lunar month and, in another context, "floating cakes in thin gruel prepared at the middle of the first moon".

As the 15th night of the New Year was later called "*Shangyuan*" and the "*Yuanxiao*" festival, so the dumplings came to be known by the name of the festival.

Yuanxiao dumplings fall into two categories.

One is those without fillings. A suitable amount of water is mixed into glutinous rice flour to make dough, which is then shaped by hand into small "solid balls". The balls or dumplings are boiled in sweetened water and, when cooked, are served in bowls. They can also be boiled in plain water and then sprinkled with sugar in the serving bowl. A third way of preparation is to cook them with dried longan pulp, candied dates or jujubes and similar ingredients to make a kind of porridge of assorted balls. Sweetened with sugar and osmanthus flowers, it makes an excellent dessert.

Another category of dumplings is those with fillings, which may be either sweet or salty in taste. For the sweet variety, the filling may be sugar,walnut meat, sesame, osmanthus flowers,rose petals, sweetened tangerine peel, bean or jujube paste, used alone or in combination. The salty variety can be filled with mincemeat, certain vegetables or a mixture of both. In either case, the materials are minced and well mixed with flavoursome seasonings.

The way to make stuffed dumplings also varies between the north and the south. The usual method followed in southern provinces is to shape the dough of rice flour into balls, make a hole in each and insert the filling inside, close the hole and smooth out the surface by rolling the ball between the hands. In the north, where sweet and non-meat stuffing is normally used, people pressed the fillings into hardened cores, dip them slightly in water and roll them in a flat basket containing dry glutinous rice flour. A layer of the flour will be stuck on the fillings, which are dipped again in water and rolled again in the rice flour. And so it goes on snowballing until the dumplings grow to the desired size.

Yuanxiao dumplings must be boiled in the right way. First bring a pot of water to a boil on strong fire. Drop in the dumplings gently and, when they float up on the water a few minutes later, keep them in the pot for a few more minutes to make the inside well cooked. But at this stage, the fire must be reduced, for dumplings boiled in rolling water may burst open. To make sure that this does not happen, some cold water may be added little by little into the pot to keep the water simmering instead of boiling.

Moon Cake

(月饼 *Yuebing*)

The Chinese moon cake is for the Mid-autumn Festival and is so called because it is made in the form of a disc representing the full moon of the festival.

The cake consists of a crust and stuffing. The crust is made in varying ways and with varying degrees of crispness, but the usual main ingredients are wheat flour, oil or fat, sugar and maltose. Part of the flour is mixed with water to make dough, and the rest is kneaded with fat. These arranged in alternate layers become the crust after baking. A wide variety of materials may be used for the stuffing; these include Chinese ham, sausage, walnut meat, pine nuts and almond. The usual flavourings are osmanthus flowers, rose petals and other natural essences.

Moon cakes are normally called by the fillings they contain—assorted fruits, five nuts, rose, ham, jujube paste, pepper and salt, and so on. The stuffing, as already shown, may be either sweet or salty or mixed in taste. There are literally a thousand and one kinds of moon cakes made in different regions of China, but it is generally agreed that the best moon cakes are produced by three schools — Jiangsu, Guangdong and Beijing.

Although the form of the moon cake is traditionally round, yet several localities have in recent years broken away from the tradition by experimenting with square, oblong and triangular moon cakes.

New Year Cake

(年糕 *Niangao*)

At the Spring Festival, namely, the Chinese traditional New Year, most Chinese families will eat the New Year cake (*niangao*) which is made of glutinous rice or millet flour and garnished with various auxiliary materials such as bean or jujube paste, assorted fruits, assorted preserves and so on. The cake is divided into two categories, the yellow one and the white one, representing respectively gold and silver. It used to be the belief that to eat *niangao* at New Year would bring good luck.

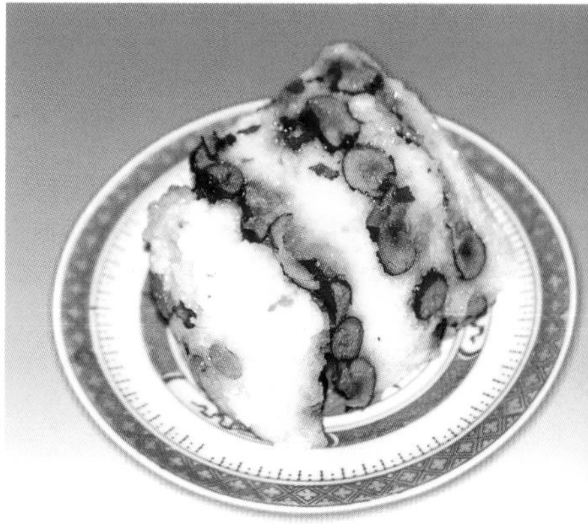

New Year cakes may be cooked by steaming or frying and are served in either case with sugar sprinkled on. Down in the south there is another way of preparation, that is, to soak a kind of plain, ungarnished cake in water and then cut it into slices, stir-fried in a cooking pot with oil and salt, mixed often with spinach or other greens.

Dough Flowers

(面花 *Mianhua*)

Dough flowers are not only a food but a work of art nice to look at. As the name implies, they are made of wheat flour, though sometimes mixed with glutinous rice flour for greater stickiness.

They are very popular in the Chinese countryside, and those made in Luochuan in northern Shaanxi Province, called *huamo* (or "flowery bread") by the local people, are particularly well-known. On the eve

figures are cooked by steaming and brightened up with colouring. Peaches made of steamed dough, a symbol of longevity for birthday parties of elderly people, are usually dyed red and yellow after the natural ones.

Dough flowers are normally sweet in taste and served at dinners between the dishes. Some are prepared by mixing natural, colourful vegetable juices into wheat flour, and they look particularly delightful and appetizing.

of festivals or ceremonial occasions such as a wedding or a funeral, the local womenfolk will inevitably turn their thought to preparing dough flowers. No patterns are needed, but their nimble fingers can in no time shape a ball of dough into a flower, a bird, a chick or a duckling. A blossoming flower is made by cutting out the petals with scissors, the plumage of bird wings by pressing with a comb, and black or green beans will make the eyes of little animals. Then the modelled

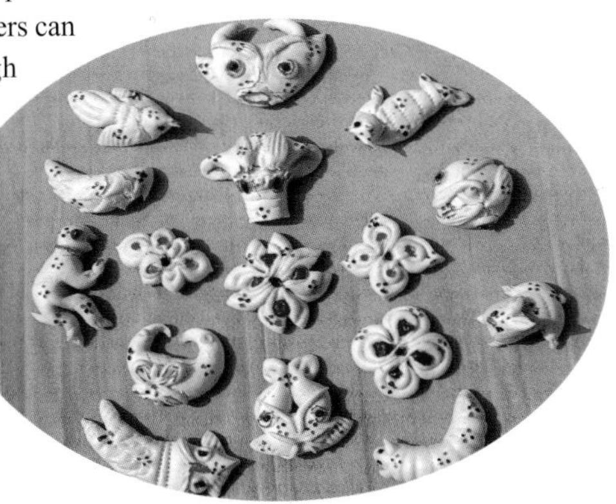

Spring Rolls

(春卷 *Chunjuan*)

Spring rolls are a great favourite with the Chinese, they are also very much appreciated abroad. At receptions given by Chinese embassies or consulates, spring rolls often prove to be a gastronomic delight to the guests. It is not without reason that they are served by Chinese restaurants abroad at many times the price they are sold in China. In China, their appearance on the dining table with their inviting brown colour has rarely failed to cause foreign tourists to click their tongues in admiration.

The principal ingredient for the fillings in spring rolls is usually bean sprouts, which are mixed with shredded pork dried mushroom plumped and shredded, vermicelli, shredded bamboo shoots and the necessary seasonings. The fillings are rolled up in thin wrappers of dough,and the resulting rolls are deep-fried in oil and served hot when the wrappers are still crisp.

The stuffing of the spring rolls is generally seasoned with salt, but there are a minority of people who use sweetened bean paste as the fillings.

Apart from being served at dinners, spring rolls are also sold as takeaway snacks in some restaurants.

Bean Curd

(豆腐 *Doufu*)

Bean curd may be justifiably called a great invention in old China.

An ancient work on medicinal herbs mentioned bean curd in these words: "The method of making *doufu* dates back to Liu An, the Prince of Huainan. It is made of soya beans, either the black or the yellow variety." Liu An (179-122 B.C.) was a grandson of Liu Bang, founding emperor of the Han Dynasty. Legend has it that the prince, in his search for a panacea to help him achieve immortality, experimented with soya beans and bittern and, through the chemical reaction, stumbled on the earliest bean curd. That was more than 2,100 years ago.

An analysis of 100 grams of bean curd shows that it contains water (85 grams), protein (7.4 grams), fat (3.5 grams), calcium (277 mg), phosphorus (57 mg)and iron (2.1 mg). As a food of high nutritive value, it has met with widespread acclaim.

Many products can be made with soya beans as the principal material. They include, in addition to bean curd of various styles, dried bean curd, bean milk and its skin, jellied bean curd, bean curd sheets and noodles, and bean milk powder.

Fermented Bean Curd (腐乳 *Furu*)

Fermented bean curd is often served as part of a Chinese breakfast.

As the name suggests, it is made from bean curd and is usually available in two different varieties, the white and the red. Bean curd, as told by the previous article, first appeared as early as the Western Han Dynasty (206 B.C.-25 A.D.), but fermented bean curd had to wait for several hundred years.

A story tells about a bean curd tradesman of the Tang Dynasty (618-907), whose business was rather slack at a time. His bean curd began to become mouldy and, to prevent it from further deteriorating, he sprinkled fine salt over it and put it away in a jar. As he opened the jar a few days later, he found to his surprise that the salted bean curd, instead of having gone bad, greeted him with an inviting smell he had never known before. Thus the first lot of fermented bean curd was born.

This food has since become very popular in China, and it is made by a rather simple process. Fresh bean curd is cut into cubes and mixed with nodule mould and left to ferment for 2-3 days until a mouldy coating appears on the surface. (Made at home, the bean curd may be left to ferment by itself, but this takes about 10 days.) The bean curd is then salted, seasoned with other condiments and sealed in jars. It is put away and kept for 4-5 months to become savoury and marketable.

Preserved Eggs

(松花蛋 *Songhua Dan*)

The proper Chinese name for preserved eggs is *Songhua* or *Songhua Dan* (pine-flower eggs)— so called because, when shelled, these solidified but semi-transparent eggs show flowery patterns like pine needles inside. The more and the prettier the patterns, the higher is the quality of the egg.

Songhua are normally made of duck eggs. The traditional folk recipe was to soak the fresh eggs in quicklime mixed with salt and water. Now the eggs are soaked, for 40-60 days, in a liquid consisting of caustic soda, salt and tea leaves. Another method followed in certain regions is to wrap the unshelled eggs individually in a clay mixture containing quicklime, salt and grain husk, and they become eatable in two to three weeks. Some Westerners have been told to call them "hundred-year-old" or even "thousand-year-old" eggs. This is definitely an exaggerating misnomer, which has unfortunately caused some visitors to fight shy of this tasty and peculiar Chinese food.

The preserved egg, when shelled, is soft and smooth but at the same time resilient, its yolk is darkened and gelatinous.

Because of the presence of sodium hydroxide and the little amount of ammonia generated by the egg itself during the preparation, the finished egg may sometimes carry a faint alkaline or stringent taste. This may be easily removed by a little vinegar with minced ginger root mixed in the soya sauce sprinkled on the cut pieces. This also helps to enhance the tastiness of *songhua* and as a matter of fact is the usual way the egg is served.

Roast Duck

(烤鸭 *Kaoya*)

The Beijing roast duck is a dish well-known among gastronomes the world over.

To cook ducks by direct heat dates back at least 1,500 years to the period of the Northern and Southern dynasties, when "broiled duck" was mentioned in writing. About eight hundred years later, Husihui, imperial dietician to a Mongol emperor of the Yuan Dynasty, listed in his work *Essentials of Diet* (1330 A.D.) the "grilled duck" as a banquet delicacy. It was made by heating the duck—stuffed with a mince of sheep's tripe, parsley, scallion, and salt — on a charcoal fire.

Today the Beijing roast duck (or "Peking duck", as it has been called) is made of a special variety of duck fattened by forced feeding in the suburbs of Beijing. After the duck is drawn and cleaned, air is pumped under the skin to separate it more or less from the flesh. And a mixture of oil, sauce and molasses is coated all over it. Thus, when dried and roasted, the duck will look brilliantly red as if painted. Perhaps that is why it is known among some Westerners as the *canard laqué* or "lacquered duck".

Before being put in the oven,the inside of the fowl is half filled with hot water, which is not released until the duck has been cooked. For oven fuel, jujube-tree, peach or pear wood is used because these types of firewood emit little smoke and give steady and controllable flames with a faint and pleasant aroma. In the oven, each

duck takes about forty minutes to cook, and the skin becomes crisp while the meat is tender.

In the restaurant, the roast duck, after being shown whole to the customers, is served in slices, which are eaten rolled in thin pancakes with a dish of *tianmianjiang* (a sweet sauce made of fermented flour) and scallion(or cucumber) cut in thin lengths. Few people, if any, could resist the temptation of the crisp and delicious taste of the Beijing roast duck.

Before the duck appears,however, various warm or cold dishes are often served,made of kidneys, hearts, livers, webs, wings and eggs, all from the duck. Even duck tongues can be prepared into very tasty dishes, and the skeleton of the eaten duck normally goes into a soup which finds few equals. A highly experienced chef of a duck restaurant can produce an "all-duck banquet" of over eighty dishes made of different parts of the fowl.

Toffee Fruits

(糖葫芦 *Tanghulu*)

Toffee fruits on sticks are popular in the northern parts of China.

They are made of various kinds of small fruits — haws, crabapples, water chestnuts, grapes or yam. First the fruits are trimmed and cleaned, they are then stringed one after another on a slender bamboo stick and coated in a bath of rock-sugar syrup. As soon as the toffee hardens, the *tanghulu* is ready. A *tanghulu* is generally made of six or seven of such fruits or, in the case of yam, one length of 5 or 6 inches. With the crisp sugar coating, it looks bright and inviting, and it generally tastes sweet and sourish.

Toffee fruits on sticks appear on the street corners in autumn and winter; sold by hawkers, they are welcomed and enjoyed by both old and young.

Chafing Dish

(火锅 *Huoguo*)

The chafing dish is a favourite with the northern Chinese, especially in winter. The main ingredient for this dish is usually mutton; however, beef, fish or prawn may also be used. It is eaten with vermicelli, fresh vegetables and sometimes dumplings.

The Chinese hot pot is different from the Western chafing dish in that its soup container is built around (instead of over) its belly-like heater. It is usually made of copper or brass, but may also be available in aluminium and burnt clay. It is called "Mongolian pot" by some Westerners perhaps because of its association with mutton from Inner Mongolia.

The preparation of the chafing dish is simple: first, water (preferably boiling water) is poured into the container and then burning charcoal is filled into the

heater from the top of the small chimney. When the water is brought to the boil again, the meat or fish slices may be put in, little by little, by the diners themselves. After a while they may be taken out with chopsticks and, before eating, dipped in a sauce prepared in advance.

The meat for this dish must be from the tenderest parts of the animal. Take mutton, the commonly used meat, for example. From a sheep of over twenty kilograms, only six to seven kilograms are fit to be eaten this way. Each kilogram is cut into at least 120 slices. They must be paper-thin in order to be cooked instantly in the boiling water and remain tender when taken out.

Along with the mutton slices, fresh vegetable and vermicelli are put into the pot, to be boiled and eaten. The dumplings, if any, usually come last.

The sauce in which the cooked slices are dipped is very important. It is a mixture of:

sesame paste (*zhimajiang*),
sesame oil (*mayou*),
shrimp sauce (*luxiayou*),
soya sauce (*jiangyou*),
chili oil, (*layou*),
chive flower sauce (*jiucaihua*),
fermented bean curd sauce (*jiangdoufu*), cooking wine, and parsley.

And sweetened sloves of garlic may be eaten for added relish.

Shashlick

(羊肉串 *Yangrouchuan*)

The shashlick is an Arab snack very popular in the north and northwest of China,where there is a sizable Muslim population. Many vendors are seen making them at street corners, especially in the cities and towns of the Xinjiang Uygur Autonomous Region.

It is made of lean mutton cut into slices. These are stuck one after another on iron skewers, which are then arranged closely on a trough-like burner and grilled over a charcoal fire. When the mutton oozes juice, salt, chilli and aniseed powders are

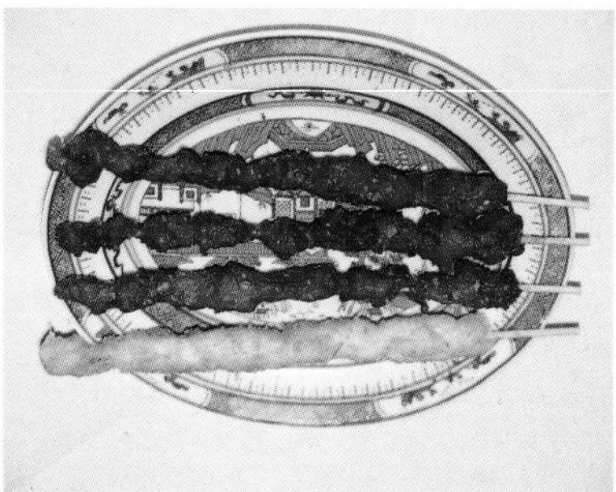

sprinkled on and the shashlicks are ready to eat. Served at a formal dinner, they are made in a more refined way, for example,

coated with sesame seeds to enhance the taste.

The shashlick is known in English under various other names and spellings — shashlik, kabob, habab, kebab, kebob and cabob, among others.

Hot Candied Fruit (拔丝 *Basi*)

This is a well-known Chinese sweet dish, and it can be made with either apple, pear, banana or yam. It is served hot and each piece should be dipped into a bowl of cold water before being put into one's mouth so that the surface is cooled and hardened while the inside remains warm and tasty.

The most important part in preparing this dish is the boiling of the sugar. Sugar is put into a round-bottomed frying pan containing hot water or oil, boiled on a moderate fire and stirred gently with a slice until the sugar melts. The syrup continues to be heated and begins to give out bubbles, which become smaller as the liquid thickens. Continued heating will cause the syrup to turn thin again, and it is at this juncture that the fruit, peeled and cut into pieces, is to be put into the pan, mixed with the syrup by stirring so that each piece is coated.

The toffee around the fruit remains sticky so that when a piece is picked up with chopsticks, flossy sugar is drawn out. To achieve this result, the fire for boiling the sugar should be well controlled, for intense fire will burn the sugar while slow fire will not make the syrup draw.

The serving dish containing the candied fruit must be smeared in advance with a little edible oil to prevent the fruit from sticking onto it.

Cake Particles in Mutton Soup
(羊肉泡馍 *Yangrou Paomo*)

Soaking cake particles in mutton soup first appeared in the pastureland in northwest China. Today it has become a special snack of Xi'an. Chunks of mutton are washed and sliced into pieces and boiled with scallion, ginger, wild pepper, star aniseseen, cumin and cinnamon. Baked wheaten cakes are then torn with hand into particles the size of soybeans and placed in a bowl. Mutton slices are then added to the torn cake before mutton soup is ladled into the bowl. The serving is thus ready with the addition of minced scallion, sliced cabbage, rice wine, bean noodles and salt. Diners may drink the soup while eating the cake particles, or allow the soup to be completely absorbed by the cake so that when the cake has been eaten the bowl becomes empty. A third method is to place the cake and meat in the centre of a bowl and inundate the mixture with soup. Some customers like to have this snack together with chilli paste and sweetened garlic.

"Cross-Bridge" Rice Noodles
(过桥米线 *Guoqiao Mixian*)

This is a special dish from Yunnan Province, a snack with rice noodles as its principal substance. It consists of: (1) a bowl of pre-cooked plain rice noodles, (2) a big bowl of rich and piping hot chicken (or meat) broth, and (3) a plate of assorted paper-thin slices of raw pork, liver and chicken with fresh vegetables. When these are served, all the diner has to do is to put the slices, vegetables and noodles, in that order, into the big bowl and the result will be a very tasty dish of "noodles in soup". But why the unusual name of "cross-bridge" noodles?

Legend has it that a scholar in the old days was jailed on an island in the middle of a lake and his wife had to cross a long bridge to bring him his meals. The food invariably became cold when she arrived at the prison. As greasy chicken broth does not get cold easily, she hit upon a solution of the problem by bringing this dish "cross-bridge" rice noodles.

"Buddha Jumps the Wall"
(佛跳墙 *Fotiaoqiang*)

This is a well-known dish of Fuzhou. It is made of an assortment of materials: shark's fin, shark's lip, fish maw, abalone, squid, sea cucumber, chicken breast,duck chops, pork tripe, pork leg, minced ham, mutton elbow, dried scallop, winter bamboo shoots, *xianggu* mushrooms, and so on. These are seasoned and steamed separately and then put into a small-mouthed clay jar together with cooking wine and a dozen or so boiled pigeon eggs. The jar is covered and put on intense fire first and then simmered for some time on slow fire. Four or five ounces of a local liquor is added into the jar, which is kept simmering for another five minutes. Then the dish is ready.

The origin of the dish is explained by a local story. A Fuzhou scholar of the Qing Dynasty went picnicking with friends in the suburbs and he put all the ham, chicken, etc. he had with him in a wine jar which he heated over charcoal fire before eating. The attractive smell of the food spread in the air all the way to a nearby temple. It was so inviting that the monks,who were supposed to be vegetarians, jumped over the temple wall and partook heartily of the scholar's picnic. One of the party on this occasion wrote a poem in praise of the dish, of which a line reads: "Even Buddha himself would jump the wall to come over." Hence the name of the dish.

Lotus Root

(莲藕 *Lian'ou*)

Lotus roots are actually the tubers or underground stems of the lotus blossoms. They may be grown wherever water exists, whether in pond, lake or marshes, and they are harvested in fall.

Lotus roots are fairly nutritive, having a good content of protein, starch, carbon hydrates, amino acids and vitamins. They are eaten in the southern provinces of China as a fresh fruit for their juicy tenderness and, up in the north, as a dried vegetable for the preparation of various dishes.

A refreshment may be made of lotus root by following a simple recipe: fill the natural holes of the lotus root with glutinous rice, steam it until cooked , cut into slices and serve with sugar. It is sweet with a fresh taste of the lotus plant.

In Jiangsu and Zhejiang provinces where lotuses are grown in abundance, starch is industrially extracted from lotus roots and is commercially packen as a special product of the region. Used as the material for an instant gruel, it is first well mixed with sugar and a little warm water into a thick liquid and, when boiling water is quickly poured onto it, congeals into a cooked paste ready to eat. It is something between a drink and a snack and helps to allay both thirst and hunger.

THINGS CHINESE 中国风物

Lucky Things

吉祥物

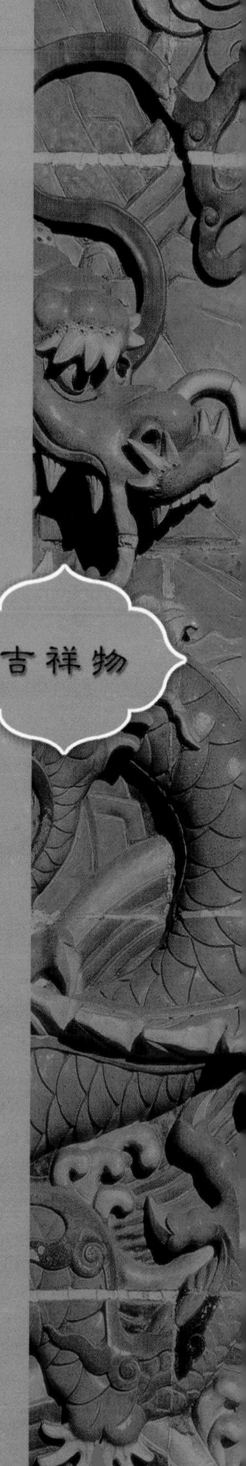

Dragon and Phoenix

(龙与凤 *Long yu Feng*)

The dragon and the phoenix are the principal motifs for decorative designs on the buildings, clothing and articles of daily use in the imperial palace. The throne hall is supported by columns entwined by gilded dragons, the central ramps on marble steps were paved with huge slabs carved in relief with the dragon and phoenix, and the screen walls display dragons in brilliant colours. The names in the Chinese language for nearly all the things connected with the emperor or the empress were preceded by the epithet "dragon" or "phoenix"; thus, "dragon seat" for the throne, "dragon robe" for the emperor's ceremonial dress, "dragon bed" for him to sleep on, and "phoenix carriage", "phoenix canopies" and so on for the imperial processions. The national flag of China under the Qing Dynasty was emblazoned with a big dragon. The earliest postage stamps put out by China were called "dragon-heads" because they showed a dragon in their designs. Even today the dragon is sometimes adopted as the symbol of Chinese exhibitions held abroad or the cover designs of books on China printed by foreign publishers. "The Giant Dragon of the East" is becoming a sobriquet for the country.

Belief in the dragon, and drawings of the imaginary animal, can be traced back to primitive society when certain prehistoric tribes in China adopted the dragon among other totems as their symbol and guardian god. Some of the recently unearthed bronze vessels of the Yin Dynasty, which existed more than 3,000 years ago, are decorated with sketches of dragons of a crude form. Earliest legends in China described the dragon as a miraculous animal with fish scales and long beards. As time went on, it became more and more embellished in the minds of the people, acquiring the antlers of the deer, the mane of the horse and the claws of the eagle — in short, appropirating the distinctive features of other creatures until it became what we see today everywhere in the palace.

The Chinese phoenix, likewise, exists only in legends and fairy tales. Sovereign of all birds, it has the head of the golden pheasant, the beak of the parrot, the body of the mandarin duck, the wings of the roc, the feathers of the peacock and the legs of the crane; gloriously beautiful, it reigns over the feathered world. An early design of the phoenix can be seen on the silk painting discovered in a tomb of the Warring States Period (475-221 B.C.) near Changsha in Hunan Province.

The dragon and the phoenix often served in classical art and literature as metaphors for people of high virtue and rare talent or, in certain combinations, for matrimonial harmony of happy marriage. As an important part of folk arts, dragon lanterns, dragon boats, dragon and phoenix dances are still highly popular on festivals among the people of all localities.

Wind-Riding Streamers
(风马旗 *Fengmaqi*)

Travellers to Tibet often espy strings of tiny flags hanging down from trees or the eaves of buildings, or fluttering on mountaintops. Made of paper or cloth and inscribed with religious incantations, they are known as "prayers' streamers" or "wind and horse streamers" because they also bear horse patterns.

A wind and horse streamer is about 10 cm square and inscribed with patterns with a strapping stud in the centre. The stud has auspicious symbols inscribed on its back and is surrounded with the likenesses of its four divine protectors: the roc, dragon, tiger and lion. These five animals are portrayed in different gestures, but they look heroic and awe inspiring. On some of the streamers the patterns of roc, dragon, tiger and lion are replaced with their names in the Tibetan language. The flags come in white, yellow, red and green colours to symbolize the four direction of universe. In the Tibetan language, "wind" means "dragon", and "horse" means

According to ancient Tibetan history books, the wind-riding horse flag was invented by Kongze Chiyai Jambo. "Kongze" is the Tibetan transliteration of "Confucius", and "Chiyai Jambo", meaning "Master of Wisdom", is a title the Tibetans bestowed on Confucius. Legend has it that in his lifetime, Confucian had served in a variety of positions such as shaman, historian, master of ceremony, and fortune teller; it was probably he who had drawn the likeness of horses and cattle on paper and burned them as sacrifices to the deceased, a practice which found its way to Tibet. In the beginning the Tibetans, too, burned the horse-patterned streamers as sacrifices to the dead; later they learned to let the streamers flutter in the wind so that the wind-riding horse could fly into the sky freely — a habit which has something to do with the Tibetan tradition of celestial burial, by which bodies are cut up and fed to birds of prey.

"smooth sailing"; thus the connotation of the flag of wind-riding horse is very much akin to the Han people's wish for good luck.

Big-Mouthed Celestial Animal
(吞口儿 *Tunkou'er*)

Travellers to Yunnan and Sichuan in southwest China are impressed by the colourfully painted wood ladles in the shape of a strange animal hanging on the front doors of the dwellings of local Miao, Yi and Han residents. The animal looks grotesque with a wide-open mouth as if ready anytime to swallow the demons and goblins that dare to invade. Obviously the wood ladle is a talisman designed to ward the dwellings of evil and disaster.

A variation of masks worn by exorcising dancers in south China, this image of big-mouthed animal was born of totemism and primitive culture. It is found in different places—glazed on eaves tiles for decorating a temple, or carved on a stone pillar that stands by the road to guarantee good luck and rich harvest for local people.

Maling, a remote mountainous county of Sichuan, is best known for its renditions of this legendary animal, which features a bizarre look and a striking contrast between bright red and green colours that is somewhat neutralized with black and white. The Eight Diagrams is painted on its forehead to render a mysterious Taoist touch to the animal. The Maling style of big-mouthed animal is one of the major rural handicrafts of Sichuan.

Hada

(哈达 Hada)

Hada, a long piece of silk used by the Tibetans and some Mongols as a gift when greeting people, worshipping celestial beings, and in daily person-to-person contacts.

According to the book *Tibetan Customs and Habits* by the Tibetan scholar Chilai Qoizhag, *hada* was invented by the Han people before it found its way to Tibet. During the Yuan Dynasty, when the Tibetan Sakya King, Phags-pa, returned to Tibet after meeting Hublai, the founding emperor of the Yuan Dynasty, he brought a piece of *hada* that was inscribed with patterns of the Great Wall on both ends and the four Chinese characters that mean "good luck".

Hada is of different lengths, but generally it is 2 metres long and 30cm wide. Most of it is fashioned out of white silk, because white means purity. There are also ones made from homespun. Red, yellow and light blue *hada* are made of fine silk fabrics and embroidered with Buddhist statues, Sanskrit messages, lotus flower and auspicious clouds, to be used for occasions of the highest grades.

When worshiping Buddhist statues,

greeting or bidding farewell to friends, or holding weddings or funerals, the Tibetans show their respects and affection to their friends or beloved ones with *hada*. Whenever they are on a trip they make it a point to bring along several pieces of *hada* to be given to friends or relatives. Tiny pieces of *hada* are attached to letters as a way of good will.

The Tibetans are very etiquette conscious when presenting hada. When the recipient is an elderly, they would bend their body and hold *hada* above their head before presenting it to the recipient's seat or feet. The ritual is much simpler between peers—you simply thrust the *hada* to the recipient's hand. When a *hada* is presented to a member of the younger generation, it is often tied to the youngster's neck, and the youngster is supposed to bend his body to show gratitude.

Spring Festival Couplets (春联 *Chunlian*)

By tradition the Chinese love to paste couplets on their gateposts or door panels when celebrating Spring Festival. The couplets are generally written on red paper and the sentences contain auspicious meanings. In the region south of the Yangtze River, couplets are inscribed on yellow paper during funerals.

The Spring Festival couplets originated in the peachwood charms against evil (hung on the gate on New Year's Eve) in ancient China. Legend has it that the names of two celestial beings who were conquerors of demons and goblins are written down on pieces of peachwood to be hung on the gate to protect a family from evil and disaster and greet the coming of an auspicious year. Later, people simply drew the images of these two celestial beings on their doors. Looking ferocious with glaring eyes and sharp weapons, they were enough to scare demons of all descriptions from intruding. Even today, pictures of the two gods can still be seen in ancient buildings. Later, people simplified the ritual by writing couplets on the peachwood to give expression to their best wishes.

In the beginning putting Spring Festival Couplets on the doors was a privilege for aristocratic families by which to sing praise of their ancestors' meritorious deeds and show off their wealth. Later they became popular among commoners. By the Song Dynasty the couplets had become part of local life.

It is no easy job to compose a good couplet because it requires symmetry in every field: sentence for sentence, noun for noun, verb for verb, and statistics for statistics. And it should sound poetic and reflect the actual situation of a family.

Today, Spring Festival couplets have acquired a new meaning — they have become a folk form to eulogize social development and people's better life.

"Fu" and "Fu" Upside Down
("福"与"福"字倒贴 *"Fu" yu "Fu" Zi Daotie*)

The Chinese character "*fu*" means good fortune and happiness, and during Spring Festival virtually every family would paste it upside down on their doors in the hope that the word could bring blessings to their families. As to why "*fu*" should be placed upside down there are three interpretations.

The first interpretation has the practice of pasting "*fu*" during Spring Festival originate in Jiang Ziya of the Zhou Dynasty (11th Century-256 B.C.). When Jiang Ziya was made a god, his wife demanded to be made a goddess. "After I married you I was always in poverty in my life,"Lord Jiang said. "Seems you are destined to be poor. So let me appoint you as the Goddess of Poverty." No knowing what being the Goddess of Poverty held in store for her, his wife was nevertheless happy about becoming a goddess. Cheerfully, she asked, "Now that I'm the Goddess of Poverty, where shall be my domain?" Jiang replied, "You are off limits wherever there is good fortune." When the residents got word of Jiang's instruction, they wrote the character "*fu*" on paper and pasted it on the doors and windows of their houses to keep the Goddess of Poverty away. Thus pasting "*fu*" during the Spring Festival became a Chinese tradition.

The second interpretation ascribes the practice to Zhu Yuanzhang, the founding emperor of the Ming Dynasty. One year, on the 15th of the first lunar month, Zhu went incognito on a fact-finding inspection tour. When he arrived at a town he saw people huddle together and watch a painting that poked fun at women of west Anhui refusing to have their feet bound by featuring a bare-footed woman holding a large watermelon in her arms. The emperor, however, misconstrued the meaning of the painting, thinking that people were laughing at his wife, Empress Ma, who came exactly from west Anhui. Returning to his palace he sent some soldiers to look into the matter. He particularly wanted to know who were those people who watched and commented on the painting, and who was the painter. He also asked the soldiers to paste "*fu*" on the doors of those who did not join in the crowd. Two days later, another team of soldiers arrived in town to arrest people from the houses whose doors were not marked with "*fu*" on charges of scoffing at the queen. Since then the Chinese have been pasting "*fu*" on the doors of their houses to shun trouble.

The third interpretation attributes the practice to Fu Jin, the princes of Gong of the Qing Dynasty. Once, on the lunar New Year's Eve, the butler of the mansion of the Prince of Gong wanted to curry favour with his master. He followed past practice and had several large "*fu*" written and pasted on the front gates of the warehouse and the mansion. One of the men sent to do the pasting was illiterate and put the character upside down on the front gate of the mansion. Enraged, the prince wanted to punish the perpetrator by whipping him. The butler, who had the gift of the gab, hastened to go down on his knees and pleaded: "Your humble servant often heard people say that Your Excellency is a man of longevity and great fortune. Indeed, great fortune did arrive today; it is a good sign." The prince was convinced. "This is why the passers-by were saying that great fortune had arrived in the mansion of the Princess of Gong," he thought. "Once an auspicious saying is repeated for a thousand times, my wealth could increase by 10,000 taels of gold and silver." He then awarded the butler and the servant who pasted the paper upside down fifty taels of silver. Since then the practice of pasting "*fu*" upside down during Spring Festival has become a tradition followed by both imperial aristocrats and commoners.

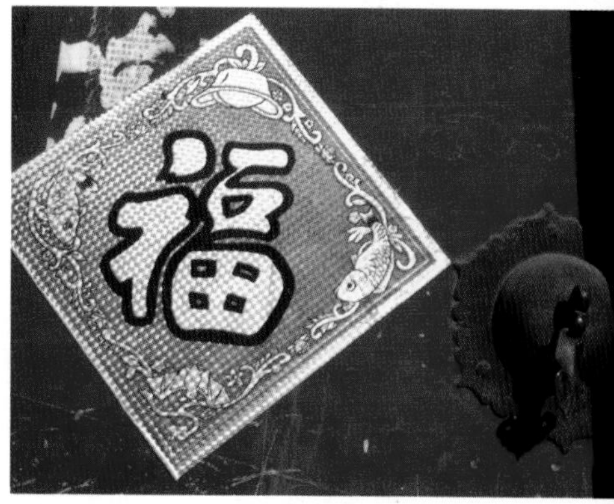

Protective Chicken Talisman (贴鸡符 *Tie Jifu*)

In old days the Chinese had the habit of pasting or painting chicken talismans on the doors of their dwellings on the lunar New Year's Day. This habit is still very much alive today in rural areas in Shaanxi Province in northwest China.

An ancient Chinese belief regards the chicken as the variant or emblem of the sun. Thus to paste a talisman in the image of a chicken is like having the sun on the door. The habit gives indirect expression to people's longing for the advent of spring. Chinese ancients also believed that the chicken talisman can help ward off the dismal impact of demons.

From this connection between the chicken and the sun, the ancients gave wings to imagination and invented the image of the Heavenly Chicken that is always the first to announce the sunrise on a daily basis. The lunar New Year's Day is known as "yuandan", or the "first sunrise of the year", and it goes without saying that only the Heavenly Chicken is capable of knowing when the sun rises for the first time of the year and reporting the news to the mundane world. Pasting the chicken talisman on the door is actually a symbolism of the chicken and sun worship.

The chicken talisman is pasted up on the lunar New Year's Day because it is also the Day of the Chicken. As the classic *The Book of Divination* puts it, "The first day is the day of the chicken, the second day is devoted to the dog, the third day to the pig, the fourth day to the goat, the fifth day to the cattle, the sixth day to the horse and the seventh day to man." This matchup between animals and time was derived from people's understanding of space. Seven is the number of the universe to indicate the east, south, west, north, middle, upper and lower directions. East takes the number one position because it is the direction in which the sun rises and because it is also in accord with the first day of the week. Wood is the symbol for east, where the divine *Hibiscus rosa-sinensis* and peach trees grow. While the sun rises over the top of the *Hibiscus rosa-sinensis* tree, the chicken perches in the peach tree. This is why east is matched up with the chicken and becomes the symbol of the day of the first sunrise of the year. In that sense, the chicken talisman entails our remote ancestors' imagination of the universe and their way of keeping time.

Tianlu and *Pixie*

(天禄与辟邪 *Tianlu yu Pixie*)

Tianlu (heavenly emolument) and *Pixie* (evil dispeller) are two Chinese mythological animals that herald in good fortune and keep evil at bay. Both look like a lion except for their wings—the one with only one horn on his head is *Tianlu* and the one with two horns is *Pixie*. During the Han Dynasty (206 B.C. -220 A.D.), the images of both animals were for ornamentation purposes. Sculptures of them were placed in front of tombs to suggest the dignity and power and authority the deceased enjoyed in their lifetime. As symbols of bravery and immunity to evil, the two animals are meant for those aspiring to ascend to heaven to ride on. Images of *Tianlu* and *Pixie* were inscribed, embroidered or carved on fabrics, army banners, bands and hooks, or the handles of seals and bells in ancient times.

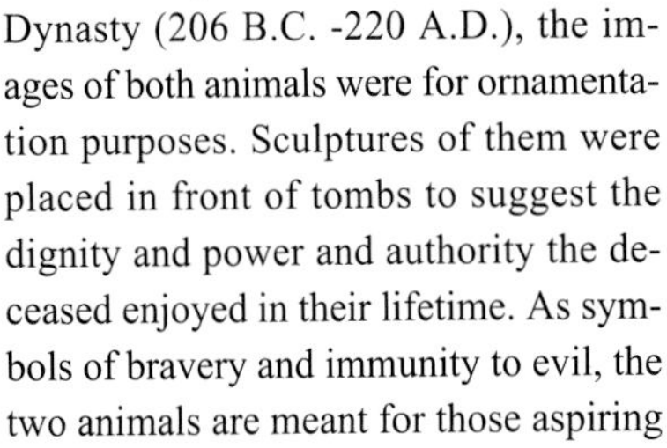

Tianlu and *Pixie* are cast in a pair of gigantic sculptures that stand along with stone pillars on the holy way that leads to

a tomb in the eastern suburbs of Nanjing. Buried in the tomb are the remains of Xiao Hong, the younger brother of Emperor Wudi of the Liang dynasty. The sculpture of *Pixie*, 3.8 metres tall, 3.8 metres long and 1.55 metres wide, has a plump body and thick and short neck, its chest puffing and its belly protruding, and walking in giant strides with its tongue hanging out of its wide open mouth. This is by far the best-preserved large stone sculpture of *Pixie*.

Xiezhi — a Mythological Animal

(獬豸 *Xiezhi*)

The Holy Way of the Ming Tombs of Beijing is franked with 12 stone men and 24 stone animals. Among them are four statues of *Xiezhi*, an animal in Chinese mythology credited with the ability to distinguish between right and wrong, and between virtue and evil.

Legend has it that *Xiezhi* is a divine goat which, upon seeing a quarrel or fight, would reach out its horn to touch the side which is wrong. It is so upright that it never compromises its principle even if the wrong side is an emperor. According to the "Records of Court Attire" in the *Book of Late Han*, "The Hat of Law is made for those enforcing the state law...It

is also known as Xiezhi Hat to symbolize justice." The Qing rule of court attire stipulated that the robes worn by royal scribes, surveillance commissioners and law superintendents should be embroidered with the pattern of *xiezhi* as an emblem of their duties. In his autobiography, Pu Yi, the last Qing emperor, also mentioned *xiezhi* by saying that the emperor had a statue of the mythological goat in front of his desk to remind himself that he should be fair and strict in handling state and political affairs.

Gourd

(葫芦 *Hulu*)

Gourd is the fruit of a kind of liana. When fresh and tender, it could be eaten as vegetable; when dried, it makes an ideal container of water or wine. Northern Chinese farmers have the habit of cutting a gourd in two to be used wine containers or ladles. Our ancestors fashioned the gourd into a wind instrument known as *sheng*, and the wayfarers loved to carry drugs in a gourd. This gave rise to the old platitude: "I don't know what he has got in his gourd." meaning somebody is wondering what's up somebody else's sleeves.

Because the gourd liana is prolific in fruits and seeds, families have regarded it as a symbol of prosperity since ancient times. Life-like green-glazed ceramic gourds were unearthed along with such burial objects as earthen kettles, ovens and

bronze mirrors from a Han tomb dating back to 3,000 years ago. This is a rare case in which gourds were used as burial objects.

In some areas, men and women in love are still observing the Mid-Autumn Festival tradition to steal gourds from the fields with the desire to have as many children as possible after they get married.

Entertainment 娱乐

Peking Opera

(京剧 *Jingju*)

As the most prestigious of all the operas in China, Peking Opera is venerated as the "Opera of China". The predecessor of it was the *huidiao* opera of Anhui some 200 years ago. In 1790, an imperial edict was issued to summon the four major *huidiao* opera troupes-Sanqing, Sixi, Chuntai and Hechun - to go to Beijing to perform and celebrate the 80th birthday of Emperor Qianlong of the Qing. The lyrics of the *huidiao* opera were so easy to understand that the opera soon captivated the audience of the capital city. In the 50 years that ensued, the *huidiao* opera incorporated the strengths of the *jingqiang* opera of Beijing, the *kunqiang* opera of Jiangsu's Kunshan which late spread to Beijing, the *qinqiang* opera of Shaanxi, and other local operas, and gradually evolved into what is today's Peking Opera.

The stage settings of Peking Opera are succinct and symbolic. Character roles are finely differentiated. Female roles are called *dan*, male roles are *sheng*; clowns are *chou*, and there are also role characters using different patterns of makeup which are known as *jing*. Among the *sheng* roles are old, young and military characters. Female roles are defined as *qingyi*, *huadan*, *laodan*, *daomadan*, *wudan*. Jing roles feature such patterns of makeup as *tongchui*, jiazi and *wu*. Clowns are either scholarly or militant. These four role models form the basis for the emergence of different schools of Peking Opera. Mei Lanfang, Cheng Yanqiu, Xun Huisheng and Shang Xiaoyun were the celebrated "Four Major Dan Roles" in Peking Opera.

Facial Makeups in Operas (脸谱 *Lianpu*)

A plastic art peculiar to the Chinese stage, the facial makeups are various designs of lines and coloured patches painted on the faces of certain operatic characters. They follow traditionally fixed patterns for specific types to highlight the disposition and quality in the personages so that the audience may immediately know whether they are heroes or villains, whether they are kind or treacherous and wicked. The following describes briefly the major categories of facial makeups:

The red face shows bravery, uprightness and loyalty. A typical "red face" is Guan Yu, general of the period of the Three Kingdoms (220-280), famed for his faithfulness to his Emperor, Liu Bei.

The reddish purple face likewise shows a just and noble

character, for instance, Lian Po in the well-known play Jiang Xiang He (*The General Reconciled with the Chief Minister*), in which General Lian was proud and impetuous and quarrelled with the chief minister to whom he was ultimately reconciled.

The black face indicates either a rough and bold character or an impartial and selfless personality. Typical of the former are General Zhang Fei (of the *Romance of the Three Kingdoms*) and Li Kui (of *Water Margin*), and of the latter is Bao Gong (*alias* Bao Zheng), the semi-legendary fearless and impartial judge of the Song Dynasty.

A green face depicts surly stubborness, impetuosity and a total lack of self-restraint.

Commonly seen on the stage is the white face for the powerful vilain. It highlights all that is bad in human nature: cunning, craftiness, treachery. Typical characters are Cao Cao*, powerful and cruel prime minister in the time of the Three Kingdoms, and Qin Hui, treacherous Song Dynasty prime minister who put the national hero Yue Fei to death.

All the above facial makeups belong to a category of characters collectively called *jing* — all males with pronounced personal traits.

For the clowns of traditional drama, there is a special makeup called *xiaohualian* (the petty painted face), i.e., a small patch of chalk on and around the nose to show a mean and secretive character, such as Jiang Gan of the *Three Kingdoms* who fawned upon Cao Cao. It is also occasionally painted on a young page or an ordinary workingman, often to enhance his wit, humour or jesting and to enliven up the performance.

Another type of players, called "acrobatic clowns" (*wuchou*), are also touched up with a tiny patch of white on the tip of the nose to show an astute mind, a keen and quick wit. Several of the stage heroes from the novel *Water Margin* are made up in this way.

The facial makeups date a long time back to the Song (960-1279) and Yuan (1206-1368) dynasties at least. Simple patterns of painted faces are found in tomb murals of that age. During the Ming Dynasty (1368-1644), improvements were made in the skills of drawing and in preparing the paints, leading to the whole set

of colourful facial patterns that we see in today's *Jingju* (Peking Opera).

As to the origin of the facial makeup, it is still largely a matter for conjecture. And there are different theories:

1) It is believed that primitive hunters painted their faces to frighten off the wild beasts, and highwaymen in the old days did the same to hide their identity and also to overawe the wayfarers they were to rob. Either practice may have led to the emergence of dramatic facial makeups.

2) It is thought that the facial makeup owes its origin to the mask. Prince Lanling of the Northern Qi Dynasty (479-507) was a good fighter but, because of his handsome features, aroused no fear in his enemy. So he had a ferocious-looking mask made and began to wear it into battles. Sure enough, he proved much more formidable and therefore ever-victorious. His followers composed a song to sing of his successes, which developed into a masked dance, showing him storming into the enemy formation. Subsequently, the mask became painted patterns for stage characters.

3) It is held that facial makeups were used for traditional operas simply because they were often presented on open-air stages to large gatherings of noisy crowds, and the characters were made to wear painted facial patterns in order to bring the drama home to the audience.

* Historically Cao Cao was a statesman of great talent and bold vision, yet through the bias of early writers, has been presented on the stage as a wicked man behind the facade of a white face.

Masks

（面具 *Mianju*）

Masks in Chinese culture are part and parcel of the world culture of masks. Masks first appeared in China during the Shang and Zhou some 3,500 years ago as a major element in Chinese shamanism. The worshipping of the god which drives away pestilence, the exorcising dances and operas, and many of the Shamanist rituals, cannot do without masks. Even today, masks are still being worn during religious rituals, weddings and funerals among nearly 40 ethnic peoples who inhabit some 20 provinces and autonomous regions. Masks are, indeed, vehicles of a wealth of historical and cultural information.

Chinese masks are generally made of wood, and worn either on one's face or head. Through colourfully painted images of people, ghosts, demons and celestial animals, they are purported to convey certain meanings. The Chinese masks fall into the following categories:

Exorcising Dancers' Masks. These masks, used at religious sacrificial ceremonies among certain minority peoples, are designed to dispel ghosts and pestilence and ask gods for blessings.

Masks for Festive Occasions. Such masks are worn by people when they join exorcising dancers during festivals or memorial services. The purpose of such masks is to pray for long life and rich harvests and keep evil spirits at bay. In many places such gatherings have become a marry-making activity.

Masks for New Born Babies. These masks are used when members of society attend ceremonies marking the birth of a baby.

Masks for Keeping Houses Safe. These masks are developed on the basis of those worn by exorcising dancers and hung on important positions of a house to scare away evil spirits.

Masks for Theatrical Performances. In the theatre of many ethnic minorities, masks are an important means to portray the images and personality of the characters. Because of this they are of high cultural and artistic value.

Exorcisers' Masks

(傩面具 *Nuomianju*)

The exorcisers' masks are a unique handicraft in Guizhou Province. Fashioned out of wood and tree roots, they range in imagery from the grotesque to the good and genuine. Such masks can be as small as several centimetres and as large as two

metres. The exorcising culture of the Miao villages in Guizhou is regarded as a gem in folk Chinese culture.

The exorcising culture first rise in central China. After it had found its way into Guizhou it was merged with the local shamanism and gave rise to a male exorciser and a female exorciser. The male was the legendary Fu Xi, a Chinese ruler who taught people how to fish, hunt and raise livestock: and the female was Nu Wa, the goddess who created human beings and patched up the sky. As the ancients believed that all the diseases and pains were caused by the onslaught of demons on the human body, so during exorcising rituals they preferred to wear masks that looked as grotesque as possible so as to dispel the ghosts and ward off the evil. The exorcising dance was invented on the basis of shamanist dance for the same purpose. With the passing of time, such dances have taken on an entertaining function. And the

exorcising opera is no longer limited to Buddhist or Taoist temples; it could be performed wherever there is an audience. It has become a traditional culture beloved by the people of different ethnic backgrounds in Guizhou.

Long White Silk Sleeves
(水袖 *Shuixiu*)

Long white sleeves are used in performances of classical Chinese operas and dances. They are 0.5 metre long but the longest of them can reach more than one metre. When being swung on stage, the long white silk sleeves look like ripples in a river. It goes without saying that our ancients were wearing loose-fitting sleeves which had no pieces of white silk attached. The long white silk sleeves on stage are a means of exaggeration to enhance the aesthetic effects on stage. The movement of

swinging such sleeves helps making up for the shortage of language, giving expression to the identity, personality and feelings of the character portrayed, and enhancing the appeals of the dancing movements. Tossing the sleeves outward means that the character is in anger; shaking them incessantly means that the character is shivering with fear; failing them skyward indicates that certain disaster or injustice has just befallen on the character; waving the sleeves to tidy up one's costume means that the character is about to see an elderly whom he or she holds in high esteem.

The use of the long white silk sleeves changes according to the changes in the character's inner world. Playing such sleeves is one of the basic skills of traditional Chinese opera.

The Change of Faces
(变脸 *Bianlian*)

The change of faces is a stunt in traditional Chinese theatre that is designed to capture the dramatic changes of mood of a character on stage. When a character's heart is going from panic to rage, he changes his face in a split second; the stunt, though somewhat exaggerating, never fails to surprise the audience and enhance the appeal of the show. The change of faces is most often used in

Chuanju Opera. In the opera *Severing the Bridge*, for instance, when the female protagonist Xiao Qing catches sight of the weak-hearted and unfaithful Xu Xian, she burst into a rage, and in her sudden transition of mode from anger to hatred, her fair face experiences a rapid succession of changes from white to red to green and black. The performer is so agile in her movement that each change is made by turning her body. This skill is acquired through special training. In some cases multiple layers of masks are used, to be torn away with each change of facial expression.

Traditional Chinese Musical Instruments (中国乐器 *Zhongguo Yueqi*)

Historical records indicate that there used to be 1,000 or so musical instruments in use in ancient times. Today, some 500 of them are extant. The earliest of them date back to more than 8,000 years ago.

Traditional Chinese musical instruments were closely associated with the rise of music in China. They are symbols of Chinese culture. In old times, they were also indicators of the level of productivity.

Our ancients divided Chinese musical instruments into eight categories or "eight sounds": metal, stone, string, bamboo, gourd, clay, leather, and wood.

Metal: referring to instruments fashioned out of metals, such as gongs, and bronze drums.

Stone: stone instruments such as chimes and carillons.

String: instruments having strings played with the fingers or with a plectrum or a bow, such as Chinese violin, 25-stringed horizontal harp and zither-like instruments with many strings.

Bamboo: instruments made from bamboo stalk, including vertical bamboo flutes and 8-holed bamboo flutes.

Gourd: wind instruments using a gourd as the resonator, such as *sheng* and *yu*.

Clay: earthen instruments, including *xun*, an egg-shaped wind instrument with one to six holes in it, and *fou*, a clay percussion instrument.

Leather: instruments using animal skins as vibration membranes, such as drums and waist drums.

Wood: instruments made mainly from wood. Common ones include wooden fish (hollow wooden block used to beat rhythm) and xylophone.

Xun

(埙 *Xun*)

The earthen *xun* is one of the oldest wind musical instruments in China. Archaeological studies indicate that some 8,000 years ago, the earthen *xun* was a hunting weapon. By the Shang (17th-11th century B.C.) under the rule of King Yin, the *xun* was made exquisitely from stone, bone or ivory. By the Zhou (11th entury-256 B.C.), *xun* became a special wind instrument in the Chinese concert.

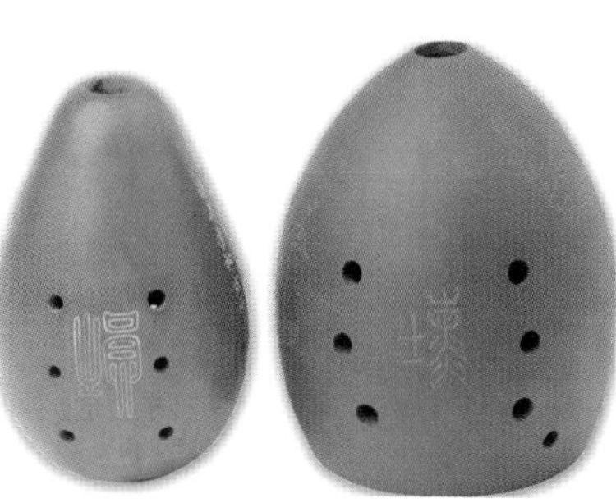

Zheng

(筝 Zheng)

Zheng is a stringed instrument with a history of more than 2,000 years. Legend has it that it was in vogue during the Qin (221-206 B.C.) in present-day Shaanxi, and thatís why it is also called *qin zheng*.

According to ancient books, the *zheng* originally had only five strings and was made from bamboo. During the Qin the number of strings increased to 10, and wood was used instead of bamboo. After the Tang (618-907), it became a 13-stringed instrument.

Today, with 13, 14 or 16 strings stretched on a large oblong wooden resonator, the *zheng* is able to emit graceful tones. Today it is still very much in use in China for solos or ensembles.

Guqin

(古琴 Guqin)

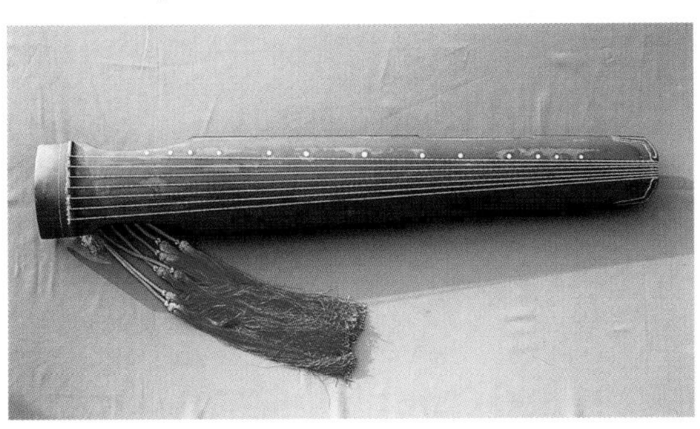

Guqin, a seven-stringed plucked instrument (similar in some ways to the zither), was a common musical instrument during the Zhou, when it was often played along with the se, another stringed plucked instrument.

Guqin features a narrow and long body made of wood, and there are 13 round marks on its surface to indicate the positions of overtones or where the fingers should be put. Generally speaking, the guqin's high pitches are clear and pleasant to the ear, its middle pitches loud and distinct, its low pitches subtle and mellow, and its overtones bright and charming.

With a strong expressiveness derived from a highly variant timbre and a good variety of techniques, the *guqin* is often played in solos and ensembles or to provide accompaniment for singing. Today, 200 or so kinds of ancient *guqin* scales are extant.

Suona

(唢呐 Suona)

Popularly know as horn, the *suona* is another ancient wind instrument most widely used in folk performing art. It first became fashionable in central China around the 16th century. As a folk wind and percussion concert or opera band, the *suona* is often used as the leading instrument in a concert. Loud in a distinct boldness, it is an ideal instrument for the playing of vivacious and magnificent numbers, and capable of the cadenza of a number and imitating the chirping of birds and insects. The *suona* is an indispensable instrument to folk celebrations and festivals.

Sheng

(笙 Sheng)

The *sheng* is another ancient Chinese musical instrument that emits sound by the vibration of reed. It became very fashionable during the Zhou, as it played accompaniment for court singers and dancers. Then it found its way among commoners, and became a common instrument in singing concerts, temple fair celebrations and other events.

The *sheng* consists of three parts: reed, pipes and what is known as "douzi", and it can be used for accompaniment, solo performance and ensembles. Highly expressive and convenient for changing the tones, with clear and distinct high pitched and graceful middle and low pitches, the *sheng* is an indispensable instrument in a folk concerto of wind and percussion instruments.

Xiao and *Di*

(箫和笛 *Xiao He Di*)

Both *xiao*, the vertical bamboo flute, and *di*, the horizontal bamboo flute, are traditional wind instruments in China.

The *xiao* enjoys an older history than the *di* because it has been around for 3,000 years, whereas the *di* found its way into China during the 2nd century B.C. from central Asia. In its early days, the *xiao* was something of a panpipe consisting of 16 bamboo pipes. Today, the *xiao* appear mostly in the form of a single flute, and, easy to be made, it is rather popular among the Chinese. The two earliest panpipes found in the tomb of Marquis of Zeng at Suixian County in Hubei Province in 1978, dating back to the Warring States Period (475-221 B.C.) consist of 13 fine bamboo pipes each, arrayed in progressively reducing lengths. The *xiao*'s soft and graceful tones are ideal for solo and ensemble playing to express profound feelings in long-drawn, soft and sentimental melody.

Pipa

(琵琶 *Pipa*)

The *pipa*, known in ancient times as "*pipa* with a curving neck", is a major plucked instrument introduced from Mesopotamia in west Asia to China towards the end of the Eastern Han (25-220), and from Xinjiang and Gansu to the hinterland during the 4th century. After the Sui and Tang (581-907), the *pipa* had become a major instrument. The preludes to virtually all the major pieces of music of the Tang (618-907) were played with the *pipa*. A versatile instrument for solo, ensembles (with two or more instruments) and accompaniment, the *pipa* is known for its high expressiveness and its capacity for both the impassioned and heroic and the graceful and subtle.

Chinese Chess

(象棋 *Xiangqi*)

The Chinese chess is a traditional game very popular among the Chinese. It is played wherever there are people — factories, schools, villages, streets, you name it. Games of the Chinese chess are often played in parks and by roadsides. A crowd appears whenever such a game is going on.

The Chinese chess is composed of chesses and the chessboard. The chess board features nine vertical lines and ten horizontal lines to form 90 crosses to govern the movement of the chesses. The middle line is known as "Chu River and Han Boundary". The section of the chessboard with oblique lines is known as "Nine Palaces", which is the domain of the command and "his" guards.

The chesses are mostly made of wood, and they are round in shape. There are 32 chesses, divided into black and red groups of 16 members each. Every group of chesses is composed of one command, two guards, two prime ministers, two canons, two horses, two chariots and five soldiers.

During the game each side manoeuvres his or her chesses to eliminate the chesses of the other side so as to seize a position in the opposite field. If one chess is in a vulnerable position, it should be withdrawn as soon as possible; if withdrawal is impossible, other chesses may be dispatched to its rescue.

The ultimate ail of a chess game is to hold the command of the opponent. The side which succeeded in a checkmate is the winner.

Mah-jong

(麻将 *Majiang*)

Mah-jong is a competitive game with a history in China. As it is played with tiles, similar in physical description to those used in dominoes but engraved with Chinese symbols and characters, mah-jong is also jokingly called a game to "move" or "lay" bricks. It is also known as a "game of encirclement". Legend has it that mah-jong was invented by an ancient Chinese strategist who used tiles to mock battle formations. A full set of mah-jong contains 136 tiles, including 36 sticks (or bamboos, numbered 1 to 9, 4 of each number), 36 dots (or circles, numbered 1 to 9, 4 of each number), 36 cracks (or characters, numbered 1 to 9, 4 of each number), 12 honours (4 red, 4 green, 4 white dragons), and 16 winds (4 east, 4 south, 4 west, 4 north winds). These do not include eight flowers, which are added in the midst of a mah-jong game.

Among the tiles, a stick represents the spear, a dot the shield, and a crack a troop. The east, west, south and north winds represent the guardian generals of the four doors. The character "zhong" denotes the commander, and the "fa" represents the officer that delivers the commander's orders. Blank tiles represent reserved forces.

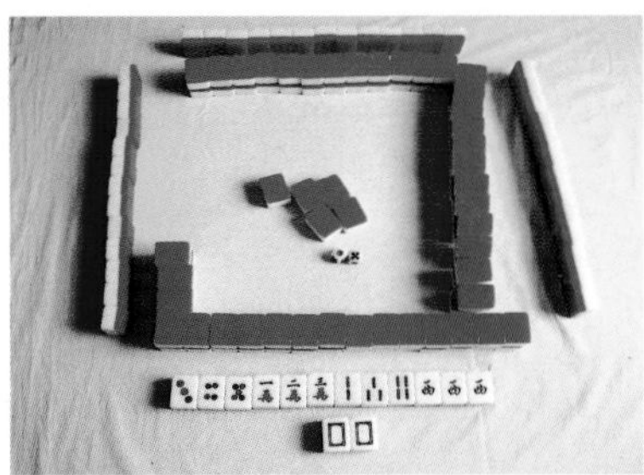

The game is usually played by four individuals each holding 13 tiles. The object of the play is to obtain sets of tiles, and the winner is the first player to hold four sets and a pair of like tiles. In old days, the mahjong was played for gambling; today it is still a fad around the country.

The game was introduced to the West and Japan during the 1920s, where it remains popular to this day.

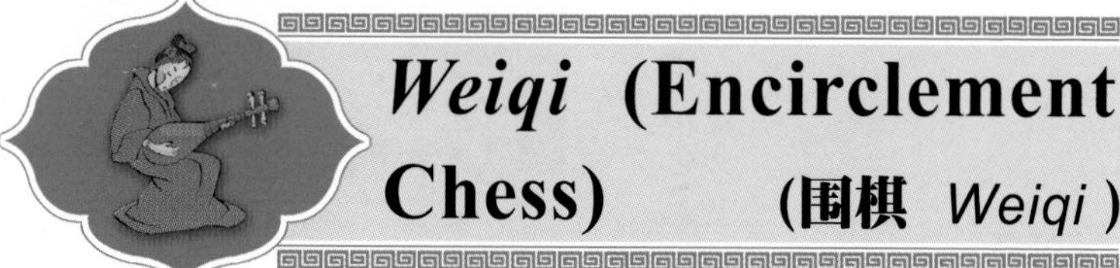

Weiqi (Encirclement Chess) (围棋 *Weiqi*)

Go is a kind of chess that originated in China. Born of war, it was probably the creation of a strategist of antiquity. In Chinese it is known as "weiqi" ("encirclement chess"), as players try to conquer territory on a square wooden board by completely enclosing vacant points with boundaries made of their own stones. Go has a history of more than 4,000 years in China, where it became fashionable as early as the Spring and Autumn Period (770-476B.C.). It found its way into Japan during the Sui and Tang dynasties (581-907A.D.). With the steady expansion of international cultural exchanges, go has spread to Europe and North America during the last few decades and is becoming a global game. The chessboard of go in its early days was checkered by 11, 15 or 17 vertical lines until it finally settled at 19 vertical lines and 19 horizontal lines to form 361 intersections. It is played between two persons, one with 181 black go-shi (flat, round pieces called stones) and the other 180 white ones. The person holding black stones makes the first move if it is a game between two opponents of equal calibre, and the person holding white stones makes the first move according to special handicap rules if the game takes place between two opponents of unequal skills. A player's final score is his number of walled-in points less the number of his stones lost by capture, and the player with more points is declared the winner. The 19-line chessboard can be seen in traditional Chinese paintings dating back to the Tang Dynasty (618-907A.D.).

THINGS CHINESE 中国风物

Medicine 医药

Traditional Chinese Medicine
(中医 *Zhongyi*)

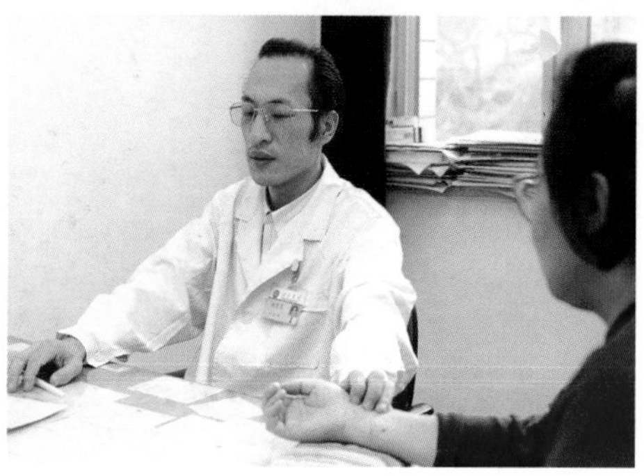

A medical science for the treatment and prevention of diseases by applying unique Chinese medical theories and prescription drugs that had been formulated as early as the Spring and Autumn and Warring States periods (770-221 B.C.). The Yellow Emperor's Internal Classic, the earliest Chinese medical book, was compiled during this period, which laid down the theoretical basis for traditional Chinese medicine.

The Chinese medical science regards the human body as an organism with main and collateral channels at the core. It also regards the human being and other things in nature as combinations of the two opposites, yin and *yang*. The loss of balance between *yin* and *yang* gives rise to diseases, and to treat a disease is to readjust *yin* and *yang* and enhance resistance to it by dispelling the pathogenic influences. Diagnosis is done by observation, auscultation and smelling, questioning, and pulse feeling and palpation. Symptoms which tell whether an internal organ is affected by exogenous harmful factors and whether a disease is caused by cold or febrile factors or by the deficiency of vital energy to ward off diseases, as well as the dialectical relationship between *yin* and *yang* and the dialectics of the viscera, are used as the theoretical basis for clinical diagnosis.

Traditional Chinese painting, Peking Opera, and traditional Chinese medicine are known throughout the world as the three national treasures of China.

Traditional Chinese Pharmaceuticals (中药 *Zhongyao*)

Traditional Chinese pharmaceuticals enjoy a venerated history, but the term itself was not coined until Western pharmaceuticals found their way into China.

Modern Western pharmacology began to spread into China during the Ming-Qing interregnum, and was coexisting with traditional Chinese pharmacology in some major Chinese cities by the 1920s. The terms "traditional Chinese medicine" and "traditional Chinese pharmacology" are coined to distinguish traditional Chinese medical science from its Western counterpart.

Traditional Chinese pharmaceuticals are made from medicinal herbs and animals, and named after the materials' names, medical effects, originality in growth, shapes, forms, and even the legends about them. Traditional Chinese pharmacology is a major contribution China makes to humankind.

Channels and Collaterals

(经络 *Jingluo*)

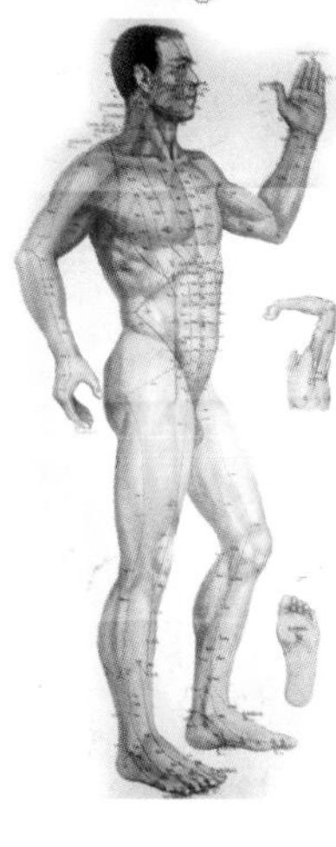

Chinese medical scientists discovered the presence of channels and collaterals in the human body as early as 2,000 years ago. They believed that a complex network covers the entire human body. Just in the same way as rivers irrigate farmlands, this network supplies vital energy and blood to every part of the human body. Running vertically in the human body are 12 channels that are connected with numerous arteries and veins. These trunk, branch and fine channels combine to form the human body's system of channels and collaterals.

If the traffic in a certain channel or collateral is jammed, it can cause pain or ailment. If this ailing channel or collateral is treated with acupuncture or moxibustion, then the role of the channel or collateral in facilitating the vital energy can be brought into play, and the ailment cured.

The theory on channels and collaterals plays a vital part in making traditional Chinese medicine work in various fields - in acupuncture and moxibustion, *qigong*, massage, and the diagnoses, treatment, and medication of both internal and surgical medicine.

Acupuncture and Moxibustion

(针灸 *Zhenjiu*)

Acupuncture and moxibustion were invented in China as means of medical treatment for more than 2,000 years. Acupuncture involves the insertion of needle tips into the skin at specific points for the purpose of treating disorders by stimulating nerve impulses. Moxibustion, or moxa treatment, is performed by burning small

cones of dried wormwood plant (Artemisia moxa) on certain points of the body, generally the same points as those used in acupuncture. Both acupuncture and moxibustion are designed to achieve the purpose of medical treatment by making sensible choice of points on the human body according to the traditional Chinese medical theory on channels and collaterals. The two methods are often used together, and that is why they are always mentioned in the same breath. They are definitely a precious medical heritage of China.

Developed on the basis of the clinical practice of killing pain by acupuncture, the technique of acupuncture anaesthesia is now used on more than 100 surgeries.

Cupping

(拔火罐 *Bahuoguan*)

Also known popularly as "cup pulling" and "suction cups", cupping is a unique old means of medical treatment that has been around for a long time in China. In the very beginning, the cups were bullhorns smoothed and perforated with tiny holes to be used to draw pus from an ailing part of the human body. Later bullhorns were

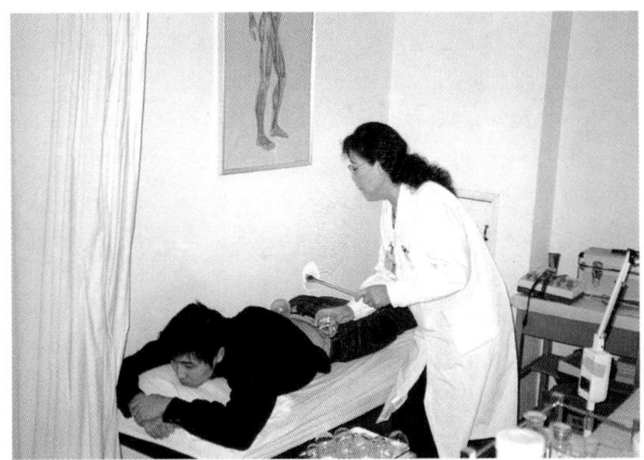

gradually replaced by cups made of bamboo, pottery and glass, and the use of the "cupping" technique was gradually developed from the treatment of ulcers to rheumatic diseases, psoatic strain, headache, dizziness, and colds. Cups are vacuumed so that they are attached tightly to the human body to cause it to be engorged to achieve the medical purpose. Simple and easy, and often with good results, the cupping technique has been handed down from generation to generation, and remains very much in use today.

Medicinal Pillow

(药枕 *Yaozhen*)

Medicinal pillows were long in use in traditional Chinese medicine. Modern medical science has proved that the efficacious ingredients of the medicinal herbs stuffed into such pillows can volatilise, penetrate the acupuncture points and be absorbed by skin or mucous membrane to cure a disease.

Natural herbal or animal medicines are mixed according to a formula designed for the treatment of a certain disease before they are stuffed into a medicinal pillow. A pillow filled with the mixture of buckwheat husk and silkworm increment has a good cooling effect; a pea-filled pillow helps cure sunstroke and dizziness; and a pillow stuffed with white chrysanthemum, pea skin, buckwheat husk, mulberry leaves and cassia seeds is used for the treatment of eye diseases.

The medicinal pillow comes handy as a medical aid. When one falls asleep with his head on such a pillow, his nose, tongue, skin and acupuncture points can absorb the essence of what is stuffed in it to prevent or cure disease or protect his health.

Ginseng

(人参 *Renshen*)

Ginseng, reputedly the "king of a hundred herbs", has been regarded as the ideal tonic since ancient times. A ginseng looks very much like the human body as it is complete with a head and limbs.

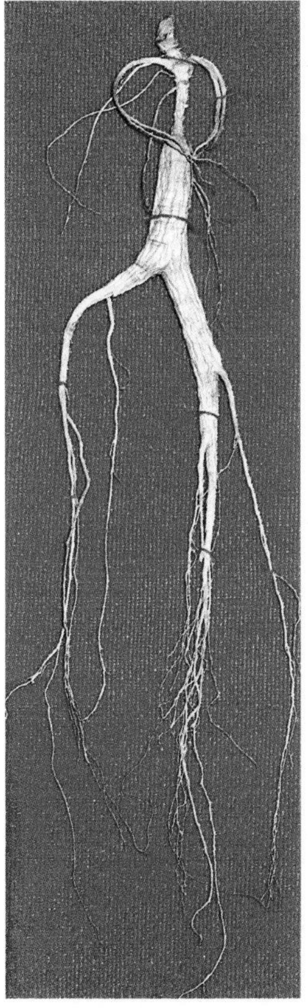

Ginseng today is either collected from the wilderness or cultivated.

The Changbai Mountains in northeast China produces the best wild ginseng in this country. It grows rather slowly, and it generally takes several decades or more than a century for it to grow up. The Changbai mountains in Fusong County, Jilin Province, made the headline in 1981 when a rare mountain ginseng, 287.5 gram in weight and 54 cm in length, was dug up from a local forest — believed to have been there for more than a century, it is regarded as a most precious treasure.

Wild ginseng is difficult to come by today, and it is too expensive to meet the market demand. That is why the Chinese were already cultivating ginseng some 300 years ago.

The medicinal value of ginseng was not lost on our ancestors. *Sheng Nong's Herbal Classic,* the earliest medicinal book in China, has this to say: Ginseng is efficacious for strengthening the heart, stabilizing the nerve system and the mind, stopping shock, improve the level of intelligence, and extend the life span. In his *Compendium of Materia Medica,* the celebrated Ming-dynasty herbalist Li Shizhen pointed out that ginseng is highly effective in replenishing the human body's vitality, making the old look young, and saving life from the brink of death. All in all, ginseng is an ideal tonic.

Caterpillar Fungus (Cordyceps Sinesis) (冬虫夏草 *Dongchong Xiacao*)

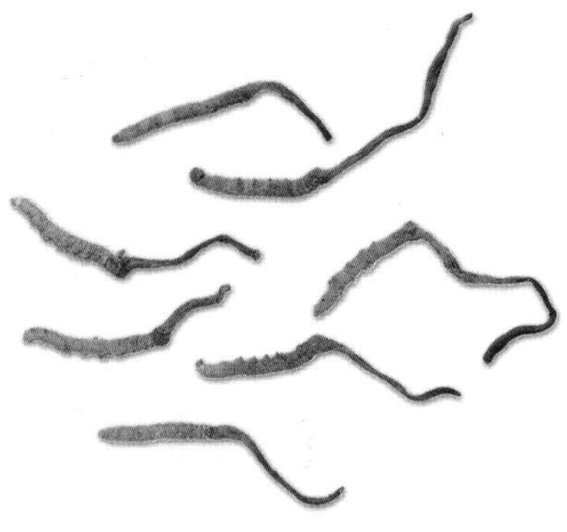

A native product of Qinghai Plateau, the caterpillar fungus is known as "Winter Insect and Summer Grass". As the name suggests, it is an insect hibernating in frozen soil in winter, and when summer begins to set in in late May and people begin to gather it, a grass has grown out of its head.

The caterpillar fungus is actually a kind of *Claviceps purpurea*. The "winter insect" is actually the larva of a moth, and the "summer grass" is a parasitic fungus living in the head of the insect. In China there are 20 or so varieties of fungi living on or in the body of an insect, and caterpillar fungus is one of them.

The caterpillar fungus grows in the meadows on the shady or semi-shady side of a mountain at an altitude of 3,500-5,000 metres. In winter, the larva is frozen solid in the soil and becomes very fragile, and it wakes up and begins to crawl about when the temperature rises. The larva has developed an unusual resistance against hunger: it can survive for 119 days without eating in a congenial atmosphere.

The caterpillar fungus is a precious traditional Chinese medicine of a sweet and warm nature. It is used for the treatment of cough and asthma, anaemia, asthenia and the deterioration of the organs.

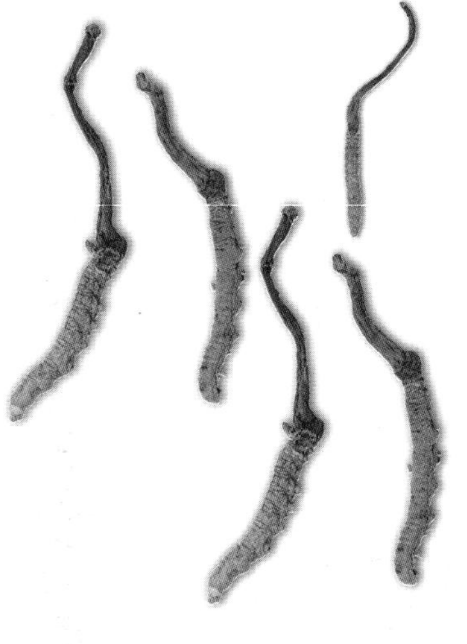

Pilose Antler

(鹿茸 *Lurong*)

Northeast China is known for its three treasures. Pilose Antler, a precious medicine, is among them. The other two are ginseng and marten pelt. But pilose antlers, which are so tender it has not ossificated and filled with blood capillaries, grow only on young stags and they are covered with down-like hair. A young stag grows its first pair of antlers when it turns two; and they are good enough to be cut in the third year. Spring and summer are the seasons for collecting pilose antlers. Another pair of antlers shall grow where the first pair were cut, which means a young stag has to endure the painful and bloody experience once a year. There are cases in which a stag has its antlers cut twice a year; and those cut in winter is known as "snowflake pilose antlers" which are very precious among all Chinese medicinal materials.

The Chinese came to know the medicinal value of pilose antlers as early as 2,000 years ago. In his *Compendium of Materia Medica,* the celebrated Ming Dynasty herbalist Li Shizhen pointed out that pilose antlers promote the secretion of marrow and other body fluid, preserve blood and increase the sexual potency, and strengthen the physique. It provides ideal cure for physical weaknesses, ear and eye diseases, and helps extend one's life span.

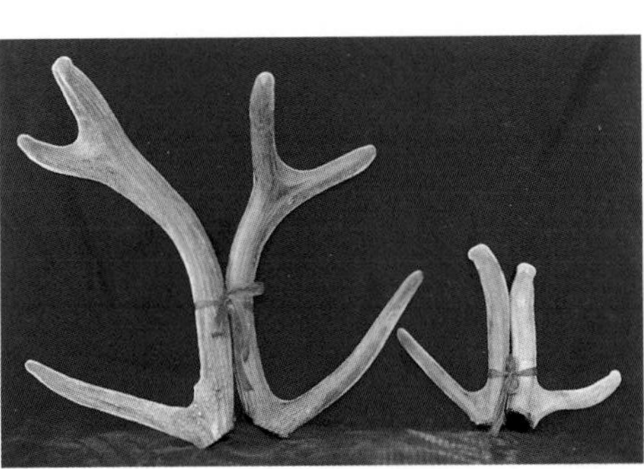

APPENDIX
A BRIEF CHINESE CHRONOLOGY

Xia Dynasty 夏	c. 21st-17th century B.C.
Shang Dynasty 商	c. 17th-11th century B.C.
Zhou Dynasty 周	c. 11th century-256 B.C.
Western Zhou Dynasty 西周	c. 11th century-771 B.C.
Eastern Zhou Dynasty 东周	770 B.C.-256 B.C.
Spring and Autumn Period 春秋	770 B.C.-476 B.C.
Warring States 战国	475 B.C.-221 B.C.
Qin Dynasty 秦	221 B.C.-206 B.C.
Han Dynasty 汉	206 B.C.-A.D. 220
Western Han 西汉	206 B.C.-A.D. 25
Eastern Han 东汉	25-220
Three Kingdoms 三国	220-280
Wei 魏	220-265
Shu Han 蜀汉	221-263
Wu 吴	222-280
Jin Dynasties 晋	265-420
Western Jin Dynasty 西晋	265-317
Eastern Jin Dynasty 东晋	317-420
Northern and Southern Dynasties 南北朝	420-589
Southern Dynasties 南朝	
Song 宋	420-479
Qi 齐	479-502
Liang 梁	502-557
Chen 陈	557-589

Northern Dynasties 北朝	
Northern Wei 北魏	386-534
Eastern Wei 东魏	534-550
Northern Qi 北齐	550-577
Western Wei 西魏	535-556
Northern Zhou 北周	557-581
Sui Dynasty 隋	581-618
Tang Dynasty 唐	618-907
Five Dynasties 五代	907-960
Later Liang 后梁	907-923
Later Tang 后唐	923-936
Later Jin 后晋	936-947
Later Han 后汉	947-950
Later Zhou 后周	951-960
Song Dynasty 宋	960-1279
Northern Song Dynasty 北宋	960-1127
Southern Song Dynasty 南宋	1127-1279
Liao Dynasty 辽	907-1125
Jin Dynasty 金	1115-1234
Yuan Dynasty 元	1206-1368
Ming Dynasty 明	1368-1644
Qing Dynasty 清	1616-1911
Republic of China 中华民国	1912-1949
People's Republic of China 中华人民共和国	Founded in 1949

Managing Editor: Tan Yan

Translators: Li Nianpei and Ling Yuan

Reviser: Ye Xinru

Designers: Wu Tao and Pang Zhuona

Photographers: Du Feibao, Mengzi and Others

(Some photos provided by China Photo Net)

First Edition in 1994

Managing Editor: Ou Xiaomei

Published and Distributed by China Travel & Tourism Press

Address: 9A Jianguomennei Dajie (Ave.), Beijing 100005, China

Telephone: (0086 / 010) 65201007 / 65201174 / 65201180 / 65201014

Printed in the People's Republic of China